From Coca-Cola to Chewing Gum

THE CENTER FOR THE HISTORY OF PSYCHOLOGY SERIES

The Center for the History of Psychology Series
David B. Baker, Editor

C. James Goodwin and Lizette Royer, Editors, *Walter Miles and His 1920 Grand Tour of European Physiology and Psychology Laboratories*

Ludy T. Benjamin Jr. and Lizette Royer Barton, Editors, *Roots in the Great Plains: The Applied Psychology of Harry Hollingworth, Volume 1*

Ludy T. Benjamin Jr. and Lizette Royer Barton, Editors, *From Coca-Cola to Chewing Gum: The Applied Psychology of Harry Hollingworth, Volume 2*

From Coca-Cola to Chewing Gum
The Applied Psychology of Harry Hollingworth, Volume II

Harry Hollingworth
Edited by Ludy T. Benjamin Jr. and Lizette Royer Barton

A REPRODUCTION OF THE ORIGINAL TYPESCRIPT,
WITH A FOREWORD BY DAVID B. BAKER AND
AN INTRODUCTION BY LUDY T. BENJAMIN JR.

The University of Akron Press
Akron, Ohio

All New Material Copyright © 2013 by The University of Akron Press

All rights reserved • First Edition 2013 • Manufactured in the United States of America. • All inquiries and permission requests should be addressed to the Publisher, the University of Akron Press, Akron, Ohio 44325-1703.

17 16 15 14 13   5 4 3 2 1

ISBN 978-1-935603-54-2

LCCN 2012938416

The paper used in this publication meets the minimum requirements of American National Standard for Information Sciences—Permanence of Paper for Printed Library Materials, ANSI z39.48–1984. ∞

Cover photo (original photo pictured above): Archives of the History of American Psychology, The Center for the History of Psychology, The University of Akron, Harry L. and Leta Stetter Hollingworth papers. Harry Hollingworth's notation reads, "On the Adriatic, 1910" and the original image can be found on page 87a of this manuscript. The image has been tinted, cropped, inverted, and repairs have been made for use on the cover. Cover design: Amy Freels.

From Coca-Cola to Chewing Gum was designed and typeset by Amy Freels, with help from Zac Bettendorf and Lauren McAndrews, in Goudy Oldstyle, printed on 60# Natural, and bound by BookMasters of Ashland, Ohio.

Contents

Foreword	*David B. Baker*	vii
Introduction	*Ludy T. Benjamin Jr.*	ix
Editorial Note		xxi
Original typescript		1
Part I, Pianissimo		1
Part II, Crescendo		44
Part III, Fortissimo		137
Part IV, Diminuendo		200
Transcriptions		247
Name Index		250
Subject Index		254

Foreword
David B. Baker

It is hard to believe that a year has passed since publication of the inaugural volume in the Center for the History of Psychology Series. The series is designed to make available unpublished primary source materials from the Center's collections. The response to the first volume, Walter Miles and His 1920 Grand Tour of European Physiology and Psychology Laboratories, has been positive and encouraging. It has provided the proof of concept that we envisioned for the series.

We are fortunate that the Center for the History of Psychology has an embarrassment of riches. It is satisfying to select the next work in the series and once again, the task was easy. We are pleased to present the unpublished autobiography of Harry Hollingworth (1880–1956). The autobiography provides detailed and descriptive information about the development of applied work in psychology. The reader will find much of interest about Harry Hollingworth, Leta Stetter Hollingworth, Nebraska history, graduate education in early twentieth century America, and the rise of applied psychology. The work is published in two volumes. This makes the size of the autobiography more manageable and most importantly, is true to the manner in which Hollingworth himself conceived and prepared the work. Both can be read in their own right, the first volume telling the story of Hollingworth's Nebraska roots and the second providing a first person account of the rise of applied psychology in the industrial northeast of America. Taken together these two volumes provide a glimpse into a transformative time in American history and psychology.

It was only natural that Ludy T. Benjamin Jr. of Texas A&M University serve as one of the editors for this volume. Professor Benjamin is recognized as a leading authority on the history of American psychology. He has researched and written extensively about the life and work of Harry Hollingworth. He is joined by Lizette Royer Barton, senior archives associate at the Center. Ms. Barton was an editor on the first book in the series and brings the skill and knowledge necessary for another successful project.

I am certain that the reader will find in these pages new insights and understandings of psychology in twentieth century America.

Introduction
Ludy T. Benjamin Jr.

This is the second volume of Harry Hollingworth's previously unpublished autobiography, which he wrote in 1940 at the age of sixty. The unexpected death of his wife, Leta Stetter Hollingworth (1886–1939), in November 1939, prompted this examination of his life. The Hollingworths had what psychologists today refer to as a companionate marriage, a relationship in which the husband and wife are wholly dedicated to one another. That does not mean that they did not value friendships, of which they had many, or that they did not value their relatives in Nebraska. It means that they had a singular devotion to one another, manifested in a very happy marriage, with professional and leisure activities typically enjoyed together. Thus the loss of his partner was especially devastating. Hollingworth was bitter and angry at the loss of someone so young (she was fifty-three) and so promising in a career that had thus far benefitted so many, especially children. Going forward with his life suddenly became much more difficult.

The first volume of this autobiography, *Roots in the Great Plains: The Applied Psychology of Harry Hollingworth*, also published by the University of Akron Press, details Hollingworth's origins in poverty in rural Nebraska and his struggles toward a life of the mind, which eventually saw him graduate from the University of Nebraska. This volume of the autobiography, which he originally titled "Years at Columbia," opens with the receipt of a telegram from New York City, offering him a position as a laboratory assistant in the psychology department at Columbia University. The telegram was from Professor James McKeen Cattell (1860–1944), one of the most eminent psychologists in North America and head of a psychology department and psychology laboratory that had few, if any, peers in terms of its excellence.

It was in this culturally and intellectually rich milieu that Hollingworth found himself in 1907 at the age of twenty-six. He arrived in New York City by train from Fremont, Nebraska, in the midst of a raging snowstorm. He walked a few miles in the storm before he found a hotel. It was an inexpensive hotel, but it still cost him most of the $3 that he had set aside for emergencies. He would find the university in the morning and begin his new life.

Hollingworth completed his doctorate in 1909 with a stellar triumvirate, James McKeen Cattell, E. L. Thorndike (1874–1949), and Robert S. Woodworth (1869–1962), at Columbia University. He accepted a position at Columbia's Barnard College, Columbia's college for women, where he remained for his entire career. Between 1910 and 1940, he published twenty books and approximately one hundred research articles and reviews. Not included in that number are the technical reports, probably more than forty, provided by contract research he did for numerous companies.

Hollingworth was well-respected as an applied experimental psychologist. His peers elected him to membership in the prestigious Society of Experimental Psychologists and to the presidency of the American Psychological Association (APA) in 1927. He was acknowledged, even in his own time, as one of the pioneers in applied psychology, largely because of his caffeine studies and his early work on the psychology of advertising, which resulted in three applied psychology books by 1917.[1] But he also wrote books on other applied topics, including vocational psychology, educational psychology, clinical psychology, judging human character, and public speaking.[2] These applied books and his many research contracts made him famous. They also made him wealthy; wealthy enough that in 1944, after having had no raise in salary at Barnard for fifteen years, he wrote a check to Columbia University for $51,000 to endow a scholarship in his late wife's name.[3]

Harry Hollingworth spent his entire professional life working in the field of applied psychology. Yet, in taking stock of that life in his autobiography he wrote, "I might as well say once and for all to the undoubted amazement of my colleagues and professional associates, that I never had any genuine interest in applied psychology, in which field I have come to be known as one of the pioneers. It has become my sad fate to have established early in my career a reputation for interests that with me were only superficial."[4]

That is a fascinating statement; to believe it is to conclude that Hollingworth spent his life working in a field that held no interest for him. Why would he do that? He offers us one possible answer in the last sentence of that quotation, that he felt trapped in applied psychology because of his early success there, successes that somehow prevented him from doing other things. Historians have written much about issues of objectivity in trying to reconstruct the past, what Peter Novick has called "that noble dream." On dimensions of objectivity, autobiographies and oral histories are especially suspect, not only because of what psychologists know about the fallibility of memory, but also because of what is known about the self-serving nature of such recall. Hollingworth also had this to say about his career as applied psychologist, "I became an applied psychologist in order to earn a living for myself and for my wife, and in order for her to undertake advanced graduate training ... Except for the revenue resulting therefrom, I found all these activities distasteful. There were plenty of interesting philosophical questions I wanted to investigate and researches I would have liked to undertake. It was disagreeable in the extreme to spend my time trotting down to these business clubs, talking the most elementary kind of psychological lore, and illustrating it with car-cards, trademarks, packages for codfish, and full color spreads. But I did it with such enthusiasm as I could muster."[5]

It is difficult to believe Hollingworth's claim—there is fairly compelling evidence that he had ample opportunities to leave applied work and pursue subjects of greater interest.

Beginnings of an Applied Psychology Career

In 1909, when Hollingworth graduated from Columbia University with his doctorate in psychology, he was a newlywed, having married his Nebraska sweetheart, Leta Stetter, at the end of 1908. Although she had a college degree from the University of Nebraska and had taught school for three years after graduation, she could not get a teaching job in New York City because of her marital status. The Hollingworths lived in a small apartment in Manhattan, surviving on his $1,000 salary from Barnard. They were in need of money, and especially so, because Leta wanted to continue her education.

In his first year at Barnard, Hollingworth got the opportunity to offer an evening course in the extension division of Columbia University, essentially a curriculum intended for the working public, especially individuals in business. Not surprisingly, many of the courses were practical in nature. Hollingworth's initial course was titled "Applied Psychology." Like the other extension instructors, he was paid on a fee basis, that is, a fee from each of the students enrolled in the course, but no additional salary from Columbia. Thus Hollingworth had plenty of incentive to make his classes popular. In his initial class, he had five students and received the total sum of seventy-five dollars.[6] A year later he also offered a similar course in the evening program of New York University.

Hollingworth's applied courses focused on the psychology of advertising. At the beginning of the twentieth century, the advertising profession in America grew considerably due to mass production and other industrial changes that allowed the mass-marketing of products. Viewed as the science most related to consumer advertising appeal, it was natural for the advertising industry to seek psychology's help. Through his contacts in these evening classes, Hollingworth was invited to offer, for a fee, a special set of ten lectures to the Advertising Men's League of New York City. The lectures, given in the spring of 1910, were eventually serialized in *Judicious Advertising*, a magazine for advertisers, and then published in 1913, in his first book on applied psychology, *Advertising and Selling*.[7]

The Coca-Cola Caffeine Studies

Another event at the beginning of Hollingworth's career, the research that he conducted in 1911 at the request of the Coca-Cola Company, had profound implications for his career as an applied psychologist, as well as for his wife. In 1911, Coca-Cola was brought to trial by the Federal Government under the recently passed Pure Food and Drugs Act of 1906 for marketing a beverage with a harmful ingredient, namely caffeine, an ingredient that the government claimed produced motor problems and impaired mental efficiency. As the Coca-Cola scientists and attorneys prepared for trial they realized that they had no behavioral or cognitive data on the effects of caffeine on humans. So they sought to contract for such research as quickly as possible, given the nearness of the trial dates. The archival record concerning who they may have contacted is incomplete, but eventually the offer went to a financially needy Harry Hollingworth.[8]

In this volume of his autobiography, Hollingworth devotes more space to the caffeine studies than any of his other research projects or books. There is good reason for such attention, because the studies can easily be seen as the watershed event of his career. How enthusiastic was he to accept this contract? He was aware that other psychologists had turned down this opportunity; he certainly was aware of the tainted nature of this kind of work. Indeed, he reported that colleagues had made clear the lamentable nature of such work, "Applications outside the school were tacitly assumed to be unclean. Inquiries and appeals for help from businessmen, employees, manufacturers, lawyers, advertising men, were often either evaded by the seniors or at best referred to younger and more venturesome spirits in the laboratory, who had as yet no sanctity to preserve."[9]

Particularly problematic was the concern about scientific integrity, raised by a company spending large sums of money for research that it hoped would benefit its legal and commercial needs. Although Hollingworth may have had some concerns about his arrangements with the Coca-Cola Company,[10] the evidence is that he was eager to accept the task. He wrote that his willingness to undertake the work was both because of the scientific value of the studies as well as the financial rewards.

Here was a clear case where results of scientific importance might accrue to an investigation that would have to be financed by private interests. No experiments on such a scale as seemed necessary for conclusive results had ever been staged in the history of experimental psychology. . . . With me there was a double motive at work. I needed money and here was a chance to accept employment at work for which I had been trained, with not only the cost of the investigation met but with a very satisfactory retaining fee and stipend for my time and services. I believed I could conscientiously conduct such an investigation, without prejudice to the results, and secure information of a valuable scientific character as well as answer the practical questions raised by the sponsor of the study.[11]

Thus Hollingworth argued that the problem was one of scientific interest which offered the prospect of valuable scientific information, namely the effects of caffeine on mental and motor efficiency in humans. There is no reason to doubt his assessment, but it seems reasonable that Hollingworth would not have taken on the research had he not so desperately needed the money.

Hollingworth's autobiography is filled with tales of poverty in his family and especially that of his wife's family. They faced serious financial crises in the early years of their marriage, particularly surrounding the death of Leta's sister in Chicago and the expenses they incurred in transporting her body back to western Nebraska for burial. To survive financially during that time, they borrowed money from several friends in New York, something that was very difficult for them.

As noted earlier, marriage barred Leta Hollingworth from some employment, at least the ones in which she was most interested. She had a genuine desire to pursue her own doctoral work and the academic talents to succeed, partly evidenced by her graduation as valedictorian from the University of Nebraska. So one can imagine the frustrations they felt—they even considered the possibility of moving back to Nebraska where both of them could teach school. They reasoned that their financial situation could not be worse in Nebraska and that at least they would be closer to family. The offer from the Coca-Cola Company ended those discussions.

The Coca-Cola funds were an economic windfall for the Hollingworths. Hollingworth noted that the funds completely paid for Leta's three years of graduate study at Columbia, where she received her doctorate in 1916, plus most of their spending while on vacation in Europe during the summer of 1912.

Other Applied Opportunities

The success of the caffeine studies, no doubt coupled with the success of the Coca-Cola Company in its case, gave Hollingworth considerable publicity within the business community. This resulted in a deluge of consulting opportunities from various businesses. By 1913, he was earning more from his consulting jobs than he made from his Barnard College salary. His account of some of the applied questions that he was invited to answer follows.

A federal department wants advice on how to interview farmers ... a perfume manufacturer wants psycho-galvanic studies of the effect of his products; a silk manufacturer wants studies of the appeal of his fabrics; an evening newspaper wants to support its advertising columns by evidence that suggestibility is greater in the late hours of the day; a famous railroad wants advice and perhaps experiments to guide it in deciding what color to paint its box cars; a city planning commission requires data on the legibility of traffic signs; a manual trainer wants to know the psychological height for work benches ... an advertiser wants to know where on the page his return coupon should appear; several people want to know the differences in buying habits men and women exhibit; more than one question concerns ... whether appeal to the eye is or is not better than appeal to the ear; a rubber company wants tests made for the better selection of clerks and other employees; and a type foundry wants studies of the legibility of different type-faces.[12]

It is not clear how Hollingworth chose among his many offers—perhaps his decisions were based on how well these consultations paid. It is also not clear how long he pursued this line of contractual research. Unlike the caffeine studies for Coca-Cola, most of the work for companies such as Grinnell Sprinklers, Savage Firearms, Gorton Codfish Company, and the United Drug Company, was not published. This contractual work was typically about improving the company's advertising. The Hollingworth Papers contain unpublished technical reports, yet information in the autobiography makes it clear that those records are incomplete. It is likely he accepted only a few of these contractual studies after 1925. By then, the financial picture for the Hollingworths was quite good; two academic salaries and book royalties and consulting income for both. However, his applied research continued until at least the late 1930s.

Following the early work in advertising, Hollingworth moved into studies of selection, especially the selection of salespeople, creating the *Hollingworth Tests for Selection of Salesmen* in 1916.[13] This work coincided with his efforts to debunk the physiognomic systems that were then popular, in which companies were urged to hire employees on the basis of facial characteristics alleged to be indicative of certain abilities and talents. He published a book in 1923, *Judging Human Character*, that was especially critical of the physiognomic system of Katherine Blackford that was used by many American businesses.[14] In his own book on judging character, he promoted a mental testing approach to selection, drawing on the work pioneered by his mentor, Cattell. His book on vocational psychology also promoted assessment using mental tests.

The Psychology of Chewing

The Coca-Cola studies have been emphasized for reasons that are obvious—they were the principal force in directing Hollingworth's feet to an applied path. As the title of this volume indicates, there is another of his applied studies that is well-known, one that occurred toward the end of his applied career—a study on why people chew gum.

In his scientific monograph on this subject, the beginning can be somewhat confusing and frustrating, due to the obtuseness of the language. Hollingworth tells his readers that the research is about a human motor automatism. Such human automatisms include head nodding, finger tapping, foot swinging, scratching, shoulder shrugging, and thumb twiddling. But, according to Hollingworth, no automatism is more com-

INTRODUCTION

mon in humans than chewing. He observed that, "This activity has the special character of being an essential feature of a fundamental vital activity pattern—eating. But it is much indulged in ... divorced from this fundamental pattern. Chewing is such a satisfying activity, in itself, that random masticatories such as straws, toothpicks, rubber bands, are utilized in order to support it. Most popular of all are the various chicle preparations. . . ."[15] Although the scientific jargon may obscure the meaning here, this was research about the effects of chewing gum.

This research was undertaken in 1934 and 1935, at the request of Bartlett Arkell, president of Beech-Nut Foods. Arkell was a friend of Hollingworth and had contracted with him for research on several earlier occasions. Gum chewing was growing in popularity in the 1930s, and Arkell wanted to know what the benefits might be. The study results were published in a ninety-page monograph which included investigations of the energy cost of chewing as reflected in pulse rate, the metabolic costs of chewing, the relationship of chewing to muscular tension, the effects of chewing or not chewing on various motor and cognitive tasks, and the influence of chewing on work output. Hollingworth found that chewing gum does provide relief from tension and that the tension reduced is muscular. Not only is there motor evidence of tension reduction, but subjective reports acknowledge the same, that is, subjects reported being more relaxed while chewing.

Arkell was very pleased with the research results and modified his advertising for Beech-Nut Gum, proclaiming that chewing gum relieves tension. Hollingworth described the tension reduction by couching it in terms of redintegration, a process by which a complex experience is generated by associations triggered by a single cue that is part of the larger experience. He explained, "Our interpretation of the mechanism ... is a very simple one ... The primary role of chewing is in the mastication of food. Eating is ordinarily a more or less 'quiet' occupation. When we eat, we sit, or otherwise repose. Random restlessness is at a low point. We rest; we relax; and the general feeling tone is one of agreeableness and satisfaction. An important item of the eating situation is the act of chewing. We suggest that, as a result of this contextual status, chewing brings with it, whenever it is sustained, a posture of relaxation. Chewing, in other words, serves as a reduced cue, and to some extent redintegrates the relaxation of mealtime."[16]

Conclusion

Harry Hollingworth claims that he had no genuine interest in applied psychology and he followed that assertion with the following, "My activity in the field of applied psychology was mere pot boiling activity, and now that it is over there is no reason why the truth should not be revealed. My real interest is now and always has been in the purely theoretical and descriptive problems of my science, and the books, among the twenty I have written, of which I am proudest, are the more recent ones which no one reads."[17]

The reference to the recent books is not clear—he wrote those words in 1940, when his most recent books were the 1939 monograph on gum chewing, a 1935 book on the psychology of the audience, and a 1933 book on educational psychology. Based on other passages in the autobiography, it is certain that the book that he felt was his greatest contribution was his 1928 book, *Psychology: Its Facts and Principles*, a general psychology textbook. This book was derived from years of teaching the general psychology course and represented his attempts to systematize the field. Indeed, he referred to this book as his "system." Hollingworth noted that he had always considered this book his masterpiece. "This volume did me personally a lot of good. It straightened out my thinking in psychology, heretofore muddled and messy, and mapped out a path for all of my subsequent work to take. But it was never widely adopted as a text. . . . One of my colleagues described the book as having been written for myself alone."[18]

The textbook was unique and its narrow approach likely ensured its commercial failure. It described most psychological processes in terms of the concept of redintegration. His utter satisfaction, indeed his joy, with his system is indicated in several places in the autobiography. He described it as bringing him an intellectual peace, allowing him to reach equilibrium in his thinking. Consider the following passage, "I had already formulated my "system" and arrived at a satisfactory *Weltanschauung* ... My frantic intellectual fumblings had all represented the endeavor to alleviate the distress of doubt and uncertainty. To be in an intellectual muddle was always for me the strongest of irritants, that is, the most powerful of motives. I had now achieved, if you like, a formula which was in my experience so uniformly applicable and relevant that intellectual distress was almost wholly abolished."[19] The system was so idiosyncratic that few psychologists found it useful as a textbook or as a system of psychology and the reviews of the book were not good.

It is also clear from the more than sixty published reviews of Hollingworth's books that the applied books reviewed quite well when compared to the books that were more theoretical in nature. Surely that was a source of considerable disappointment for him. Clearly this textbook was critically important to Hollingworth—with it he had achieved an understanding of psychology that had evaded him for the first twenty years of his career. The book afforded him a vision of psychology that bordered on certainty, yet he seemed to be the only one who saw it that way. How would that affect his evaluation of his work?

Hollingworth could draw the conclusion that his theoretical work was of little value and that the real contributions he made in psychology were represented by his many applied works. That view might have been endorsed by many who knew his work. Or he could conclude that he had been typecast as an applied psychologist in the early years of his career, which made it impossible for his nonapplied work to be taken seriously. Or he could conclude that his system was misunderstood because he had failed to present his theoretical ideas appropriately. That is precisely the claim he made—that he resurrected a historical term, "redintegration," which carried historical baggage with it and led to misunderstanding; that he gave too much emphasis to the cue-reduction process in his theory, which was his use of a redintegrative idea; and that he should have devised a clever name for his system as some kind of "ism" rather than portraying the system as psychology.[20]

To maintain faith in his theoretical work, Hollingworth might have been inclined to devalue his commitment to the applied work. But what of his work did he consider applied? Consider the following passage in which he discussed the caffeine studies and other studies he did on alcohol: "Although both of these investigations were sponsored by industrial interests, I have never considered them to lie in the field of applied psychology. They were from the beginning straightforward efforts to discover the nature of certain facts and relationships, and the chief interest of the findings has never been in any industrial or commercial application of them."[21]

Clearly, he found those studies interesting. Further, he recognized them to be excellent experimental work. Yet this passage indicates his penchant for splitting hairs, arguing that they did not represent applied research. The studies were done for specific applied purposes and he took the money to work toward those purposes. He enjoyed the chewing gum research as well.

Hollingworth was educated at a time when the distinction between pure versus applied science were made evident and students were encouraged to walk the path of academic truth doing "pure" research and to avoid the temptations of real-world riches from applied work, a distinction still evident in psychology and other disciplines. Academics in Hollingworth's time might have accepted applied work in educational and clinical settings, but when the work was funded by businesses with a clear agenda for the outcome of the research, then the work was open to serious questions about its scientific merit. Hollingworth's writings, both published and unpublished, indicate that he was well aware of what academic sanctity was about.

Perhaps Hollingworth felt himself to be a failure as a scientist because certain key markers of accomplishment had alluded him. For example, he was never elected to the prestigious National Academy of Sciences, whereas many of his contemporaries were, including eight of the twelve APA presidents surrounding his election year. Further, he never held a faculty position in a graduate research department. Although he was a member of the Columbia University faculty for his entire career, his assignment was to an undergraduate department at Barnard College, meaning that he could not leave a legacy of doctoral students he had trained. In evaluating Hollingworth's autobiography it is important to remember that those words were written in the months after Leta's death. So perhaps his disclaimer about his interest in applied psychology could be attributed to his grief.

In conclusion, it could be argued that at the age of sixty, Hollingworth doth protest too much. If he became an applied psychologist to make a living and to aid his wife in going to graduate school, then he could have abandoned that work by 1925. Although it does seem that he stopped the small contract studies by then, he continued to publish books on applied topics and continued to work on other large-scale, commercially-funded projects until near his retirement. Why would he have continued that work for all those years if indeed it was of no genuine interest? If the theoretical and philosophical problems of his discipline interested him more, then why did he not work on those? Perhaps he followed the rewards, and not just the financial ones. That is, he continued to do the work that earned him good reviews and brought him attention, which was his applied work.

In summary, Harry Hollingworth was a creative applied psychologist. He was an experimentalist who brought his science to bear on real-world problems in rigorous and imaginative ways. He was arguably one of the best of his day at what he did. Yet his comments at age sixty—and there is no evidence that he retracted those statements in the remaining sixteen years of his life—express dismay and maybe even shame about his applied work and perhaps about his career. It is disappointing that at the end of his career he could not be comfortable with his place in psychology's history as one of the individuals whose work expanded the domains of psychological science and practice beyond the boundaries of the academy. This volume of his autobiography, from the Coca-Cola studies to the investigations of chewing gum, tells the fascinating story of a pioneering psychologist whose work and reputation helped open a vast field for those psychologists who would follow.

Notes
1. Hollingworth, H. L. (1912). The influence of caffeine on mental and motor efficiency. *Archives of Psychology*, No. 22, 1–166; Hollingworth, H. L. (1913). *Advertising and selling: Principles of appeal and response*. New York: D. Appleton; Hollingworth, H. L. (1916). *Vocational psychology: Its problems and methods*. New York: D. Appleton; Hollingworth, H. L. (1917). *Applied psychology*. New York: D. Appleton.

2. Hollingworth, H. L. (1920). *The psychology of functional neuroses*. New York: D. Appleton; Hollingworth, H. L. (1922). *Judging human character*. New York: D. Appleton; Hollingworth, H. L. (1930). *Abnormal psychology: Its concepts and theories*. New York: Ronald Press; Hollingworth, H. L. (1933). *Educational psychology*. New York: D. Appleton; Hollingworth, H. L. (1935). *The psychology of the audience*. New York: American Book Company.
3. A typed and handwritten page in the Hollingworth Papers at the Center for the History of Psychology at the University of Akron shows that Hollingworth's Barnard College salary reached a high of $9,000 in 1929 and remained at that figure each year until his retirement in 1946. Documents concerning the Leta S. Hollingworth Fellowship at Columbia University are also in the Hollingworth Papers.
4. "Years at Columbia" (1940), p. 56.
5. Novick, P. (1988). *That noble dream: The "objectivity question" and the American historical profession*. New York: Cambridge University Press; "Years at Columbia" (1940), pp. 56, 58.
6. Hollingworth, H. L. (1938). Memories of the early development of the psychology of advertising suggested by Burtt's Psychology of Advertising. *Psychological Bulletin, 35*, 307–311.
7. For information on the conjoined rise of experimental psychology and advertising in America, see Benjamin, L. T., Jr. (2004). Science for sale: Psychology's earliest adventures in American advertising. In J. D. Williams, W. N. Lee, & C. P. Haugtvedt (Eds.), *Diversity in advertising: Broadening the scope of research directions* (pp. 22–39). Mahwah, NJ: Lawrence Erlbaum.
8. Benjamin, Jr., L. T., Rogers, A. M., & Rosenbaum, A. (1991). Coca-Cola, caffeine, and mental deficiency: Harry Hollingworth and the Chattanooga trial of 1911. *Journal of the History of the Behavioral Sciences, 27*, 42–55.
9. Hollingworth (1938), Memories of the early development of the psychology of advertising, p. 308.
10. According to his autobiography and the preface to the published account of the caffeine studies, Hollingworth said that his contract with Coca-Cola called for the studies to be published regardless of their outcome. Further, Coca-Cola was barred from using the research in its advertising or from using Hollingworth's or Columbia University's names in advertising. No copies of this agreement were found in the Hollingworth Papers or in the Coca-Cola Archives in Atlanta, Georgia.
11. "Years at Columbia" (1940), p. 65.
12. Ibid., pp. 111–112.
13. *Hollingworth Tests for Selection of Salesmen* (1916). In Hollingworth Papers.
14. Katherine Blackford was an American physician who developed a nonscientific characterological system for selecting employees. Her system was popular with American businesses from the publication of her books around 1915, into the 1930s. Blackford, K. M. H., & Newcomb, A. (1913). *Analyzing character: The new science of judging men, misfits in business, the home and social life*. New York: The Review of Reviews Co.; Blackford, K. M. H., & Newcomb, A. (1914). *The job, the man, the boss*. New York: The Review of Reviews Co. The Blackford system was a frequent target of psychologists who lamented the common acceptance of such pseudopsychologies in business and industry.

15. Hollingworth, H. L. (1939). Psycho-dynamics of chewing. *Archives of Psychology*, No. 239, pp. 5–6.
16. Ibid., p. 90.
17. "Years at Columbia" (1940), p. 56.
18. Hollingworth, H. L. (1928). *Psychology: Its facts and principles*. New York: D. Appleton; "Years at Columbia" (1940), p. 196.
19. Ibid., pp. 207–208.
20. Ibid., p. 200.
21. Ibid., p. 178.

Editorial Note

Harry L. Hollingworth's two volume autobiography is part of the Harry and Leta Stetter Hollingworth papers housed in the Archives of the History of American Psychology at The Center for the History of Psychology located on The University of Akron campus. The manuscript is reproduced here as an archival facsimile. The original is available for viewing at the archives by appointment.

The manuscript has been reproduced in its original typescript. Hollingworth included numerous photographs in his autobiography and many of the images appear throughout the facsimile. Please note that a few images are missing and appear to have been lost to history as they could not be located within the Hollingworth papers.

Page numbers have been added to those pages that Hollingworth did not number. The original manuscript does not include pages 121a or 128.

Hollingworth typed the manuscript and later penciled in page numbers, photograph descriptions, and additional notes. Over time, the writing has become very faint. Despite our best efforts, much of the handwritten script remains difficult to read.

These pages have been modified in the following manner: the scale has been reduced to fit within the pages of this book and section pages and headings have been added to enable the reader to navigate this work.

PIANISSIMO

When juvenile back-sliding saved me from this fate there was none of the emotional conflict that is sometimes experienced when the faith of childhood collapses under sceptical insight. Instead, my solution was a more or less humanistic interpretation of the theological dogmas. It may be that this preoccupation developed an inclination for philosophical reflection. It seems more probable however that this very mode of solution of the intellectual conflicts of adolescence grew directly out of an original predisposition for abstract speculation, verbal manipulation, and psychological analysis.

It must be borne in mind that psychology as we now know it is a new subject. Psychology and I are really contemporaries, for the first psychological laboratory was established by Wundt in Leipzig in 1879, this being the year in which my parents married and in which I was conceived. The first man to be called a professor of psychology was the same Cattell whose assistant I was to become at Columbia. I must therefore have found my way into the subject before it became widely known, and long before it was heard of in our town.

I seem to have been from the beginning headed for philosophical pursuits. It was the heavy and serious essays and the volumes on abstract topics that I bought from Montgomery Ward and Company as a boy and which constituted for me the introduction to the world of books. Boyish papers published for me in the magazine Word and Works were on definitely psychological themes, although I did not then know it,- "The Unconscious in Education" and "The Optics of Life". The earlier religious attraction was more to theology than to practise. I was granted permission to study history of philosophy while still a preparatory student, at my urgent request. At the University of

From Coca-Cola to Chewing Gum
The Applied Psychology of Harry Hollingworth

Copy No. 2
complete with photos

Copy No. 1 has
better photos. I

YEARS AT COLUMBIA

by

Harry L. Hollingworth

(A Sequel to Born in Nebraska)

This story runs in sweet and tender ways,
For always and forever roses die
And all about us fragrant petals lie;
The remnants of the precious, perfect days
Which come and pass.. But mem'ry still may lend
A fragrance sweet to gladden to the end.

                                        Leta Stetter
                                        1906

CONTENTS

Part I PIANISSIMO

Overture
Taking New York by Storm
The Doors of Schermerhorn
Circumstances and Personnel
The Staff at Columbia
A Summer on Fort Defiance Hill
On the Trail of a Research Problem
The Local Atmosphere
A Dissertation Develops
False Leads Tempt the Scholar
Galloping Over Europe
We Pitch Our Tent Together
I Become a Doctor of Philosophy
Professorial Personalities

Part II CRESCENDO

Gasping for Breath
Why I Became an Applied Psychologist
Psychology of Advertising,—Early Memories
The Caffeine Investigation
The Trial at Chattanooga
Professional Activities
Platform Adventures
Life in the City
Off to Europe Again
The Progress of L.S.H.
The Aftermath
Labors of a Psychotechnician *(A Forgotten Page in Applied Psychology)*
We Join the Montrose Colony
Life in the Country
Colony Characters
The Plattsburg Episode
Why I Developed a Ruby Rash
A Theory of the Neuroses

Part III FORTISSIMO

Pause for Consideration
Certain Temperamental Traits
More "Impudent Letters"
The Next Five Years
The Alcohol Experiments
On the Witness Stand Again
The Gay Decade
A Systematic View Point Develops
Three Fundamental Principles
The Decade Sobers Up
We Become Permanent Country Folks
A Study of Psycho-dynamics
Associations at Barnard College
The Spirit of Columbia

Part IV DIMINUENDO

Our Subjective Climax
Back to Nebraska
The End
Postscript
~~Postscript No. 2~~
Appendix

Perhaps all illustrations should be omitted.

ILLUSTRATIONS

Part I

The Library of Columbia University
The Doors of Schermerhorn
James McKeen Cattell
Robert S. Woodworth
Edward L. Thorndike
Two Early Columbia Playmates
    (Poffenberger and Strong)
Wandering with the Montagues
Vagabonding through Europe

Part II

Barnard College
With "The Folks" on the Campus
On the Adriatic, 1910
L.S.H. and Her Sister Ruth
At 417 West 118th Street
A Tri-furcated Personality
The Colony Assembles for a Tournament
A Corner of the Colony Lake
Our Original Home at Montrose
A Glimpse of Road Day
Some of Our Dogwoods
We Build Our Own Canoe
Associate Professor, 1916
Chief of Educational and Psychological Service
Officer of the Day

Part III

Josefine and Virginia
A Glimpse of Ancestral Derbyshire
Somewhere in Ireland
The House at Hollywyck
At Hollywyck
Leta Stetter Hollingworth
Measuring Reactions in the Psychological Laboratory

PART I
PIANISSIMO
~~TRANSITION~~

PART I
PIANISSIMO
~~TRANSITION~~

Overture

My life falls naturally into two sections, the break coming in the spring of 1907 when I left my native state of Nebraska and came to New York City. This was in the middle of my twenty-seventh year. The Nebraska period is of little general interest although to me of course its incidents are full of significance. Personal curiosity about the influences and events operating in those developmental years has led me to write about them in detail in another manuscript, which bulks larger than does this volume. There is no reason to suppose that it will ever be published and for the purpose of the present volume all that is required is a brief, objective account of what happened before the "Years at Columbia" began.

The little town of DeWitt, where I was born in May, 1880, had been in existence only a few years. It was but a few miles north of Homestead No. 1 whose claim by Dan Freeman has become the subject of an oft repeated bit of pioneer history. From a population of about 1,000 in its most prosperous days, it has declined now to about half this size. It was in an agricultural area and depended for its existence chiefly on the trade of farmers within a radius of five or six miles. These farmers now whirl past the little town in their motor trucks, headed for some distant but more animated metropolis.

To the northeast was a thrifty colony of German farmers. Northwest the region was occupied chiefly by Bohemians who carried their liquor less easily. To the south lay an extensive area populated for the most part by English immigrants of good quality and their descendants. Straight east of town lay "Scully land", owned by a British absentee landlord, rented to tenants who were responsible for their own improvements, and managed by an agent. I became acquainted with the people in all these sections by building barns and houses for them and teaching their one room schools.

The period from 1880 to 1907 lay between two celebrated eras,- the sod house frontier and the machine age. Life in Nebraska then was plain and frugal. My father was a carpenter and we were always "hard up". In the endeavor by all members of the family to achieve jointly our fuel, clothes and food we children acquired many practical skills the possession of which we have never regretted. But our memories of those days are chiefly of hardships, frustration, and high mortality rate.

Kept out of school by a family feud until I was eight years old I then progressed rapidly enough through our ten-grade school. Although little was known of colleges in our town I aspired to occupy myself with books and ideas. It was however six years after finishing the local school that I managed to get far enough away from home to find a college. There it was necessary wholly to earn my way and first of all to complete two years of preparatory work. Two years enabled me to meet the entrance requirements and also to accomplish most of freshman year. Three years at the State University then enabled me to achieve my bachelor's degree and this was conferred with honors.

During the six exasperating years referred to I had worked at carpentry, clerked in stores, taught rural schools, dug graves in a cemetery, been janitor of various buildings, built crooked brick chimneys, peddled newspapers; there are in fact few necessary things that I have not done at one time or another. Similar activities, especially in summers, enabled me to live during the winter months of study. Economically and socially these were miserable years but there is no need here to rehearse their plethora of chagrin and embarrassment.

Entering the University of Nebraska as a sophomore in 1903 I majored heavily in philosophy and psychology, revelling in the freedom of an almost wholly elective curriculum. After the first semester I became assistant in the psychology department under T.L.Bolton and served in this capacity throughout the rest of my course. It was during these years that I met Leta A. Stetter and we became engaged toward the end of our junior year. She was a Chi Omega; I joined a fraternity, borrowed a few hundred dollars, and we had a good senior year.

Upon graduation we were both interested in prospects for scholarships or fellowships for graduate study in eastern universities; but we had no luck. We therefore found jobs as teachers in the public schools. My own appointment was as principal of the high school in one of the larger towns of the state. A lively and interesting year was getting under way and I seemed *destined* to live the hard pressed life of a school executive. But near midyear a telegram came from Prof. J.McK. Cattell of Columbia University asking if I could come January 1st to be assistant in psychology.

Since I could not drop my responsibilities on such short notice I expressed my ~~interest~~ interest in the opportunity provided that I could postpone arrival to March 1st. Happily this compromise was accepted. I resigned, paid off my debts so far as possible, bought a day coach ticket for New York City and boarded the train when the first of March drew near.

It now seems incredible that I could summarize in these few paragraphs the bulky manuscript that describes the days of my childhood and youth. But for the present purpose the significant facts appear to have been indicated.

That purpose is of course not to report the history of Columbia University for any period of time, but to sketch my own activities there during a period of forty years. In the history of the institution these activities were minute and little official record was made of them. Thousands of scholars during those two score years pursued in this locus their scientific work, some of it destined to shake the foundations of knowledge. If each of these should write his autobiography no one would be able to read them all, but each author would find genuine satisfaction in his enterprise. Several have actually done this and I have read their accounts with lively interest.

That is the only justification to be given here for this account of the most active forty years of my life,—since the day when I boarded a train in Fremont, Nebraska with a ticket for New York City and a job as assistant in Columbia University.

TAKING NEW YORK BY STORM

The details of that tiresome trip eastward in the day coach have almost entirely disappeared from my memory. I recall that packages of letters, from the faculty, students and friends in Fremont, were opened from time to time at points on the journey which the writers had designated as appropriate,- "On crossing the Mississippi", "At Niagra Falls", "When you get into New York State". They were kindly, cheering messages, which I kept for years and only recently had the heart to dispose of.

A chief difficulty on the journey was getting sound sleep while sitting upright in the stiff coach seat; occasionally I was fortunate to have the whole seat to myself and could flatten out in a half-coiled position, resting my head on my overcoat placed on the hard seat arm. But I managed to pass the two nights thus without serious distress.

Another difficulty was finding things to eat, since I was not financially in position to take advantage of the dining car. Stops at stations were short and uncertain and often there seemed to be no readily accessible lunch counter at the depot. Sometimes sandwich and fruit vendors would be on the platform or pass through the train, and at one or two points such as Chicago and perhaps Albany there was time to stock up from outside on crackers, cheese, and bananas.

So far as I now recall only one acquaintance was made among the passengers,- a young and talkative salesman who was going part way East, who had been in New York City, and had many tales to tell me about the life there.

FROM COCA-COLA TO CHEWING GUM

In some respects I was glad not to be able to patronize Pullman and dining car for these were both new to me and I was green, wary, and indisposed to tackle too many new things all at once. The strange country through which we passed was enough to keep me occupied,- it was so different from the prairies I knew so well.

In my childhood our family had, it is true, made one or two expeditions afield. We had made one trip by tourist car to San Francisco and up into Washington, where my step-mother's people were living. But we took our food all prepared in a big clothes basket, and I was too young to remember much about the country or the trip. Vague pictures of the Garden of the Gods, the Cliff House and sea lions, and the dense pine and spruce woods in Washington have long been with me, but it is likely that these pictures originated in the many stereoscopic slides we brought back from that expedition. The stereoscope was a familiar instrument of diversion then and many college boys, I came in time to learn, made their living by selling these to the farmers and small-towners during the summer months.

I also have a few scrappy memories of a short time we spent in Colorado Springs, where my father had been sent for the restoration of his health or for treatment, after a nervous attack. But none of these memories either were of much use in preparing me to adapt to unknown features of my journey westward. They are mainly memories of the landscape and of efforts to protect my young brother from the attacks of a neighboring colored boy who persisted in teasing him.

Having been told to alight at Harlem, 125th Street, upon reaching New York City since that was closer to the University campus, this was done, on the evening of March 4, 1907, in a raging snow storm. A short-spoken policeman, when asked where Columbia University was, told me to take a street car and go in a direction to which he pointed. Although this direction, as I later learned, was westward, it seemed to be southward, and has seemed so all through the 33 years that I have come to know 125th Street so well.

New York City has always been 90 degrees displaced on my mental compass. I came to the city from the West, and that brought me straight down the Hudson River, which must therefore be flowing due east. It still seems to me to flow east and its current to head straight out for Europe. In order to become oriented in the city at all I have had to adopt quite arbitrarily the quaint conception of the inhabitants that the Hudson River comes down from the north. Of course I now know that I had over-looked the right-angled turn made by the New York Central when it hits Albany and turns southward for the metropolis. But even today, and in spite of that knowledge, if I were asked to point to Portland, Maine, I should point square ahead into the heart of the Atlantic Ocean.

At any rate the policeman showed me the direction to go and clambering on the car I asked the conductor or motor man to let me off at Columbia University. He mumbled something about getting off at some place, and I asked him to repeat his statement but could make nothing out of it. The car stopped, however, at what I later learned to be Amsterdam Avenue, and I was beckoned off.

FROM COCA-COLA TO CHEWING GUM

1gA

Nothing that I could see looked anything like a university, and in the falling snow, since darkness had fallen too, there was little enough to see anyway. Some passerby told me to walk down the street and I would find the University, so down it I went although it seemed to me I was climbing <u>up</u> all the time. I carried my paper telescope bag in my hand and looked right and left for the stretch of campus and ivy covered buildings I had pictured. All I could find was what I called "store buildings" and there seemed even to be no houses for people to live in.

Finally, deciding that I was on the wrong road, I asked another passerby,-"Where is Columbia University ?".

"Why, right here," he replied. "This is Columbia University."

The "This" to which he referred must have been the corner of Amsterdam Avenue and 116th Street, for after turning off as he directed I came to the bare paved space in front of Low Memorial Library, with just glimpses of 'campus' here and there.

Since it was getting late and there were no hotels in sight I inquired of still a third passerby which way the 'business district' lay. He pointed down a street along which cars were moving, and this turned out to be Broadway. I had heard a great deal about Broadway, but nothing that I saw fitted the descriptions that had been given of the "Great White Way" except the snow which still fell and accumulated.

I decided just to get on a street car and keep on going until I could see a hotel. We travelled for what seemed like miles before, off to the right, appeared a well illuminated and impressive structure with the sign "Hotel Belleclaire" emblazoned thereon. This hotel still stands, not many blocks above Columbus Circle, and there I spent not only the night, but most of the two or three dollars I had saved for emergencies.

It seemed to me an unwarranted presumption when a fellow behind the desk made me sign my name before letting me go upstairs; and when a dapper uniformed chap tried to grab my telescope bag out of my hands I tightened my grip on it, bearing in mind the tales about bandits and hold-ups and confidence men in the eastern cities. Except for the little commercial places in the hamlets of western Nebraska, on my bicycle trek across the state, I had never spent the night in a hotel. The awe inspiring Lindell at Lincoln was the only place of this sort I had ever been in, and then only reverently to eat a meal in the dining room. I was raw and green and naïve, but doors in the East had opened, and in the morning I should set out to find them.

THE DOORS OF SCHERMERHORN

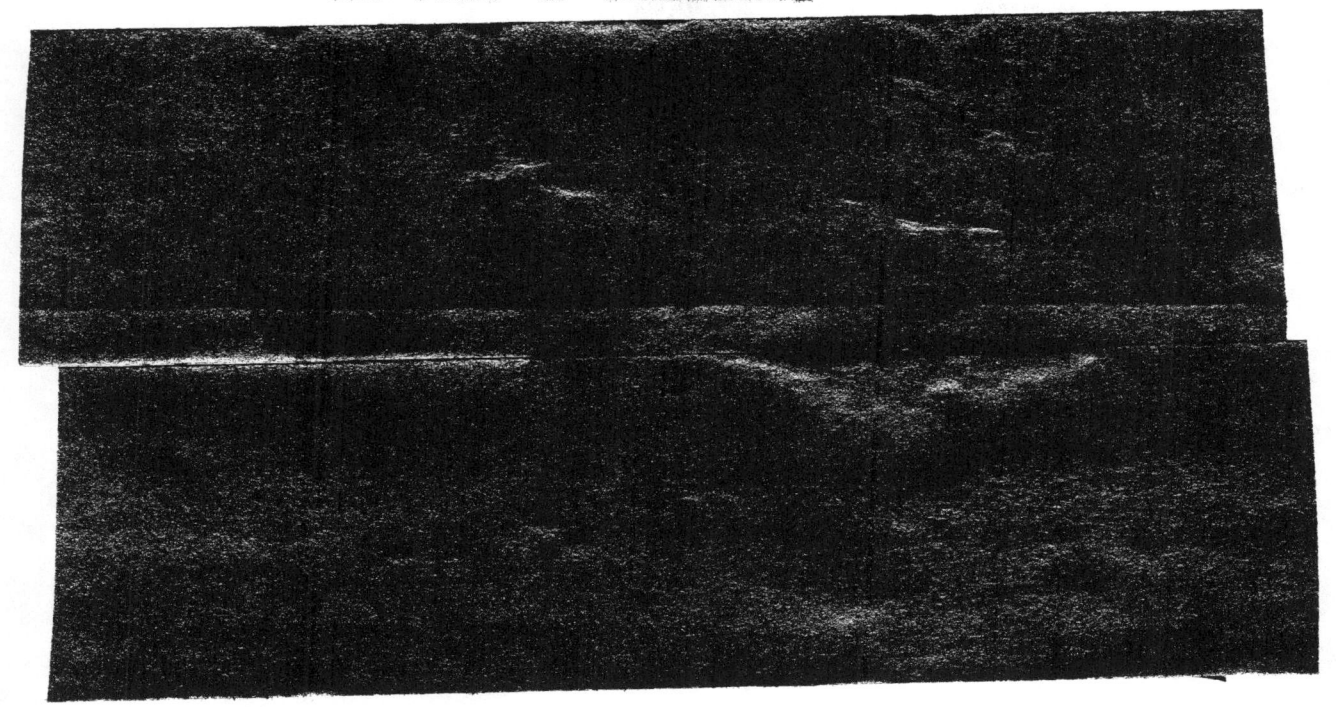

The doors that opened in the East were the tall and ponderous oaken doors of Schermerhorn Hall. There as now the Department of Psychology of Columbia University was located. From March 5, 1907 to yesterday, which was April 8, 1940, a third of a century, I have passed in and out through those doors, and how many more years they shall admit me I do not know.

For a year or two my passage through those doors was lone and solitary. Then for more than thirty years my wife and I passed through them often together, in our joint and mutually interesting activities. Now again I pass through them in solitude and loneliness, and with a bitter heart.

Those ponderous doors have shadowed us from the beginning of our life together to the very end of our companionship. On the wall at my home hangs a photograph of those noble doors, framed in mahogany by my Chi Omega, the scarlet Tam-O-Shanter girl, after their opening had enabled us to be man and wife. To our friends the picture means little enough. To us it was always a tiny symbol of the things we jointly held most precious.

Passing through the doors of Schermerhorn Hall on the morning of March 5, 1907, I went up the broad granite stairway to a long balcony, at one end of which the word PSYCHOLOGY was painted, and behind this sign lay a suite of rooms. I looked about for some one resembling a professor, but nowhere was anyone in sight. At smaller doors, bearing the names of Cattell and of Woodworth respectively, no one answered my knock.

PIANISSIMO

The Doors of Schermerhorn
A.T. Beals
N.Y.

But a voice was coming from behind another door, as if a lecture were in progress. Opening this door, there appeared a large room, with seats and a long demonstration table at one end, and in the other end tables, chairs, cabinets, and apparatus, all of which looked much like the familiar objects in the laboratory at Lincoln. I slipped into the room, took a back seat and quietly listened to what the man at the desk was saying to the group of students occupying the seats. The speaker seemed youthful and easy-going, and was quite indifferent to my presence, but he was clearly enough talking about psychology.

"This must be one of the young fellows", I said to myself, "giving the students some instructions. I cannot remain here for I am already several days late, and must find the professor." So as quietly as I had come in I now slipped out of the room, and renewed the search for the department chiefs. In due time the class adjourned and all filed away except the young and easy-going man who had been talking. I told him who I was and for whom I was looking. To which he replied, "Oh, yes. You must be the new man. I'm Professor Woodworth, and you are going to be my assistant." And he added, "That was the class you are to help me with. They will come for laboratory this afternoon. Are you ready to take charge of them ? I'll be pretty busy myself for I'm behind hand with instruction sheets for the experiments and must do a lot of mimeographing."

And so thus shortly, before I had even found a place to sleep that night, my period of service in Columbia University began. This period is still, I hope, far from terminated; at least these words are being written in my office in the department of psychology. Although the street cars on Amsterdam Avenue have now been abandoned, they still run up and down Broadway, up and above 125th Street and down, past and beyond the Hotel Belleclaire, in which I have never since set foot.

By evening the laboratory class had finished its work. In the absence of instruction sheets, not yet mimeographed, I found out from the boys (these were all Columbia College students apparently) what they had been doing and what experiment was due for today. Fortunately it was in a field familiar to me and oral instructions enabled us to proceed. After adjournment I hastily made arrangements at the University offices to occupy a tiny room in one of the dormitories, with no payment until the end of the month, when I should have my first pay check. The "Commons" must have extended me credit too on a meal ticket, for after the Belleclaire episode I had no cash to live on during that month.

The room turned out to be too small for comfort, too noisy for reflection and study, and too full of grit and dirt from Amsterdam. Shortly this room was abandoned and down on 124th Street I found a hall bed room, in the apartment of one Mrs. Beach. This was dark and gloomy, but it was cheaper and it appeared to be quieter. Alongside me in another room was a dignified and grave young man, whom I came in due course to know. I predicted then that he would become either a bishop or a college president, although he was heading for a major in history. He was Dixon R. Fox, later professor of history in the University, and president of Union College.

In this room I lived, when in New York City, until the last day of 1908, when upon our marriage my wife and I moved into a newly built apartment house on West 136th Street, and began those peregrinations that constitute the alleged "life" of the chronic apartment dweller.

In this way began a change of residence that was to last for forty years or more. Before pursuing further the vicissitudes of those years it may be appropriate to raise briefly a question that others have often asked, namely,—"How did I come to be a psychologist?" If the answer is to be found in any external circumstances or in early experience it ought to refer to influences operating in the years described in an earlier volume, describing my youth in Nebraska. But I think one may search those pages without finding any clarification; of course it is possible that the effective factors were not clearly recognized, and escaped report. But such considerations as the following seem more relevant.

I had been discouraged in my teens at not being able to get my education under way more expeditiously. Even when this had been achieved it seemed likely that the delay would be a serious handicap to achievement, since others would have such an appreciable head start. In maturity, however, I felt grateful for the obstacles that had impeded my early intention to become a theologian. It seem likely to me now that, had my college years come earlier, they could only have misguided me either into wasted effort, later to be atoned for, or into a precarious career as a half-hearted preakher or a hypocritical bishop.

When juvenile back-sliding saved me from this fate there was none of the emotional conflict that is sometimes experienced when the faith of childhood collapses under sceptical insight. Instead, my solution was a more or less humanistic interpretation of the theological dogmas. It may be that this preoccupation developed an inclination for philosophical reflection. It seems more probable however that this very mode of solution of the intellectual conflicts of adolescence grew directly out of an original predisposition for abstract speculation, verbal manipulation, and psychological analysis.

It must be borne in mind that psychology as we now know it is a new subject. Psychology and I are really contemporaries, for the first psychological laboratory was established by Wundt in Leipzig in 1879, this being the year in which my parents married and in which I was conceived. The first man to be called a professor of psychology was the same Cattell whose assistant I was to become at Columbia. I must therefore have found my way into the subject before it became widely known, and long before it was heard of in our town.

I seem to have been from the beginning headed for philosophical pursuits. It was the heavy and serious essays and the volumes on abstract topics that I bought from Montgomery Ward and Company as a boy and which constituted for me the introduction to the world of books. Boyish papers published for me in the magazine <u>Word and Works</u> were on definitely psychological themes, although I did not then know it,- "The Unconscious in Education" and "The Optics of Life". The earlier religious attraction was more to theology than to practise. I was granted permission to study history of philosophy while still a preparatory student, at my urgent request. At the University of

Nebraska I had been fully as interested in Philosophy as in Psychology and I had gone there chiefly to find better instruction in these two subjects. It was I who had picked the professors, not they who influenced me toward their subject matter.

Upon graduation I had applied for fellowships in either of these two fields, for psychology was still a part of philosophy and this affiliation was recognized in the organization of university departments. Had a fellowship or an assistantship in metaphysics, or epistemology, or logic rather than in psychology been available, I should undoubtedly have siezed the opportunity. But in these fields nothing but a tuition scholarship in Cornell had been made available.

The doors that opened, when this finally happened, were those of a psychological laboratory. That is surely the chief reason why I became a psychologist rather than a philosopher. But I have no good explanation to give for the fact that from early childhood I was headed for these general fields rather than for any of the things that my friends found to do and appeared to enjoy. So far as I can tell the predilection represented a native taste or constitutional predisposition and was not due to anything that happened to me or that was taught me. I seem to have been born that way and to have persisted in it in spite of obstacles. This volume is in fact the story of those vicissitudes.

CIRCUMSTANCES AND PERSONNEL

The place as Assistant which I assumed had been opened in the middle of the year by a somewhat complicated chain of circumstances. V.A.C. Henmon, now long a prominent educator and Dean in the University of Wisconsin, had been, in his capacity as Assistant giving a course in Experimental Psychology just started in Barnard College. He had accepted a call to a professorship in Colorado College at mid-year. F.L. Wells, then Assistant in the Columbia department, and since well known for his work in clinical psychology and psychopathology, undertook to continue the course in Barnard in place of Henmon. That left the Assistantship unoccupied in Columbia, and it was this place that Prof. Cattell had offered to me. In the meantime, since I could not come until March, a man who was just taking his degree, Sven Froeberg, since then professor in St. Olaf's College, was designated temporary Assistant until I arrived.

A number of other people were about the department, finishing or just having completed their work for the doctor's degree. Among these were W.C. Ruediger, M.T. Whitley, Abram Lipsky, F.M. Hamilton. Philosophy and Anthropology also mingled freely with Psychology in those days and among the advanced students in these fields were A.A. Goldenweiser, Howard Woolston, Max Eastman, H.C. Becker, Elsie R. Clapp, Wyllistine Goodsell. Nearer the beginning of their work, like myself, were A.E. Rejall, D.O. Lyon, Lawrence Hill, A.E. Chrislip, J.W. Todd, A.J. Culler. The next year appeared also H.H. Woodrow, J. Breitwieser, and soon thereafter A.T. Poffenberger, J.F. Dashiell, D.E. Rice, J.P. Turner, E.K. Strong. Many of these are now familiar names in psychology or in allied fields.

Clearest of all in my memory, so far as those days are concerned, is the personality of Warner Brown, among these advanced students. He also was first a Fellow, then Assistant in Schermerhorn. He was a year or so ahead of me in his work and we occupied adjoining offices on the floor above the laboratory. But for his fund of information and experience and his kindness in giving me the frequent benefit of all these I might well have come to an unfortunate end . Especially when in the following year I became the Assistant to Prof. Cattell in the Advanced Experimental course, would I have had trouble.

My own laboratory experience was all on the elementary level. We had neither the equipment nor the time at Nebraska to set up the elaborate apparatus of some of the more advanced experiments, even had we had graduate students, in any great number. But Cattell of course assumed that I was ready to do what was needed. He might leave on Tuesday, instructing me that on Thursday he would like to have the Hipp chronoscope set up in line with Wundt's fall hammer, all activated by a gravity cell battery, and there I was. What or where these things were or how to know when they were in line, these were wholly beyond me. Brown always knew; what is more, he would without any apparent scorn show me all I needed to know, answer all my questions, and finally set the whole business up with such dispatch and precision that when Thursday came the professor never had any fault to find with my work.

In a selfish sort of way I must say I was glad that toward the end of the year, when his dissertation was in press and ready for proof reading, Brown came down with scarlet fever and had to be isolated somewhere down town in a ward for communicable diseases. It was possible for me to get through the lines, wearing the gowns provided, and taking other precautions. Thus I could bear to him the installments of his proof, which he could read, and then when it had been duly fumigated I could bear it back again to the printer.

The dissertation therefore appeared and he received his degree in time to take the position in the University of California that had been offered him. He has been in that university ever since. The little that I was able to do for him during this critical period has done something to efface the chagrin I might otherwise have retained over my own ignorance and incompetence in those early days when he so often came to my rescue. Once more my reach was exceeding my grasp.

I recall also with gratitude a useful hint volunteered by F.L.Wells who turned out to be a fraternity brother of mine. We became well acquainted during the next year and he remarked one day that the department had little interest in what courses I might take,- the chief concern was that I should get busy with experiments and investigations of my own. This observation gave an appropriate turn to my immediate activities and later experience confirmed its soundness. It was a useful thing to know at that early stage of my career, acquainted as I then was chiefly with undergraduate assignments and examination grades.

Harris & Ewing　　　Edw. L. Thorndike　　　Washington, D.C.

THE STAFF AT COLUMBIA

When I now consult the current announcement of the Department of Psychology of Columbia University I find thirty-seven Instructors and Professors listed, in addition to a group of Assistants. The change since the day I arrived at Schermerhorn is truly amazing. Then there were in Psychology only Cattell and Woodworth at Columbia and Thorndike and Norsworthy at Teachers College, to which Rueger had just been added. It is true that C.A. Strong also had an appointment in psychology, but just after my day he was on more or less permanent leave of absence.

Philosophy was then a strong department. There were Dewey, Woodbridge, Montague, Fullerton, Lord, Adler, Pitkin, Bush, Miller whom I remember promptly and there may have been others. Of these Montague alone is still on active duty. He is clearly enough America's ablest active philosopher, but the others now comprising the department, perhaps because they are still young, or perhaps only because I am old, do not impress me as did that group I found on arrival at Columbia in 1907, when William James was also scheduled to give a series of lectures.

Although Anthropology was more or less closely allied with these two groups and Boas and Farrand were not uninterested in psychology, I never carried any work in that department and hence came to know little about it, and am even not now well acquainted with my colleagues in that field. The philosophers, on the other hand, I continued to team up with to some extent, and have retained my original amateurish interest in their work.

Since so much of the work in Education in Teachers College rests on psychological foundations, it was natural enough that there should have been close affiliations from the beginning between the educational and the psychological groups. In my memory there was a joint Seminar, for advanced students doing their work in psychological fields, and Thorndike and Norsworthy along with Cattell and Woodworth conducted this Seminar together.

The group in Teachers College began to increase even more rapidly than the group in Schermerhorn, and the ties have now become less intimate, although many of the Teachers College people are well known psychologists. When these two groups, and others groups later originated, are listed together, it becomes clear that never in the history of man was such an imposing group of psychologists permanently gathered together in one place as at Columbia University in the year in which this is being written.

My own associations with the psychologists of Teachers College have been closer than would ordinarily have been the case, because a few years later my wife, upon receiving her doctor's degree, was appointed to a place on that faculty and continued her professional work there, with distinction, to the end of her life. Not only did I thus indirectly become acquainted with the course of events in that institution, but many of the people on the Faculty have become my closest and most valued friends. To list the names of this large group in this connection would be to go too far afield, but some of them, as the Thorndikes, Gates', Jersild, Pintner, Reisner, all of whom I came to know early and well, should not be omitted.

A SUMMER ON FORT DEFIANCE HILL

The university year at Columbia is fairly short and compact, with few long vacations. By the middle of May classes are usually over and the examination period under way. Since I arrived during the first week in March the spring term was already nearly a third over, and it was too late to make any formal registration, although, as Assistant, half of my time was available for study. I "sat in" on various courses of lectures, read widely in the journals and books to be found in the reading room, and set about improving my French and German in which examinations would have to be passed as part of the requirements for a degree.

Shortly Professor Cattell inquired whether I should like to come to his place for the summer, to help him with a biographical dictionary he was editing and publishing, and to act as part-time tutor to his children. I had already begun to worry a bit about the coming summer, and had secured tentative information concerning the qualifications required for a job on the city traction lines, which seemed to be about the only obvious thing I might work my way into as a transient laborer. The prospect of working for this period with my major professor, of living in a camp on his wooded hill, four miles inland from Garrison, N. Y., and of receiving for which had been my salary also as principal of the Fremont High School, soon put a stop to my plans to be a street car motor-man or conductor. In the middle of May I once more boarded a New York Central train, this time going up the river, reversing the route that had only recently brought me to New York City. Alighting at Garrison, which is on the Hudson River just

PIANISSIMO

12/276A

With two Early Columbia Playmates, — E. K. Strong and A. T. Paffenberger.

12A

across from the West Point Military Academy, I found my way
through the wooded country, to Fort Defiance Hill.

At Fort Defiance I lived in a small frame camp on the hillside, below Cattell's house which came to be known as "the castle". The house stood on the very point of the high hill, several hundred feet, perhaps 800 or 1,000, above sea level, looking out in all directions for many miles over the surrounding country. Once more "baching" became my mode of life, although tea was served in late afternoon up at the house where my work was done, and Sunday dinners with the family often introduced variety into the bill of fare and were in themselves particularly pleasant and interesting occasions. At the foot of the hill, and squarely on the Albany Post Road stood ~~the little house~~ the Hill Country House, ~~~~~~~~~~~~~~~~~ a summer hotel for New Yorkers who preferred the mountains to the seashore.

Automobiles, although they existed in 1907, were not common, and a team of oxen was in fact still in use in the neighborhood. Being four miles from the station, this hotel was quite isolated. If the food had only been better, the place would have been an inviting spot. Even as it was I shortly gave up preparing my own meals, taking breakfast and evening meal at the hotel and carrying back up the hill with me the inedible fragments that were provided for my lunch. One advantage to this arrangement was that I got acquainted with the summer boarders and learned a good many things about New Yorkers in that way. Through the kind offices of one of these, a political leader of some sort in the city, I was invited to a "clam bake" given on

Long Island by a Republican Club. This festivity, staged near the seashore, was a new experience for the boy from the prairie.

Human nature appeared to me in new guises as I watched these summer people from the city and came to know them. In the West that I knew there had been little pretense. People were just what they were, and everyone in the community knew just what this was. But here I found all the boarders playing a role, in which their status represented a 'wish fulfillment' rather than their actual life.

A broken down chorus girl paraded as a "retired prima donna"; a medical student, serving as time keeper on an aqueduct project in the neighborhood, was always called "the doctor"; a cash boy in a down town store became over night a "jewelry salesman"; the decrepit rig that the hotel used to transport groceries and occasionally the boarders, was the "coach"; and the humble laboratory assistant from Columbia shortly became "the professor". These gratifying pretenses were not only indulged in and tolerated, there was even mutual encouragement in their development as for a few short weeks all these plain citizens enjoyed to the utmost the vacation funds they had so carefully saved during the preceding year. I began to see more clearly why, when delusions develop in the mentally unstable, they are so much more likely to take the grandiose form, rather than the self depreciatory.

FROM COCA-COLA TO CHEWING GUM

*Wandering with
W. P. Montague*

As for the work on "the hill", I felt myself not to be much of a success, although I was invited back again for a repeat performance, and have ever since made at least an annual pilgrimage to Fort Defiance. The biographical dictionary, which was a directory of the world's psychologists, went well enough, so far as I could see. But the tutoring of the children kept me guessing.

There were six children, but only the older ones were being given instruction. According to the professor's educational theory, they were not actually to be "instructed", but rather, led to discover useful knowledge and acquire valuable techniques in the course of more directly and strongly motivated activities. Arithmetic was not to be taught as such, but incidentally acquired in keeping records of the various collections the children had become interested in making, in timing themselves in certain physical feats, such as running, and plotting graphic records of improvement and fluctuation, and so on. All this I recognize as a note then new, but now common, in progressive education, with some psychological justification; but I was poorly fitted to execute it in spite of my four years of teaching.

We had nevertheless many good times together. We swam vigorously in the lake, one side of which Cattell owned. We played tennis barefooted on the grass court, sometimes joined in this diversion by the equally barefooted professor. We made innumerable wooden cages, with doors hinged with leather, for the colonies of white mice the children were raising and, to some extent studying. We played croquet on the tiny area of lawn left on top of the hill after the castle had been built. And ever and anon I managed to stir a faint interest in problems of percentage or in Woodrow Wilson's "History of the United States" (which I personally abominated). But I often detected a quizzical gleam in the eyes of Professor or Mrs. Cattell as they stood in the doorway observing the course of our "lesson hour", and knew full well that this was not occasioned by the sight of the huge bull snake that often crawled lazily about on top of the long rectangular table about which we sat during such study periods.

In spite of the irregularities of their elementary and secondary education, these children grew up to occupy themselves with editorial, scientific, educational and publishing enterprises. This has always been a consolation, because it has encouraged me to believe that my tutorial bungling during that summer with them worked no irreparable damage.

Among my most pleasurable memories of that summer on Fort Defiance Hill, aside from the personal associations that still attract me to it when the conflicting rush of many busy lives makes a visit possible, are the evenings and nights in the cabin on the hillside. This well watered country, where trees had almost to be fought against, instead of tenderly nursed, as was the case in so many parts of Nebraska, was most welcome to me, for I had always loved the woods. The chill evenings, even late in May or June, when I had to have a fire to keep comfortable, were also a novelty, for spring always came early in Nebraska. There was moss, which was new to me, on all sides; and whip-poor-wills, which I had never heard, kept calling and were close at hand.

When the day's work was over, and a fire going, and heavy volumes pulled down from the shelf, or a letter started to a Nebraska girl who, I devoutly hoped, might before long be with me in the East, the same spiritual quality permeated the place that I had heretofore known only in the little school house in District 149. It was a quality that, for me, was always worth struggling for, or waiting for.

ON THE TRAIL OF A RESEARCH PROBLEM

In September, after returning to the University, the uppermost problem became that of finding a topic for investigation that promised to yield a doctor's dissertation. Of course, along with my work as Woodworth's assistant, I carried now a full load of courses, splitting my field into a major (psychology) and two minors (philosophy and education). But there was nothing new to taking courses and this part of life was tossed off lightly enough, and well enjoyed.

During that year and the one following I was in classes under the instruction of Cattell, Woodworth, Thorndike, Monroe, Woodbridge, Dewey, and C. A. Strong. All of these men were stimulating, and some of them I understood. In Education as such my interests were decidedly minor; I had already had severe doses in that field, and did not intend to go into it unless it should offer opportunity to do reasonably "pure" work in science, rather than in administration and teacher-training.

In Philosophy I think I never made any advance beyond the point to which Hinman had brought us in his final seminar. There were certain new notes that were being faintly struck. Pragmatism was in the air, but we had already wrestled with it at second hand. The new Realism was in the making, but this, so far as I comprehended it, and found it to my liking, was but the reaffirmation of a position into which I had already worked. And much of the philosophical teaching I encountered seemed to me to be light hearted, jocose, and not animated by a serious concern over the profound problems to which the tomes in our old stack room had been dedicated. Already the social slant was creeping into philosophy in America, and although Dewey, for example, did lecture from time to time on logic, it was in terms of "instrumentalism", and he seemed preferably to give courses on ethics and on social psychology. There was a robust heartiness about the points of view advocated by Woodbridge, but Dickinson Miller came nearer to being the kind of person I had pictured as a philosopher, and even he was drifting off into what seemed like a theological direction. C. A. Strong brought into his teaching of psychology (the more systematic or theoretical variety) an analytic approach that I welcomed. But there were only three or four students who seemed to care for this sort of thing, and since the instructor was likely to weep if we put up any strong opposition to his doctrines, we made little progress in that field.

In psychology the quantitative and statistical approach was being emphasized by Cattell and Thorndike, and the physiological by Woodworth. The historical "Freshman tests" were still being given and one of my annual jobs was to spend an hour on each of 100 Columbia freshmen, giving them these tests and recording the results. The record sheets were stored along with a musty pile of earlier ones that Wissler and Farrand had made some use of; but so far as I know those I diligently accumulated were never put to any use.

I must record the fact that I did not take kindly to the instrumental and statistical type of psychology. I revolted, inwardly, against so much preoccupation with probable errors and coefficients of correlation; these measures, and others like them, had only lately turned up and everyone was excited over them. It seemed to me that too much attention was being given to the mere instruments and apparatus of research, and too little to the possible significance of the problems toward which they were being directed.

This business of a problem was what chiefly engaged me at the moment. It appeared obvious that no one cared very much what courses, if any, I took. The main thing was that I should experiment and turn up some interesting and "reliable" results. Research rather than study seemed to be the keynote of the department of psychology, so I began at once to investigate some leads that had grown out of the experiments with Bolton at Nebraska.

In a conference with my major professors they asked me what studies I had already carried on, and these were briefly described. "Those studies seem to be familiar" said Professor Cattell. "Did you publish the results?" "I presented a paper before our state Academy of Sciences," I replied. "Maybe there was a report of it, but only in SCIENCE, or some such journal as that." And my tone disparaged all journals of such an ilk. Cattell and Woodworth exchanged amused glances, for which I saw at the time no occasion, and I felt a bit hurt. Only later did I realize that Cattell himself not only edited, but owned and published SCIENCE, to which I had so slightingly referred.

Well, the earlier studies at Nebraska, of such acts as walking, stepping, standing, had suggested that discrimination of distance and position was better the greater the activity involved. So I set out to discover whether active movement might be better discriminated than passive movement. It seemed to me that this, if true, might have certain pedagogical implications. There was already a slogan to the effect that "Only activity educates," but I could find no experimental demonstration of this faith. It also seemed likely that I was on the threshold of an experimental investigation of "The Will," and so I read widely on all these and related topics.

Active and passive movements were studied in a great variety of ways. I rigged up a planchette, suspended from the ceiling, and with my subject's arm resting thereon, made experiments. I made angled grooves in doubled heavy cardboard, put graphite on the track and had my subjects move a pencil or stylus about these figures, or else I moved the hand about the track while they made no active effort. The angles or the length of lines, or what not, were then to be reproduced, or compared with others, and so on.

From time to time I would report progress in the Seminar; if I had apparent results, it would turn out that the probable error of the difference was too small, and I was advised to secure more measures and to make more computations. For a good half year I followed up, experimentally and theoretically, this comparison of activity vs. passivity, and "Evermore came out where in I went." But on the way, certain other curious observations were made, and eventually I abandoned "The Will" and set about the investigations that led easily enough into my doctor's dissertation.

The negative results of these experiments on active and passive movement were never recorded in the literature, although in some ways negative findings are as significant as any others. In time one comes to realize what a large number of scientifically motivated adventures in curiosity are never reported. They are like inventions that fail to materialize and are not advertised; like expeditions that fail to discover any new islands and are therefore treated as if they had not been. And yet, to discover that there is no island is a result not to be ignored, if one can be sure of it. I remember in this connection an experiment in which I assisted Warner Brown, a time consuming project and yet one of which the world at large knows nothing.

Brown was a keen critic of conclusions and sceptical of interpretations, with a passion for matter of fact. I still remember his scorn of one of my unstudied remarks. We had been mixing hot and cold water for experiments on the temperature sense. It was observed that a little cold water would chill a bucket of hot, whereas it took a large quantity of hot water to warm a bucketful of cold. My simple verdict was "Cold is more power ful than hot." This animistic conclusion provoked his withering rebuke, and a ~~[illegible]~~ rehearsal of facts about the physiological zero, adaptation, and thermal thresholds.

But the experiment to which I refer was not this one. It dealt instead with the apparent size of the moon on the horizon and in the zenith. Brown surmised that current explanations were pure chatter; that actually the lens of the eye falls into a different position when one looks upward. This might change the distance of the lens from the retina and thus produce the illusion physiologically rather than psychologically. We found in Hamilton Hall a deep stair well, stretching the full height of the building. We cut artificial moons out of card board, determined their apparent size when the observer lay on his back on the ground floor and stared up at them through the deep stair well. These estimates were then compared with similar judgments when the moons were seen at the end of a hallway as long as the stair well was deep. The experiment was accomplished some 35 years ago but no report of its outcome has ever crept into the literature. To understand this I need only recall my own experiments on the thresholds of active and passive movement.

THE LOCAL ATMOSPHERE

University life at Columbia in those days was more like the traditional European pattern than appears now to be the case. There were relatively few women among the graduate students and student relaxation was inclined to be alcoholic. Greenwich Village was in its prime; Riverside Drive, instead of a row of apartment houses along an express highway, was fairly rural. Some of the blocks had groves and gardens and in the center a restaurant and bar. Student clubs would sometimes meet in these gardens for beer, food, singing and discussion. Adjoining the campus were small farm areas with chickens and goats, but the region was beginning to be built up rapidly. The subway under Broadway was just being built and trolleys were still the chief mode of transportation. From the campus to the down town section was a long trip, but in many ways a pleasant one.

Harlem, and especially 125th Street, was a busy up-town center, much more like a separate community than now. There were good stores; theatres which showed the good plays after their initial run on Broadway; several famous variety shows. The bars usually offered a generous free lunch and some of them became favorite student resorts. The black belt had not yet completely engulfed this region.

Students and faculty became more easily acquainted than now, partly because there were not so many of either. Seminars and departmental clubs often met in the evening, usually with beer and smokes, and after the meeting might adjourn to the Fort Horn Cafe for an aftermath of beer and argument. We would then usually return to our offices in Schermerhorn and work till late hours. It was on such an occasion that a graduate student, too hilarious for academic effort, tried to slide down the long and curving stair rail in Schermerhorn Hall. He made the first curve but overcompensated in recovering his balance and plunged headlong down the stair-well. He landed first on the reconstructed horns of the dinosaur skeleton that was the pride of the geology department. His own principal injury was a broken leg. We knew of no doctor readily available at midnight on a Saturday, but through eloquent explanations managed to get him admitted to St.Luke's Hospital. The dinosaur, as it was later revealed, also suffered major lesions, but both patients were ultimately rehabilitated.

What is now the Eastern Psychological Association, with hundreds of members, was then a small group of psychologists from New York, Philadelphia, Princeton and NewHaven, meeting as a section of the N.Y. Academy of Science, often along with anthropologists and philosophers. After the evening program in a small room of the American Museum of Natural History, reached by street car on Amsterdam Avenue, this group likewise adjourned to a near by bar and held informal parties. I was made secretary-treasurer of the group, this being the only office that seemed necessary, and in this way became quickly acquainted with the elder members and was included in the parties.

These meetings were occasions not easily duplicated now. There around three or four tables in the "family parlor" of the bar, would often assemble a group containing such people as Franz Boas, W.P.Montague, F.J.E.Woodbridge, John Dewey, J.McK.Cattell, E.L. Thorndike, R.S.Woodworth, Clark Wissler, Howard C.Warren, Thomas McComas, H.D.Marsh, Alexander Goldenweiser, Robert Lowie, Henry Rutgers Marshall, perhaps Fernberger, Scripture, Judd, Wallin, and such younger men as Wells, Henmon, Brown, Woodrow, Eastman, Rejall, Hamilton, Lyon, Turner, Parmelee, Rowe, Bell, Pitkin. The tables were full and an hour passed quickly in animated and sometimes profound conversation.

A DISSERTATION DEVELOPS

During the course of these misguided experiments on active and passive movement, and certain others on free and blocked arm movements, I had been struck by certain "constant errors" made with great uniformity by my subjects. Small movements were likely to be made too long, when reproduced, and longer movements reproduced too small. A certain average movement would show no clear constant error of estimation. This fitted in with previous reports concerning the estimation of time intervals, for which there had been reported a certain interval (varying to be sure with different investigations) that was estimated without constant error.

But I noticed that my most "favorable" extent varied with the particular "series" with which I was working. Whatever the series or range of movements employed, the longer were underestimated and the shorter overestimated. A stretch that would in one series be subject to underestimation, would in another series, of greater magnitude, be overestimated. If I made it instead approximately the middle magnitude of a series or range, no constant error would be found.

Clearly enough the judgment of a magnitude appeared not to be solely a function of itself, but to some extent a function of the company it kept, of the context in which it appeared, of the series of magnitudes of which it was a member. And in any such series there was a tendency to mistake either extreme for the middle magnitude, that is, to make the longer movements too short and the shorter too long, so that all tended to be more nearly like the central value than was actually the case.

Varying my initial series in certain ways, as by extending it at the upper end, or by curtailing it at the lower end, or by gradually and unknown to the subject introducing larger and larger magnitudes, I could shift the "indifference" magnitude up and down the scale at my pleasure. I was discovering a general law of perception, which I christened "The Law of Central Tendency," or "The Central Tendency of Judgment." The exhibition and demonstration of this law became the core of my Ph. D. dissertation. I was able to show, moreover, that in the studies of the "time sense" and other topics such as memory the same law had been operating, although not hitherto noted and formulated.

Certain incidental topics were also reported in my first volume as an experimental psychologist. A new illusion, which I called the "illusion of impact" had been observed and this I was able to show had an important bearing on all studies in which movements were subject to investigation. I also investigated the role played by time perception in the judgment of extent of movement; further studied an already described illusion due to the degree of muscular contraction present at the beginning of a movement; made some observations on the effect of practise on an illusion, and on the memory for the extent of movements that had once been made.

This study appeared, under the title "The Inaccuracy of Movement," as No. 13 in the Archives of Psychology, and as No. 3, Vol. 17, of the Columbia Contributions to Philosophy and Psychology. In connection with that first research project there have been two experiences which have always seemed to me to be valuable, from the point of view of a student who is beginning research, probably in any field.

The first experience was connected with a visit to our laboratory by Professor Titchener of Cornell, commonly referred to as "The Dean" of American psychology. In my capacity as Assistant I had led him about the place, showing him whatever might interest him. Finally he politely asked me about the topic of my own research, and I took him into the room where my home-made apparatus was set up, and explained that I was studying the perception of the extent and duration of arm movements.

His response was discouraging in the extreme. That was all well and good, he said, but it had all been thoroughly explored already and it seemed unlikely that I should turn up anything of much interest. If I insisted on studying movement, why not follow up some curious observations of 'phantom movement' that had been reported in one of the German periodicals, instead of going on with this old Cattell-Fullerton apparatus, which I had adapted to some of my own problems? To a raw recruit it was at least disheartening to have his efforts thus disparaged right in the middle of their course.

The other experience was many years later, when Professor Koffka came to America, as one of the heralds of the new and vigorous gestalt psychology, which Titchener among others had been much interested in having introduced to American students. When he met me and learned my name, he beamed with joy. "Ah," said he. "So you are Hollingworth. You are one of my familiar names. For many, many years on the wall of my laboratory there has hung the graph of your experiments showing how the judgment of a magnitude is modified by the field or series in which that magnitude lies. That early experiment of yours is one of the corner stones of the gestalt psychology!" In due course appeared a survey by him, in the Psychological Bulletin, reciting my results, among others, and showing their significance when interpreted in the light of the newer formulations of principle. I have said that these two experiences seem to me valuable from the point of view of a beginning research student. All I mean by this is that even the Deans of science cannot always predict what is going to emerge out of an investigation, and that the student can well afford to think twice before he abandons some project of his own in which he has an intrinsic interest, for a small bite of some other project to which his major professor is already dedicated.

One of the wholesome things about the atmosphere at Columbia has always been the absence of dictatorship in research, or in systematic thinking about the field of psychology. Students were always encouraged there, and still are, to stand on their own feet, to find their own problems if they could, and to make the most of them, even if they appeared quite irrelevant to the current interests of the professors. No doubt some students flounder under such freedom, and such absence of supervision and minute direction; it is just possible that these are the ones who should flounder and that it was good for them to be detected at an early stage. At any rate there have always been enough survivors so that contributions of the Columbia laboratory to American psychology have been both impressive and substantial.

As for myself, my topic had by the end of the year 1907-08 developed to a point where enough data were on hand so that I prepared a preliminary report as a Master's Essay, in case I should for any reason have to leave Columbia at the end of that year. And the project so formulated itself that, if I should be there for another half year, I should have my dissertation in final shape, just a year and a half after matriculating in the department.

In case anyone with technical psychological interests should become occupied with this narrative, it may be well to point out here also that in connection with the main topics of this dissertation there appeared certain further suggestions that seem to me now to have been the beginning of a systematic view point. These subsequently expanded and became generalized into at least two of the three fundamental principles that have given my work in psychology a theoretical skeleton. There will be more to say about this systematic view point later on, but I must briefly indicate at this point *its* emergence in this earliest piece of my experimental work.

On the basis of my analysis of the experimental results I concluded that there is no one-to-one relationship between inner sensory data and the external events of which these are in perception the signs. For each feature of a movement, such as its duration, speed, extent, force, I concluded, specific cues are established through experience. "Movements are judged equal that have been <u>learned to be</u> equal," with no question of equality in the sensory patterns by which we know them. These may be equivalent, but not necessarily equal.

Furthermore, I realized, the sensory pattern is always a context , not an "elementary sensation". The correct judgment of our own movements involves the synthesis or comprehension,into a single pattern, of this context. Verdicts touched off by details not thus contextually checked are likely to be wrong. In psychophysics this leads to error; in perception it leads to illusion; in clinical behavior it is the picture of the neurosis.

Thus two significant principles emerge.One is the use of partial sensory details as signs for situations first experienced more completely.The other is the factor of scope,that is, openness to the total context of signs presented by a given situation. In both these there is emphasis on cue or symbol , and on context or pattern,insistence on a multiple-cue theory, and rejection of a one-to-one doctrine of perception .

Not only have these two principles received later elaboration in my own work. They are also, as others have recognized, basic to the newer formulations of gestalt psychology,in so far as that doctrine emphasises the importance of context (field) and repudiates the one-to-one theory (constancy hypothesis). But ## my own elaborations have, I believe, successfully escaped the demonology with which the gestalt psychology soon became infected.

FALSE LEADS TEMPT THE SCHOLAR

When the end of this university year approached, in May of 1908, I began to experience a certain restlessness, not unfamiliar to young men who have for two years been engaged and have had only occasional glimpses of the subject of their affection. During my service at Fremont, Leta Stetter had been teaching in my home town; the school there had added an eleventh grade by this time, but the general conditions of life were still as they have been portrayed in *Born in Nebraska*. Before this year was over I had left for New York, and meantime we had seen each other but infrequently.

During my first matriculated year at Columbia she was in a better location, as a teacher of subjects in which she had specialized, in the Mc Cook High School, this town being a thriving place not unlike Fremont. It had now been two years since we graduated together at the University, and nearly three years since we had determined to lead our lives together as soon as that could be accomplished. I wanted to be with her, preferably in New York so that we could build up some common memories of that place before leaving for Oskosh or Kalamazoo or elsewhere if some young Ph.D. should be needed.

For us to be married and start life in New York on the $41.66 per month which was my stipend as Assistant, plus such pickings as might accrue during the summer, was out of the question. The only alternative was to be with her elsewhere than in New York, by finding a position immediately, taking my Master's degree for the time being, and postponing further study until we could go on together. Leta Stetter also wanted to study, and probably to write; but as a heavily loaded High School teacher she was not able to make any headway toward this ambition.

I therefore became responsive to any opportunities that came along, and several showed their heads. There was a possible place in a normal school in Arizona; an opening for one year in a school in Indiana as substitute for the professor who was to be on leave; there was an invitation to apply for a place in one of the New York City training schools for teachers. None of these seemed quite to fill the bill, however, and after careful consideration of them all, and much correspondence between us, we decided to let these go and continue as we were for the time being if it must be. Pitiful enough were those recurrent bursts of hopefulness, uncertainty, and decision, always with defeated longing on the part of both of us.

Finally a brighter light appeared. Inquiry was made whether I would come back to the University of Nebraska as an instructor, to develop there the work in experimental psychology. We both agreed that in that place we could profitably continue our aims and work gradually toward the things we had in mind; we should be together; and we should have a living wage, although a modest one. Thus it was therefore arranged, and a confirmatory letter of appointment was received from the Chancellor. We were to begin in the following September.

In high glee we both began our preparations, and both relinquished the positions we were then holding, so far as the next year was to be concerned. I spent such extra dollars as I had for a few standard texts that I knew I should need for my work. We began to write to each other with zest concerning our impending marriage and our future life.

Suddenly, out of the clouds, came a telegram from the University recalling the appointment, with "letter to follow." The letter was a profound apology from the Chancellor, with genuine regrets, and with offers to make good such expense as I might have been put to in connection with my preparations for work there. At a meeting from which he had been absent because of illness the Regents had turned down his appointments; they had turned him down too, and a new Chancellor was to be found.

Thus crashed the first definite plan that we had made for the pitching of our tent together, and for the beginning of our "forty years" with each other. We hastily recalled our own resignations and clung to the posts we had previously occupied, claiming them, if it should be permitted, for the year to come. Fortunately in this we were not too late, but another year of separation now appeared to stare us in the face.

Our letters from those days disclose with what heavy hearts we turned to face this prospect. But we were jointly determined to see life in long stretches , and firmly resolved that however strong our longing to be together, that should not and must not be allowed to interfere with the struggle for other good things which, we insisted, must also be added unto us.

There were other like disappointments in connection with job finding then and later that need not be rehearsed in detail. Some of them, especially long remembered, involved simply being rejected in favor of some other candidate. It is of course but a silly pride that leads one to identify his successful rivals, to watch their subsequent careers intently, and to anticipate their ultimate mediocrity. But there is a petty pleasure of this sort, nevertheless, and I must confess to a morbid satisfaction in contemplating the miserable destinies of some who were thus favored, especially if my own qualifications seemed to have been carelessly regarded by the authorities.

Resentment at such carelessness by the Chancellor of the University of Kansas endured a long time. He invited me to make a 100 mile trip to interview him in a New York hotel, at a specified hour. Upon arrival at that time I was informed by the desk clerk that the gentleman in question had checked out several hours before, leaving no messages. When written to for an explanation the debonaire Chancellor blandly wrote that on the day previous to his appointment with me he had interviewed a satisfactory candidate, given him the appointment, and therefore found it unnecessary to await my visit. Not only was I happy to read of this Chancellor's subsequent death; some of the dislike spilled over, as emotions will, onto the person of the rival whose interview had been so persuasive. It was not a matter of indifference to me that he remained forever a non-entity in the field of psychology, although he may well have been in other respects a most estimable man. Thirty years after another rejection in favor of a rival candidate a shameless childish gratitude was experienced when a distinguished and in part responsible administrator, reminded of the episode, remarked that the authorities had at that time made a serious mistake.

Of course one endeavors to repudiate such paltry affronts to self esteem during his professional life. But one's memories are incomplete without them. Since those days, fortunately, the vocational prospects for aspiring psychologists have materially improved. It has even come to be the rule that young Ph.D.'s look with scorn upon many opportunities offered them, and are able to pick and choose to suit even the most capricious taste. But I have never wholly recovered from the insecurity attending my own early search for a job and have always experienced a certain distress at not being able to appoint all the available candidates for places in my own department when such openings occurred. From this distress I have sometimes been saved by the captious stipulations and expectations exhibited. There even seems to be today a growing attitude of indifference to opportunity which might be expressed by some such assertion as "The world owes me a living now that I have my Ph.D. and if your university or normal school job does not suit me the P.W.A. will always take care of me". In the days here written of there was no P.W.A., no social security budget, no old age pensions, and the world owed no one a living. Deplorable as it may now seem, this brutal fact appears to have colored heavily the greater part of my life, and given it an intensely private rather than a thinly social motivation.

GALLOPING OVER EUROPE

In all our disappointment we had overlooked one fact,- namely, that we were living in a Republican administration, one of those periods in which the industrious and the intelligent are favored over the shiftless, the improvident and the dull. Although we were not far from the panic of 1907, in the midst of which I had arrived in New York, things were looking up. A prosperous business man had an only son who did not seem then to be making effective adjustment to the difficult conditions of his motherless life. It seemed desirable for a young man with psychological insight to be found, to become his companion for the summer. The two were to seek new surroundings, preferably abroad, to thresh out together such intellectual and attitudinal problems as arose from time to time, and thus if possible achieve better adaptation.

Under the advice of Pearce Bailey, a distinguished neurologist, this lot fell to me. Preliminary contacts showed that we might get along well together and I was engaged for the summer. We were to travel in Europe, with expenses taken care of, and there was to be a wage that, if thriftily saved, would enable me to invite the girl of my choice to come to New York after we had come back in the autumn.

To get a little acquainted before going so far afield, we put up at a hotel in the city and did a little studying and a good deal of roaming through the parks, which were our laboratory. For we were studying "trees", and thanks to the Phi Beta Kappa requirements at Nebraska I had chosen as my Botany course with

Dr. Bessey the subject of "Woods", or as we preferred to call it (for L.A.S. joined me in this delightful course) Xylology. The young man and I found ourselves congenial to each other; he was bright, gentlemanly, serious minded, and had a good sense of humor. Shortly he expressed himself as ready to go to Europe (there had been some talk of an expedition westward into the cattle country instead) and our transportation was secured.

In the brief interval between the close of school and joining my young companion I managed to slip in a hasty trip back to Nebraska, to have a brief visit with my Chi Omega, and to say farewell to my 'folks' who were on the point of leaving Nebraska to take up residence on the Pacific coast, where they subsequently lived.

Sailing for Europe a little late in the summer, we had decided that the therapeutic plan would be to lead as extrovert a life as possible. We set out to see as much of the world as we could in the time at our disposal, and also to swim in the lakes, climb the mountains, survey the cathedrals, master the art museums, and learn something about European history as well.

We landed in England and made London our first long stop, studying English history and seeing the sights. Then we jumped the Channel for Holland, which we intended to survey on foot. We actually did walk from one city to the next, but there was dust, and the heat was discouraging, so that thereafter we rode.

FROM COCA-COLA TO CHEWING GUM

Vagabonding in Europe

From Holland we took a boat up the Rhine; we saw Cologne; we went farther up the river and over into Switzerland, where we found Zurich an ideal place for swimming, tennis, climbing and other extrovert activities. I also took occasion there to visit Dr. Carl Jung at his clinic, to inspect the laboratory at the University, and to purchase some interesting books by a man named Freud, which had recently come on the market and of which I had not yet heard much.

We saw Lucerne and Geneva; we went up into the mountains; we climbed the Jungfrau one night by moonlight, roped in between two guides and wearing ice-creepers. We went on down through Verona and into Venice and rode about in gondolas during a festival. Then we came back into France where we made our headquarters in Paris and did what everyone who goes to Paris with adequate resources wants to do. Then, the summer being spent, we returned home.

In subsequent years I saw a great deal of my young friend and was pleased to see the progress he made in his studies and in his adaptation to life. We sometimes went on shorter vacation trips together, or I visited him at his home on the Sound and we sailed or ice-scooted, depending on the weather. The following summer, in order again to replenish the exchequer, I went again with him to Europe. The summer after that five of us went together,- the friend, his father and aunt, my wife and I. But to bring these trips into the picture is to run ahead of the story.

These expeditions into Europe were as full of instructiveness to the naive prairie boy as they were of therapy for his companion. Particularly striking at that time was the stratification of society there as contrasted with the fluidity of our own social organization, especially in the West. This was illustrated by the bewilderment of a courier whom we had hired in Zurich to accompany us on trips and talk German. On the way to visit Carl Jung's clinic at the sanitarium just out of town we passed a house in course of construction. My attention was caught by certain details foreign to my own carpenter techniques, and I remarked on them. We paused for a moment to inspect the structure more closely.

The courier did not know what to make of this interest. "But how can you know of building work ?" he asked; "You are a student". Well, I am also a carpenter", I said; "at least I was for many years." "And how then are you now the student ?" was his response; "It could not be in our country." His high opinion of me seemed suddenly to slump.

When we arrived at the sanitarium the clinic was in session and Dr. Jung came to the door. I gave him my card and he invited me into the room. The courier and the young man were on the point of entering also when Jung turned to me and asked, "And are these gentlemen doctors ?##No?#" They will have to remain outside ." And so the still further bewildered courier returned to town, along with the young client. "It is very strange, that man", he said. "He is a carpenter. He is a student. He is also a doctor. I have lived here always and they do not admit me. I do not understand how it is in America."

Since when the summer began we could not know how it might turn out, Leta Stetter and I could lay no definite plans for our immediate future, and she had perforce to accept again a contract to continue teaching in her High School at Mc Cook. Public schools in Nebraska began even earlier than the date of our return, somewhat late in September. Some delay was therefore necessary, even after the accumulation of University wages and summer earnings had made our projected marriage feasible.

There had to be time for decent withdrawal from work already started, for a new teacher to be found to carry the work in the Mc Cook High School, to gather things together, bid farewell to family and friends, and get under way for New York City. In each of these there was unavoidable delay, so that when all had been taken care of we fixed upon Dec.31, the last day of 1908, as the date on which we should begin our life together,— no longer to be L.A.S. and H.L.H., but hereafter Mr. and Mrs. H.L.H., or, as it turned out in our professional writing, L.S.H. and H.L.H.

WE PITCH OUR TENT TOGETHER

A minor characteristic of our relationship had always been and was to the end of our companionship that we did not call each other by our first names. No one ever had called me "Harry" except my parents and teachers. To everyone else I was "Holly". This was true not only in our home town; it was the same in the Academy and at the University of Nebraska; it was true also at Fremont, at Columbia, and even my most dignified associates now call me thus. This was the name by which I was always known to Leta A. Stetter, both in our earlier contacts and throughout our married life.

Apparently because others did not call me by my first name, I have been indisposed to use theirs. At any rate I never learned to call my wife "Leta" except in referring to her when talking to others. Even then it was just as likely to be "Mrs.Holly", which was the name by which she was most commonly addressed by all our friends after our marriage.

In college she was most often called L.Stetter, this being a common way of addressing girls then on the campus. In little notes we often called each other L.A.S. and H.L.H.. but I soon fell into the habit of using for her a pet name which was all my own, and which is not to be used in these pages. For the present I shall use our initials and this will enable also the use of the third person, for a change.

While L.A.S. was arranging her affairs so that she could leave Nebraska and come to New York, where she was to live for the next thirty-one years, H.L.H. was busily engaged trying to find a suitable place for the two of them to live. This was far from easy, for the day of small apartments had not yet arrived in the city. Small apartments, or at least cheap apartments, could be found, but they were "cold water flats",- not tempting places in which to begin one's married life. For a long time it seemed that the only alternatives were either to take a place much larger than was needed, or else to take rooms in the apartment of some one else, and neither alternative had the right appeal.

At last a place was found. A brand new apartment house, walk-up style, with four room (more strictly roomlet) apartments, had just been finished on West 136th Street, near City College. This was nearly a mile from the Columbia campus, but the place was fresh and clean and it seemed that the walk up and down Amsterdam Avenue would be nothing to people just arrived from the great spaces, where miles scarcely counted.

A rear apartment in this building, on the second floor, was rented to be our first home. Enough second-hand furniture of a simple sort was secured to see us through the remainder of the academic year. Who knew where our next tent would be pitched ? Perhaps way out in Tempe, Arizona, from which place inquiries were already coming . By Dec.31 all was in readiness, even to an imposing mantle clock which J.Breitwieser had brought up to the apartment as a wedding present.

FROM COCA-COLA TO CHEWING GUM

All this was a third of a century ago but the memory of my naive struggles to find and equip this apartment on a few dollars still makes me smile whenever I review the arrangements. A pair of straight backed chairs and a matching settee, a little center table, along with a red rug bearing the green figure of a tiger, seemed to equip the sitting room. But I added a wooden rocking chair, encrusted with varnish. It was even then an old object but it is the one piece of this original furniture that I still own and cherish, now that the varnish has been scraped off.

It seemed to me that the bare dining room floor ought to be covered, and this was done by tacking down strips of reed matting over the whole expanse. I had once rented a bed room thus carpeted in my earlier days, and had liked it; but the dining table and chairs soon tore it to shreds.

A young woman clerk in a little Amsterdam Avenue hardware store showed me the minimum and cheapest essentials for the kitchen and a few dollars secured them. A bed, chair, and bureau, with an extra cot for the dining room, and a home made book case, completed our equipment. One day we found a ten dollar bill under a layer of newspaper in this bureau. But it was a fresh layer of paper and the source of the windfall we never discovered.

The only doors inside the apartment were to the bed room and bath. The sitting room, on a rear court, was entered by passing down a narrow hall, through kitchen and dining room. Since this apartment house still stands, someone is probably living there even now, with few of the privileges of privacy, using a communal dumb-waiter outside in the stair hall-way. Up that hard-worked dumb-waiter came all the ice and groceries, and down it went all the garbage and refuse, of the four apartments on our floor. There was also a community telephone, located in the basement in the janitor's rooms.

During the Christmas holidays H.L.H. was in Virginia on a therapeutic trip with his young friend, thus further replenishing the exchequer. And while L.S.A. rode eastward from Chicago, H.L.H. was rushing up from Norfolk so as to be at Albany in time to meet her train at that point and usher her into New York City.

December 31 of that year (1908) was on Thursday. Since Friday was New Years Day, Saturday also had been declared a holiday so far as municipal offices (such as the marriage license bureau) were concerned. And then came Sunday. We were therefore hard pressed, for on three days following the date of the expected arrival of L.A.S. no marriage license could be secured, this act requiring the presence of both parties.

The license clerk, when visited beforehand, had promised to keep the office open to the latest possible hour on December 31, and really seemed to sympathize with our difficulty. The train was met in due season, and there was L.A.S. on it. From the Grand Central station in New York we went direct to the license bureau and found the friendly clerk still waiting to serve us, although the hour was late.

H.L.H was supposed to have made arrangements with one Rev. Martin Walker, who had charge of a little Lutheran church not too far from the apartment, to perform the ceremony. All friends were out of the city for the holidays, and nothing but the legal minimum had been arranged by way of a ceremony. Bride and groom knew not a soul in the city and had no one to call upon for witnesses. They were counting on the pastor to provide these.

After finding an evening meal in an Amsterdam Avenue restaurant, the apartment was exhibited to the amazed and somewhat dubious L.A.S. who was as new to the arrangements for living provided for the citizens of the metropolis as the prospective groom had been on the night he first tried to find Columbia University.

At any rate, we decided, if other people can live in such little boxes, so can we, at least for the rest of the school year. We settled down to wait for time to go to the more or less similar dwelling of the Lutheran minister. Upon our arrival there we learned that the pastor was engaged in holding an evening prayer meeting, and would not be free until ten o'clock, some two hours behind our schedule. We were furthermore told that he had been engaged to marry us on the evening of Dec. 30, and this was the 31st.

The groom in his excitement had hastily run through the jingle verse that had hitherto been a sufficient guide, but had apparently made it-

        Thirty days hath December,
        April, June and November.

So we sat on a stone coping outside the church, hand in hand, and patiently waited for the prayer meeting to be dismissed. The Rev. Martin Walker was surprised enough to see us. He had assembled suitable witnesses the night before, but all had been disappointed. Tonight, at the late hour, he was not wholly ready for us.

But we had our license in hand, tomorrow was Sunday, and the next day was a holiday, and we wanted to go home man and wife. So two satisfactory witnesses were found who had not yet retired for the night. Except for a little awkwardness arising from the failure to know that Lutherans expected both bride and groom to have rings, and to exchange them, whereas this bride and groom had but a single ring between them, the ceremony went off without a hitch.

At last the longed for day had come. Leta Stetter and Harry Hollingworth were married. We had pitched our tent, alongside the waters of the Hudson, after three years of more or less patient waiting. The dream we had dreamed, on a tiny bridge over a little stream in North Lincoln in the early part of our Senior year, was fulfilled. We had crossed one of the "long stretches" we had foreseen, and we had not hesitated to recognize it for what it was. Our hoped for "forty years together" were at least beginning, and thereafter our two lives were to be as one.

I BECOME A DOCTOR OF PHILOSOPHY

The remainder of that academic year moved swiftly and smmothly. The dissertation had already been completed and was ready for press. A period of reading and review, in preparation for the final oral examination, in major and minors, as well as on the dissertation, followed.

In this period of review L.S.H. was a great help because of her ~~greater~~ familiarity with German. Certain sections of Ebbinghaus's volume it seemed desirable to read, but it was in German, which I read haltingly. So while I read on in such English references as seemed appropriate, L.S.H. wrote out translations of vital sections of the Ebbinghaus, which I could then more quickly master.

My main trouble in connection with the Ph.D. requirements turned out to be the languages (French and German) in which my preparation had been all too scant. The examination in German I had managed satisfactorily. Immediately upon arriving from the gallop over Europe I had repaired to the head of the French department and, fresh from daily reading of Paris newspapers, satisfied him. All this had been a good year before the date scheduled for my oral examination on the dissertation.

What was my dismay, a few weeks before this scheduled date, to be informed by the office of the Dean of the Graduate School that they had no records of my having passed these examinations. Since they had been duly filed by the examiners, they had been lost in the administrative office, and I had to make good for this blunder.

The German professor remembered me and in the most gentlemanly way sympathised with my difficulty and immediately signed a new certificate of proficiency. The French professor merely said "Ah, yes ? They have tried that story on me before!" And the old scoundrel, whose name I do not hesitate to record was Cohn, compelled me to face another examination, although I had read scarcely a word of French during the time since passing his first examination. Perhaps all this was just, but it made the language examination one of the incidents of this period of review that still stand out in my memory.

The oral examination itself I remember well enough. It was very different from the present examinations, which are on the dissertation topic alone. This examination, as was the custom then, covered the entire field of my major in Psychology, my minor in Philosophy and my minor in Education . Several representatives of each field were thereto quiz me, and I can still recall a number of the questions they were able to think up for my discomfiture. Still they were tolerant enough and clearly did not really expect me to know everything about everything.

A Japanese graduate student, Tsuru Arai, who was working on the topic of mental fatigue with Thorndike, had arranged to give me a one hour series of efficiency tests before I went into the examination room, and to repeat these when the examination, which lasted some three hours, was over. She was discouraged, or at least surprised, to find that the presumably fatiguing experience had improved (!) my efficiency in her tests. She was, I think, inclined to conclude that there is no such thing as mental fatigue. Perhaps not. But she had also to reckon with the fact that before the examination I was full of anxiousness, and after it stimulated with elation and wholly ready to give my exclusive attention to whatever might present itself. Furthermore, in my second trials at her tests, I had the advantage of previous practise in her first set of measurements.

On Commencement Day when the Ph.D. degree was to be conferred, we did not attend the exercises. Instead, we found Thaddeus L. Bolton who was for the time being in the city, and we three together, in memory of Tau Psi Xi, made a "spaziergang" through Harlem and spent the day in the Bronx Zoological Gardens.

The beautifully engraved diploma, all done in Latin and signed by the hand of the President of the University, as was still the quaint custom in American institutions of learning, was subsequently recovered from the Bursar's office. The recipient had just accepted an appointment as instructor in Psychology and Logic in Barnard College for the ensuing year.

We were man and wife; one of us was a Ph.D.; and there was a job in the offing. Practically on Commencement Day, as ever after, we celebrated our birthdays together. On May 25th, 1909, my wife was 23 and on the next day I was 29 years old.

PROFESSORIAL PERSONALITIES

Having been a teacher myself since the age of seventeen, I have had a special interest in the traits and attitudes of my own professors. On the whole my teachers have been disappointments, in spite of the fact that many of them have been distinguished exponents of the art of instruction. Being clearly conscious of my own pedagogical weaknesses, this judgment is not merely a captious verdict. Instead, it raises the whole educational issue of the function and qualification of educational leaders, an issue that may merit more honest discussion than it is likely to be accorded.

My teachers in the grades were women who made little impression. Some of them are forgotten and I can name only two of the four or five there must have been. The men, from later years, I can name, but only the high school principal in my last year (10th grade) exerted an enduring influence. Most of what he taught is lost and some of it was undoubtedly in error. But his manifest integrity, his grave poise, his enthusiasm for manly bearing, his effective physical health, his voice, his zealous encouragement of our meager musical talents, are still lively memories.

My college teachers, in undergraduate years, I scarcely came to know personally, nor did I expect to. For the most part their instruction was necessarily the routine drilling of large classes in the more elementary parts of their specialties. Most of the subjects I studied were intrinsically interesting and all that was required was that the instructor know his stuff. This they effectively did, and outside of class hours most of them were unknown and unobserved.

Some of them, however, exceeded the minimum requirement and I am grateful for the nuances of feeling revealed by F.A.Stuff, the robust heartiness of Charles Fordyce, the eagerness of Bell, the timid enthusiasms of Alway, the philological raptures of Fossler and Thompson, the benign nature lore of Bessey, the original epigrammatic quality of Ross, the sarcasm and hard polish of Ward, the dry ~~~~~~~~~~ humor and scholarly precision of Louise Pound, the deft athleticism of Clapp, the apparent erudition of Fling and Taylor, and the friendly encouragement of Harvey Cox, Robinson and Patterson.

Hinman and his critical insight introduced me to such inviting fields that in another volume a section is devoted to him. Bolton, finally, I really came to know, and this fellowship has continued through all the succeeding years, over a third of a century. We have remained friends and his early support of my aspirations has made me eternally indebted to him. We have enjoyed many pleasant social occasions, week ends, and trips. But we were from the beginning temperamentally in conflict and never managed to hold a sustained conversation on any serious topic. In deference to his early loyalty it has been necessary, though often trying, to suppress over evaluation of his attitudes and pronouncements. It has therefore been as a friend, not as a teacher, that his influence has endured.

My professors in the graduate school were not what I had expected them to be. Temperamentally each was unique, but their personal patterns lacked freedom and scope and the content of their lectures was seldom inspiring and often not instructive.

One of these had done original work as a young man and he made frequent reference to these ancient studies. In psychology he had done little since then but he had the prestige of being one of the earliest workers in his field. He was energetic, acid, crotchety; his disposition put him at odds with constituted authority and his academic life was terminated with a law suit. He gave most of his time to organizing societies, building up a publishing and printing business, establishing journals, and urging others to advance science. His activities as a politician in science and as an editor and publisher of directories and journals were a useful contribution to the general cause but they could have been accomplished equally well by a chemist or a congressman. He was therefore not a model for a young psychologist to emulate. A foreign born graduate student when the professor's name was mentioned said in surprise "But I have never heard of him! What is his book?" And there was none to be named. But he was a man of unique even if aggravating character; I like to think he was a good judge of men for it was the invitation to be his assistant that enabled me to leave the prairies of Nebraska to undertake my own graduate work. His students will cherish his memory as they do that of a character in a Dickens novel.

Another professor in my major field was versatile, judicious, modest and intellectually keen. When he wrote he was at his best and his fair evaluations of the work of others were admirable, as were the range of his own expertness, his originality, his wide acquaintance with the literature, and his aptitude of verbal expression. But he was strongly introverted, hesitant, made feeble social contacts and was a poor speaker. He was gorgetful and found it difficult to reach decisions even on trivial matters. I have seen him hesitating interminably when sorting a pile of stones into two sizes, because he could not decide whether the one he held in his hands was a small one or a large one. As much as I admired his knowledge and insight I did not get along comfortably with him and regretted the false impression of ineffectualness that his personality made on first acquaintance. Our relations were always tentative and reserved, although cordial enough, and I enjoyed him most not on the campus but when we were neighbors together in the country.

A third, among my major guides, was the most aggressive of all. His intellectual appetite was voracious, his capacity for work prodigious, and he was impulsive, restless, almost explosive. Even in occasional moments of play and social contact he was tense and strenuous, although he could be gay and was always likely to be the center of the group. He had marked originality and ingenuity and opened up many new fields, often in unexpected and dramatic ways. The cultivation of these fields he preferably left to his disciples, of whom he had many. So rapid were his own mental acts, so brusque and confident his own verdicts, that he seldom allowed others to finish a sentence; in its middle he nodded or shook his head with vigor as if to indicate that he knew beforehand what you would say and whether it was right or wrong. He was in many ways the most influential of my teachers in the general fields in which his work lay. Although a great admirer of his energy, his loyalties and his achievements, in all the years I knew him as teacher, neighbor and friend, we never carried on a conversation on any one topic for more than 60 seconds.

The professors in my minor fields were in some ways more satisfactory, perhaps only because I did not take them so seriously and expected less from them. None of them, however, did anything to quicken my initial lively interest in philosophy. These were the high days of pragmatism and empirical realism and leaders in these robust movements sooner or later joined the Columbia faculty. I attended the classes of two of these who were already better known to me through their publications than were any of my major professors.

One of them was a hearty, jovial person , with an admirable presence, a forthright delivery and a more or less jocular enthusiasm. Beyond occasional candid articles on consciousness and knowledge, and editorship of a journal , he left little record of his thought. He professed, in fact, a certain scorn for the very things he was doing. He had never taken the trouble to achieve a Ph.D. for himself although he was charged with responsibility for the dissertations of others. He would begin his class with the declaration that the reason he was teaching philosophy was that people paid him for doing it. Although this jesting tone was in time neglected his students remained with the conviction that their own philosophic interests were more genuine than those of the master.

Another philospher had a distinguished reputation and achieved a remarkable following of economic left wing groups and educational radicals. He wrote profusely and most of his ideas, even when striking, were garbed in a heavy burden of obscure sentences . In spite of the difficulty of understanding him he came closer ####### than any other American philosopher to the status of an idol. The very obscurity of his declarations seemed in fact to encourage this outcome, for enlightened ambiguities can be interpreted to fit almost any recalcitrant taste. I sat with diligence through several lecture courses given by this man and "ever more came out where in I went." He seldom faced the audience, but sat sidewise, looking out of the window and occasionally running his fingers through his long hair. Meanwhile he talked on, as if thinking aloud, with little or no concern for the presence of his auditors. I still wonder at the prestige of this man's words for the power behind them seemed ineffectual. The best explanation seems to be that at heart he sympathized with all rebels and malcontents and occasional clear expressions found in his writings, supported by some of his practical and social activities, gave the impression to others that his insight would provide the philosophic platform for any impending revolution.

If my major professors exerted any marked influence on my own scientific development it was chiefly at a distance and in extra-curricular ways. There was even a latent hostility in my reactions that I often discerned and sought to inhibit. I wonder if some such antagonism does not usually creep in between teacher and pupil, just as it so often does between parent and child, lender and borrower, between any benefactor and beneficiary.It seemed to me however to be due to the fact that the things overtly taught by my teachers were less satisfying than the spectacle of their individual activities as investigators and sometimes as scholars and writers. For nearly all that they taught , by way of general principles and viewpoints in psychology, turned out to be unconvincing and even unpalatable. In a way this was a virtue for it drove one to formulate objections and to try for a more constructive platform. I have liked occasionally to stop experimenting and think things over, trying to see in them whatever systematic relationships might be present. This called for verbal statement rather than a mere array of numbers and measures. For such enterprise my instructors happened to have little enthusiasm.

Another circumstance has had something to do with our relationships. I became a teacher in the institution that had trained me and given me my professional degree. My teachers became my colleagues while I was still an academic fledgling and I never quite lost the deference a pupil has for his masters. This obstructed the free give and take of argument so that often I resorted to inner negativism rather than to overt contradiction when we disagreed on policies or principles. This has had two results. It has prevented frank expression of opinion and intimate acquaintance, and it has given me a juvenile complex. Although now the academic senior of the three departments of psychology in our institution, I feel neither the prestige nor the responsibility that this aged status implies. Internally at least I still feel myself a stripling and a junior, not far removed from the boy I was when my revered and always friendly professors conducted my Ph.D. examination and appointed me to a minor position on the staff, along with them. So I have fully explored and experienced the heirarchy of the inner circle without ever genuinely acquiring its dignity. It is likely therefore that although my elementary students and undergraduate majors may have been satisfied with my teaching, the more advanced graduates and research students would probably give a more disparaging characterization of me than those just sketched of my own teachers. I can but hope that, like these latter, my own example of industry and scientific activity may weigh more heavily with them than the effect of my personal contacts and the impression of my more immediate instruction.

PART II
CRESCENDO
~~PULLING UP STREAM~~

PART II CRESCENDO

GASPING FOR BREATH

The account of my life reveals two dominating goads that prodded me on. To a considerable extent moreover these two goads interfered with each other. One was the goad of <u>poverty</u>, leading to the furious scramble for the wherewithal to eat, be decently clad, and to participate in life. The other was <u>intellectual hunger</u>, a craving for knowledge about the world and a desire to occupy myself with activities of a mental sort.

Except for the latter of these, I could comfortably have taken a job with the wholesale grocery firm, or gone into a local bank when opportunity offered. Except for the former, the economic want, the intellectual pursuit could have gone on freely enough. The great difficulty was in making intellectual activity contribute directly toward the relief of physical hunger as well as to that of spiritual thirst.

Both Leta Statter and I had renounced the life of the public school teacher and administrator on the ground that although by this route we might readily enough solve our immediate economic problem together, the drudgery and routine would surely thwart our impulses toward more intellectually creative things and might even, if we should have children, block the exercise of these impulses forever..

During the first months of our marriage, aside from the small savings from summer earnings, most of which were consumed in the initial act of getting married and setting up housekeeping, we had only the $41.66 a month, which was the stipend of the Assistant in Psychology. And we had also to defray the diploma fees and, worst of all, the printing costs of the Ph.D. dissertation. Even when the next academic year began and the new salary as Instructor in Psychology and Logic in Barnard College began to come in, this was but $83.33 monthly, for the salary was $1,000 a year.

These were our only resources; we had no assistance from our families, nor ever did or could have, and no one else to call on in case of emergency. To think of bringing children of ours into the world under these circumstances was wholly out of the question; if nothing else had done it, the misery of our own life long poverty would have deterred us. So that this issue was immediately disposed of. The problem of being able to continue to live ourselves still confronted us, and continued to do so for many years.

We had chosen one of the cheapest apartments to be found, and paid but $19 a month for it; later when we moved into a front apartment the rent was but $30. In these years my wife did all of the housework for us, including most of the laundry. Being also a good seamstress she made her own clothes, even to her winter coat and tailored suits, and trimmed her own hats. Some of my shirts, and general things like our bathrobes we came into possession of only through the work of her busy fingers.

The only actual record of living costs for us in those days is a weekly record kept for our own guidance over a period of six months from Oct. 1 1912 to the end of March 1913. This **was** during my fourth year as Instructor at Barnard College, by which time my salary had been advanced ~~to $1000 a year~~ to $1200, that is to say exactly $100 per month. This economic business has been so important a factor in my life that I shall here give a somewhat detailed analysis of our living costs during that six-month period and then consider what we could do to meet them on our university income. By this time my wife's sister had become an invalid and was living with us, so that we had to secure a larger apartment, nearer the university, at $40 a month.

Cost of Living, 6 Monthly Periods

1912-1913	Oct.	Nov.	Dec.	Jan.	Feb.	Mch.
Groceries	32.51	28.94	29.29	26.38	26.63	28.50
Meat	14.50	15.00	15.00	13.50	13.00	13.00
Laundry and Service	11.08	10.05	8.22	11.23	8.43	8.78
Rent and Telephone	40.10	40.25	40.55	40.20	40.00	40.00
Ice, Heat and Light	4.46	2.88	4.94	6.88	6.12	8.08
Outside Meals	9.00	10.45	16.30	9.80	10.45	8.40
Clothing	32.27	15.88	9.90	8.00	9.63	24.59
Entertainment Gifts, Amusements	.50	10.25	21.01	1.20	15.00	8.50
Stamps, Fare, Books, Drugs, Paper	9.75	4.75	7.60	6.00	9.00	6.00
House Furnishings	11.48	8.50	1.25	1.25	2.50	7.10
Dental and Medical	0	0	0	10.50	15.00	3.00
Monthly Totals	165.65	146.95	154.06	134.94	155.76	155.95

Inspection of this table of living costs in the fourth year of service at Barnard is instructive, and it explains many features of my subsequent development, as well as much of the character of my earlier professional activity. We were healthy, and at first there were no dental or medical expenses in this table. Later on, after the invalid sister had come, for whom we were fortunately able to care during the rest of her life and provide such medical and sanitarium attention as was needed, medical expenses began to feature.

Some months we managed to get along without any use of the telephone, as the table shows. Clothing for the two of us was kept close to $15 a month. As for house furnishings, it is clear that scarcely anything of this sort was attempted. We were still for the most part getting along with the second-hand things I had bought four years before. One month we got along on just half a dollar's worth of entertainment, amusement and gifts, but when the Christmas season came and our numerous relatives had to be remembered, the amount rose to the unprecedented height of $21.

We were gasping for breath, but we were pulling on upstream. In the brief breathing spells L.S.H. tried her hand at writing, and short stories were sent from time to time to the magazines, which did not seem to want the kind of story that she wanted to write. For her own pleasure she wrote verses from time to time. We much desired that she be able to go on with her own higher education, but where was the tuition to come from ?

FROM COCA-COLA TO CHEWING GUM

49a

MILBANK HALL, BARNARD COLLEGE

The Doors of Milbank

A single episode, related not to our personal privations but to our responsibility for others, will serve to illustrate the degradation into which our penury threw us. The sister of L.B.H. had come to live with us, having no other place to go, to recover if possible from pulmonary tuberculosis. Little was to be gained from sitting on the fire escape, wrapped in an old quilt, although this was her mode of life for a time. Finally we managed to get her to a sanitarium in the Catskills, but before long her malady proved fatal. We had in some way to meet her funeral expenses, the sanitarium expenses, and to take her body back to Nebraska for burial. No one was available to help us in this, and we had just no savings at that time. We finally managed it by arranging thirty days credit with the undertaker and getting my publisher to advance a few dollars on royalties which might accrue in the next six month period on the one book I had published by that time. Both the undertaker and the publisher kindly cooperated and we were able to get tickets and a single berth for the long trip back to Nebraska. Few people have ever been told of our misery during this predicament, but we never forgot it. If in spite of it we persevered in the life of scholarship this was a sign only of the firmness of our purposes.

We never lost our optimism, at least for any length of time. There were a few occasions during this first period when L.S.H. would unaccountably burst into tears. In those days she was never quite able to tell me why. Later on she said it was because she could not bear being strong and able, with a good mind and a sound education, and yet being so unable to contribute materially toward our welfare. This was only part of it, I know well enough. For now L.S.H. was "caught in a trap". This time the trap was not due to ignorance nor to misguided faith, but solely to poverty. She was as full as I of the urge toward intellectual endeavor, but for these five years she had been condemned to forms of housework which a ######### ###### woman could have done without any of her training. And it did not yet appear how soon, if ever, it was going to be her turn to get her feet on "the glory road."

When morning came the first one to awake would call out- "Come on ! Got to pull on our pants and get great !" and this was our mutual slogan for a long time thereafter. We had no special longing to be 'great' as such; what we meant was that only by becoming 'known' could we finally reach a place where the things we were both wanting for both of us could be realized.

It was still our joint belief that writing was to be the ultimate activity of L.S.H. But in our present circumstances there was no time to write, even if it had been felt that further study and instruction were not needed for this. The things she did write during these early years when we were gasping for breath are to me the most precious things she ever did, and my first zeal since her loss has been in getting these things on record so that her many friends can know and enjoy them. They are especially a volume of verse and a collection of stories.

As the foregoing budget table shows, then, my economic problem during these earlier years quite over-shadowed any professional problems that might have shown themselves. Only twice during this sample period, in my fourth year of teaching, did our frugal monthly expenses run under $150; usually they were around $155. And how was I to meet this minimum requirement, and also be prepared for such unforeseen emergencies as my life-long catastrophobia kept bringing into my fancy ? How could a man, on a salary of $83.33 to $100.00 monthly meet minimum living costs of $155 and still devote himself, as he desired and as was expected of him, to a life of research and scholarly endeavor ?

Although my appointment as instructor was only on an annual basis, with no assurance of tenure, I was lucky to get it, for so far as I can recall no other openings appeared and I had been seriously considering the possible necessity of going back to Nebraska to engage in public school work again, with carpentering in the summer. The position had just been vacated by H.H. Woodrow (whose middle name, curiously enough was Hollingsworth) upon his appointment to an assistant professorship elsewhere. He had been at Barnard as tutor, after having studied at Michigan, Princeton and taken his degree at Columbia.

In spite of the uncertainties of this job, it seemed to me to be a good gamble, even had other alternatives appeared. There had been a plan of bringing to Barnard a well established man as professor of psychology, and Knight Dunlap had been suggested in this connection. He was a prominent psychologist and was also an old friend of Montague, who was chief of the joint department of philosophy and psychology. Another man who had been suggested was Frank Freeman, since a well known psychologist and educator and now Dean of the School of Education in the University of California.

I continued to accept the re-appointment from year to year because students were increasing and there seemed every possibility that a permanent job there might develop if I could make good. It was therefore necessary to do successful teaching in my courses and to build up a following in the college and to establish favorable relations with my colleagues and the administration. Besides this it was necessary to do research and to publish my results so as to establish my own reputation as a "coming psychologist". And added to this was the necessity, just outlined, of in some way making money.

There is more to be said about the economics of the academic life in American universities than I have here expressed. I am not sure just what the conclusion is but it has something to do with lightening the burden and uncertainty of instructors who in later life are going to be able teachers and active scholars. Just how these individuals are to be identified is of course half of the problem. But once this is achieved the curve of increasing compensation should be definitely flattened out. It should be raised in the beginning to at least a living wage that will enable the young to express the faith that is in them. It could easily enough be dropped to below its maximum in the last ten perfunctory and arthritic years of service ,when most responsibilities have been met and a modest pension accumulated. Professors might be retired,at least the more somnolent ones, ten years earlier on half pay,the savings to be added to the pay of young appointess. There is even something to be said for breaking abruptly with the old folk-way of our economic life and paying a teacher his highest salary in his earliest years, requiring him to provide for his own pension. I expect little sympathy with this suggestion; however I should have been glad to have had my salary during the last ten years cut in half if a portion of this deprivation (say half of it !) could have been added to my initial years. The Dean of the graduate school in my day had a solution that satisfied him. He said that only those should be made instructors who had sufficient private income to enable them to live in comfort. That way surely lies aristocracy,-but not necessarily the aristocracy of intellect.

WHY I BECAME AN APPLIED PSYCHOLOGIST

Such odd jobs as came along were eagerly accepted. One of these, a terrible torture as it turned out, was proctoring for the examinations given to Columbia students in the big gymnasium. The proctors marched up and down the aisles, in their academic robes, eyeing the men, distributing question sheets and answer books, and guaranteeing honesty and orderliness. For this they received 50 cents an hour for the time spent. Although my arches troubled me a good deal, I marched and marched on every examination day that came along.

But the real solution was hit upon when I turned applied psychologist. I might as well say once and for all, to the undoubted amazement of my colleagues and professional associates, that I never had any genuine interest in applied psychology, in which field I have come to be known as one of the pioneers. It has been my sad fate to have established early in my career a reputation for interests that with me were only superficial. Often enough I have met a new person who promptly said, "Oh, yes. You are the author of ....",- naming with apparent enthusiasm one of my books of which I was the least proud.

My activity in the field of applied psychology was mere pot boiling activity, and now that it is over there is no reason why the truth should not be revealed. My real interest, now and always, has been in the purely theoretical and descriptive problems of my science, and the books, among the twenty I have written, of which I am proudest, are the more recent ones which no one reads. I became an applied psychologist in order to earn a living for myself and for my wife, and in order for her to be able to undertake advanced graduate training, for which she was just as eager as I had been.

The first step consisted in developing in extension teaching (for which additional stipend was paid to an instructor) courses in Applied Psychology. Business men became interested in these activities and in turn courses were organized for them in various parts of town. I spent many a night, after a full day in the laboratory, trudging down town to some hotel or to the Aldine Club, with my arms full of car cards or other collections of advertising copy, to give these series of talks to groups of men self-organized for this purpose.

The extension courses at Columbia were enlarged and increased in number. Many students came to them, and the instructor's pay was on a fee basis,- that is it depended on the number of students drawn to the course. In time New York University asked me to give similar courses there in the School of Business, and I did so. I even attended a Commencement Exercise at that university at which the Chancellor introduced me, hailed my appointment as a token of the friendliness of the two sister institutions, and asked me to give a speech. Here I was at one and the same time an Instructor in two institutions, repeating in one of them the courses I was giving in Extension in the other.

In time this duplicity, if such it was, came to the attention of the authorities at Columbia and I was asked to a conference with two of them, who shall go un-named. They told me they disapproved of my arrangement and asked why I was doing it. To which my simple reply was "To make a living." When it was suggested that the amount paid me by the "sister institution" might be added to my stipend for the Extension courses, if I would give them only in the one place, I readily agreed.

By the time this arrangement had been made I had already, in 1912, published a book on "Advertising and Selling", having first sold it for serial appearance in a business magazine. Royalties were coming in; I was earning as much from my Extension courses as I was being paid for my day time work at Barnard; there were consulting jobs that began to come my way, and "industrial investigations" were requested. Our monthly budget began to be taken care of, small savings began to accumulate, and L.S.H. enrolled in the Graduate School of Columbia University.

Except for the revenue resulting therefrom, I found all these activities distasteful. There were plenty of interesting theoretical questions I wanted to investigate and researches I should have liked to undertake. It was disagreeable in the extreme to spend my time trotting down to these business clubs, talking the most elementary kind of psychological lore, and illustrating it with car cards, trade marks, packages for cod-fish, and full page color spreads. But I did it all with such enthusiasm as I could muster. It went over well enough, and perhaps in all this I did my bit toward creating the boom that psychology in later years came to enjoy.

In connection with a recent review I took occasion to survey historically some of these activities in the psychology of advertising. Perhaps the story can be told as easily by simply incorporating that book review here, or at least that part of it which refers more especially to the history of my own work in that field.

PSYCHOLOGY OF ADVERTISING,- EARLY MEMORIES

Upon writing a review of a recent volume on the psychology of advertising for one of the technical journals,* old embers were fanned into flame.

Just a quarter century ago the reviewer's own book, now an antique, on that subject was published, after having first run serially in an advertising magazine. In these twenty-five years the psychology of advertising has developed into a substantial and accepted body of material. No field of applied psychology can point to a more consistent and cumulative growth, in which later steps confirmed and incorporated earlier findings, with a minimum of theoretical disputes.

Many of the incidents of this growth have not been recorded, just as perhaps a good half of the investigations conducted have never been published. The latter is a fact because they were often sponsored by business interests who found the results too valuable to be made immediately available to competitors who had assumed none of the initial expense. The former is true chiefly because few who have more recently written were in the arena when the game began.

Each of the earlier workers in this field could probably narrate interesting incidents of those days when applied psychologists were pariahs whom the anointed would scarcely tolerate in the temple, especially if these latter were not themselves psychologists. It required just these twenty-five years for applied psychologists to form a national order of their own, with their own sacraments and taboos. It would be interesting to collect the memories of these early adventures in business psychology and patch them together into a picture that could otherwise only be guessed at. Some historian should assemble such records before they oblivisce.

Twenty-five years ago there had been exhortations to make practical applications of psychology, and prophecies of what portentous outcomes might result. In education, which was considered a more or less sanctified field, real progress had been made, and in this dis-

---

* Psychological Bulletin, XXXV, 5, May, 1938

cussion I wish specifically to exclude educational psychology from any of the comments made. Applications outside the school were tacitly assumed to be unclean. Inquiries and appeals for help from salesmen, employees, manufacturers, lawyers, advertising men, were often either evaded by the seniors or at best referred to younger and more venturesome spirits in the laboratory, who had as yet no sanctity to preserve.

In the years just preceding the quarter century now closing Gale had reported in an inconspicuous way his pioneer experiments with advertisements. Scott had published a volume on advertising, in the title of which, at the publisher's insistence, the word "Theory" was substituted for the word "Psychology." Muensterberg had preached the "psychology of the market place," but the triviality of his experiments gave the wrong chroma to the topic.

In 1910 there was given in University Extension, then supervised by Teachers College in Columbia, what was perhaps the first regular course to be called "Applied Psychology" (outside the field of education) carrying university credit. It was a one semester course, offered by a man who had just received his Ph.D. and had been designated "tutor in psychology" in Barnard College. It was attended by five students and the instructor's "honorarium" was $75. Among other topics, each of which has since become a book, there were included three meetings devoted to "psychology in advertising."

The Advertising Men's League of New York City had recently organized to put their work on a respectable and professional basis, and they were conducting two lecture courses, on "English in Advertising" (Hotchkiss) and "Art in Advertising" (Parsons). Learning that somebody was to give three lectures on "Psychology in Advertising" at Columbia, they delegated a committee of three to attend and report on this dubious proceeding. The committee endured the lectures and the League requested that they be expanded into a series of ten and given to their members on their own premises. This was agreed to, with stipulations of coöperation and access to files, records, materials and campaign plans.

This series was given many times and to varied groups, at "Round Tables," in hotels, at the Aldine Club, and elsewhere. Interest was lively, and the program of investigation outlined was welcomed after a few preliminary samples, to the extent of raising funds to support a full time graduate research fellowship for the investigation of problems in the psychology of advertising. This fellowship fund was offered to Columbia University. It is worth recording that the Trustees of this institution refused these research funds, for this is a concrete illustration of the dread of industrial contact prevalent in educational circles at that date.

The idea of "sponsored" or "subsidized" research had not yet stifled individual initiative and made spontaneous effort appear trifling. Industrial provision of research funds and of personal stipends for investigations conducted by men also engaged in academic activity was definitely under suspicion. At this same time the writer, in publishing the report of his caffeine experiments, felt it necessary to introduce the volume with a justifying preface which now sounds abjectly apologetic. Nevertheless, at a subsequent meeting of the American Philosophical Association a Johns Hopkins professor whispered in scandalized breath to a philosopher from Columbia—"Did you know that Hollingworth received funds for his caffeine experiments?!!" Perhaps these early insinuations die hard. At any rate, in the quarter century since that time Judas has never been able to secure research subsidies from any source except the hard-headed business man.

Subsequently the Columbia trustees' blockade, wherever it was located, relented. The fellowship fund was accepted by the University and in similar overtures since that time there has always been cordial coöperation in ethically conceived plans for the business endowment of research. E. K. Strong, then or recently assistant in the Barnard laboratory, was appointed to the fellowship. His "Relative Merits of Advertisements" was a startling title in the sober *Archives of Psychology*. This fellowship was continued by larger organizations of advertising men with whom the pioneer League merged, and Strong under these auspices carried through extensive researches, which are well known to later workers in this field.

My own *Advertising and Selling*, embodying the course of lectures referred to, was published in 1913 by Appletons for the Advertising Men's League, which shared in the royalties so long as there were any. Its chapters had, during the previous year, appeared serially in "Judicious Advertising," a magazine for the trade, published by Lord and Thomas of Chicago.

In time the League's organized educational program, including a later course on "Economics in Advertising" (Tipper) was taken over bodily by the School of Business of New York University, and this was one of the steps in the development of its vigorous Division of Marketing. The "four horsemen," as they were then called (Tipper, Hotchkiss, Hollingworth and Parsons), were appointed lecturers and collaborated in the production of *Advertising, Its Principles and Practice* (1915), which attempted to put in a single volume all the aspects of advertising except the office details.

Local developments proceeded at such a pace that it would be tedious to chronicle them. My own work in this field was shortly limited to the extension courses in Columbia, where a course in vocational psychology was also developed, along with a more general course in applied psychology. Poffenberger entered the field and soon assumed entire responsibility for these developments; the work in advertising was then taken over by Nixon, with a more elaborate program in the School of Business. Franken carried on the psychology of advertising at New York University, and also took over certain consulting connections which I had engaged in up to the time of the War. The fellowship ceased and Strong's work was continued elsewhere.

Similar developments were in progress in other centers, and memories of these could profitably be recorded by those in touch with them or responsible for them. Scott's second book dared to use the word "Psychology" in the title. Starch, Adams, Kitson, Burtt, Poffenberger, and more recently a host of active and prolific younger men too numerous to list could all contribute memories of early adventures in the rather remarkable story of the development of a well-knit and substantially scientific chapter in the history of psychology. Some of these memories might antedate the events here sketched. A rather surprising group of psychologists have somewhere published a single paper in this field. The circumstances of this isolated act might be interesting. A few examples from memory are Brown, Dorcus, Knight, Laslett, Langfeld, Newhall, Thorndike, Yerkes, Warden. The submerged reports of investigations "not for publication" (there are at least 40 in my own files) would provide a mine of material if they could be excavated.

Actual developments took what was for some an unexpected and even an unwarranted turn. There seemed to be a feeling among the old masters, even those whose tolerance overlooked the practical character of the activities, that the youngsters were overstepping the bounds of propriety in presuming to instruct and correct advertising men in their practices. The writer, for one, was warned that psychologists could more profitably *use* the advertiser's materials as *illustrations* of psychological laws. "One could show how Weber's Law and the Curve of Forgetting are demonstrated in these practical things."

But for these youngsters the mere finding of lively examples wherewith to illustrate armchair lectures was trifling with an opportunity. The viewpoint and technique of the laboratory were carried over bodily into the print shop, the copy room, the studio, the factory, the consumer study, the sales and marketing program. Trade-marks, slogans, packages, headlines, copy, cuts, letter series, magazine dummies and car cards were dragged into the laboratory to replace the sacred lifted weights, series of grays, and nonsense syllables. The psychologist became an expert adviser rather than a mere camp follower and often found enough extracurricular activity and consultation to take the place of more scholarly diversions such as billiards and chess. Whatever the impropriety of such behavior, that is what gave the psychology of advertising a substantial foundation. Its observations stand and cumulatively grow while structuralism, organicism, anthroponomy and topology in turn flare up and expire.

The Economic Psychology Association was formed in these days, for the support of research in applied psychology by industry. In this organization the writer was psychological instigator, as well as being responsible for its dissolution. Experience in that connection induced an initial sceptical attitude toward the destiny of the Psychological Corporation, established years later with the same aims, but by an earlier scientific generation. The old guard have probably never quite understood the lukewarm enthusiasm of younger and actually active applied psychologists for paper organizations that do not embody the consecrated energy of some individual.

THE CAFFEINE INVESTIGATION

These activities in business psychology constituted a logical and psychological unit and there was a definite continuity in their development. But they by no means represented the only applied endeavors. During the second or third year at Barnard College an opportunity came, by somewhat devious channels, to combine applied and pure research in a most interesting way. This led to the "caffeine investigation" which, I have been told by others, has become a sort of experimental classic in the field of psychology.

A well known Company had been accused, under what was then I think called the Pure Food and Drug Act, not only of marketing a harmful beverage but of adding thereto "deleterious ingredients." The particular ingredient referred to was caffeine. The case was being tried with the aid of an imposing array of lawyers, and a still more impressive array of experts. On the side of the government, and under the general direction of Dr. Harvey Wiley, various specialists had conducted experiments, with guinea pigs, with rabbits, with chopped liver, and so on, calculated to show the damaging influence of caffeine. An equal number of specialists, retained by the Company, had matched these experiments or performed others.

In general command of the Company's experts was Dr. Hobart Hare, a distinguished pharmacologist and toxicologist. The specialists engaged represented many of the universities and medical schools of the country; their evidence had been assembled and was under review with the impending trial in mind. Dr. Hare at this point realized that they really had no direct experiments on the use of caffeine by intact human organisms, and proposed that a psychologist be retained to conduct investigations to discover whether human behavior was in any way measurably affected by the ingestion of this substance in such quantities as were contained in the soda-fountain drink.

As nearly as I can now recall the circumstances Dr. Hare approached Prof. Dickinson Miller, of Columbia University, who was a friend of his, and asked who should be requested to do such a piece of work. Miller suggested Prof. J. McKeen Cattell, head of the department of psychology, whose Assistant I had been in the early days. Who else was approached I do not know, but none of these wished to undertake such an exploit. Miller then suggested me, and Dr. Hare and I went into conference.

Here was a clear case where results of scientific importance might accrue to an investigation that would have to be financed by private interests. No experiments on such a scale as seemed necessary for conclusive results had ever been staged in the history of experimental psychology, and as I have shown in the foregoing section on advertising, to accept private business funds for the prosecution of research seemed to be considered by my colleagues a somewhat shady business.

With me there was a double motive at work. I needed money, and here was a chance to accept employment at work for which I had been trained, with not only the cost of the investigation met, but with a very satisfactory retaining fee and stipend for my own time and services. I believed I could conscientiously conduct such an investigation, without prejudice to the results, and secure information of a valuable scientific character as well as answer the practical questions raised by the sponsor of the study.

With some trepidation therefore, since older psychologists had adopted a policy of "hands off", I drew up a contract according to the terms of which I would be willing to undertake this study. The results were to be published, no matter what the nature of their outcome; no use of these results was to be made by the Company in its advertising; no mention in the publicity for the product was to be made of me or of the University; and the details as to periods covered by the work, financial arrangements and responsibilities, were all included.

The technique of the investigation has been what has given it its historical place among laboratory experiments in this field, especially the large number of control conditions introduced and the scale of its operation. But it seems to me that the most important thing about it historically was the way in which it set its face against the ethical taboos and brought industry and science together in a common enterprise. The sensed danger of this undertaking is so well expressed in the apologetic "Preface" to the volume reporting our results that it seems useful at this point to reprint that historical Preface.

PREFACE

In the spring of 1911 the writer was called on by the Coca-Cola Company, of Atlanta, Ga., for an opinion as to the influence of caffein on mental and motor processes. In the absence of adequate reliable data (see discussion of previous investigations) it seemed necessary to conduct a set of careful experiments before any opinion could be rendered with either fairness or certainty. Such an investigation was made possible by an appropriation by the Coca-Cola Company sufficient to cover all the expenses of the experiments. A later appropriation made possible the publication of this monograph, which presents in full the results of that investigation, a preliminary oral report of which was made by the writer in the U. S. Court at Chattanooga in March, 1911.

The writer is well aware of a popular tendency to discredit the results of investigations financed by commercial firms, especially if such concerns are likely to be either directly or indirectly interested in the outcome of the experiments. He is also aware of a similar human impulse at once to attribute interpretative bias to the investigator whose labors are supported and made possible by the financial aid of a business corporation, and hence do not represent a vicarious sacrifice of time and effort on his own part.

From the point of view of the immediate data any such bias can easily be avoided by having the measurements made and recorded by assistants who know neither the experimental conditions under which the records are being made nor the direction in which the facts may be pointing. If these data are then presented in full they may receive independent interpretation by any one who is inclined to take the pains to examine them. Such conditions were adhered to throughout the experiments to be reported here, and the immediate data are given in full. Thus in no case did any assistant know whether the measurement being made was a caffein record or a control record (see chapter on method), and separate tables are given which present all these records.

But the monograph would be relatively useless were no attempt made to interpret the data. The writer has therefore given the conclusions based on his own careful study of the records, and these conclusions are, to the best of his ability, free from all suggestion of prejudice or bias. While he was compensated for the time given to

(over)

PREFACE

the experiments themselves and to the preliminary oral report, the considerable labor involved in preparing the results for publication is entirely his own contribution, and was undertaken on his own initiative. The invitation to direct such an investigation provided opportunity for a most valuable addition to scientific knowledge of the effects of the substance specifically studied; for a careful examination into the value of various sorts of tests for the purposes of such study; and for the accumulation of a great mass of data on a variety of problems of intense psychological interest. To have refused this opportunity to make a useful contribution to knowledge, and to hesitate to interpret the results of the study, simply through fear of the suspicion of bias, would have been nothing less than an evasion of scientific duty.

In the light of these statements the reader must place his own estimate on the ability of the writer to free his interpretation of all suggestion of bias. The complete data are given. They have been compared from several points of view and by various methods of computation. The conditions of each experiment are explicitly stated. Conclusions can thus be checked up without difficulty by reference to the records themselves, or somewhat more inconveniently by a repetition of the experiments reported.

H. L. HOLLINGWORTH.

COLUMBIA UNIVERSITY.

THE TRIAL AT CHATTANOOGA

One of the most amusing notes to me now in this Preface is the ringing challenge at the end, in which those who distrust my conclusions are invited to repeat the experiments and find out for themselves. Actually to do this would be no small feat. A half dozen trained assistants were secured, including a physician. An apartment was rented for use as a laboratory, on the ground floor of a house where there was also a dining room, so that all the subjects could, if necessary, be served the same meals. Sixteen men and women subjects were hired, the men being university students, the women the wives of graduate students.

L.S.H. became Assistant Director and since the laboratory was in constant session during day time hours, she was in command alone while I was away about my college duties. Various experimental materials were secured and set up in the various rooms, and each day, for some six weeks, these subjects were given a schedule of doses in appropriately controlled ways, while their performance in various respects was being measured from hour to hour. The details of these experiments need not be rehearsed here, since in conformity with the terms of the contract the results were published. They appeared as No. 22 of the Archives of Psychology, a volume of 166 pages, published in April, 1912. This was the same year that "Advertising and Selling" was first published, and the two projects were running along simultaneously. It is little to be wondered at that H.L.H. began to develop tremors and twitches in his fingers and to lose weight.

At night another group of assistants, working on the daily records, (duplicated because of my catastrophobia) kept up with the course of things so that by the end of the experiment we were able to formulate our results in a preliminary way. These were dictated by me to D.E.Rice in long night sessions while the other men, especially Poffenberger, Strong and Dashiell, were drawing up the curves, and making charts.

For we were expected almost immediately to appear before the court at Chattanooga, there to report our findings and to consult with the lawyers for the defence and with the other experts. Both L.S.H. and H.L.H. attended the trial, taking with them all the apparatus, which was to be set up and demonstrated in the court room, before the Judge and a most dumbfounded jury.

On one side of the room sat the prosecuting attorneys and their experts, all present in person. On the other side sat the defendants, with attorneys and experts. Then the battle of scientific evidence began, and a most interesting and often amusing conflict it was. And how different were our carefully controlled experimental findings from much of the anecdotal and misguided testimony that appeared, on both sides.

One man reported that caffeine did this and that, and upon questioning admitted that the only evidence he had that it was caffeine he used was that "It said so on the bottle". Our own dosages had been bought on the open market, then independently analysed and identified by the department of Chemistry.

Another man reported that the drug produced congestion of the cerebral blood vessels in his rabbits, and when interrogated admitted that he had killed these creatures by hitting them over the head with a stick, and he had no control animals who had been thus killed but had no caffeine.

In our own experiments we had not only administered the doses in gelatine capsules ,interspersing caffeine doses with innocuous doses of sugar-of-milk , but we had also run squads for days at a time , giving them capsules daily, in varying sizes,but always containing nothing but the control dose.

Derelicts,on other grounds,were exhibited individually as evidence of the disastrous effects of using caffeine; they were easily matched by other individual exhibits,in rugged health, who had used the drug all their lives; and so on.

This was my first experience in appearing in court as an expert and submitting to cross examination. The examining attorneys in the front of the room received a constant flow of notes and memoranda from the experts seated behind them, suggesting queries and catch questions,and traps for the unwary.

It is probable that our results contributed little if anything toward the verdict, which was favorable to the Company, for we specifically admitted that our studies had reference solely to the immediate effects of small doses and that we had no evidence on matters that we had not directly investigated. At any rate everyone concerned appeared satisfied with our work.

The effects of caffeine were only a small part of the valuable material accumulated in this investigation. Actually there was a barrel of material available for answering other questions that could be raised, and many of my articles in the technical journals in the years immediately following were based on the data secured primarily in the study of the effect of the drug,but lending themselves equally well,when adequately analysed, to a variety of other problems.

I have always been glad that we took on this project, which in the beginning appeared to all concerned to be a somewhat dubious undertaking. It did yield results of scientific value and they have stood the test of time and of/repetition [such] as has been accorded them. It yielded, as already described, much valuable information in the form of records and measurements that could be used for the investigation of questions remote from those originally raised. It yielded me a reputation for work of that character and "repeat performances" dealing with other problems but by similar techniques will come to the front in their due place in this narrative. The investigation, and its report, did I believe its bit to break down some of the taboos then prevalent and to encourage cooperative investigation in which science provides the insight and technique and industry offers the problems and the means. Last, but far from least so far as L.S.H. and H.L.H. were concerned, it was one of the various things that cancelled the deficit appearing monthly in the table of "Living Costs" presented on an earlier page.

PROFESSIONAL ACTIVITIES

It must be borne in mind throughout this part of the narrative that during the five year period in which we might correctly be said to be gasping for breath, my main work was the instruction in Barnard College. There was a single departmentment of Philosophy and Psychology, of which W.P.Montague was chief. There was a required course for all students, one term psychology, one term logic. The other people in the department were professional philospphers; all of us taught sections in both terms, so that some of the students learned their psychology from the philospphers, and others learned their logic from a psychologist.

In addition I was responsible for the course in experimental psychology, which in the beginning had only a few students but quickly increased to 75, so that we had to have new rooms assigned and a student assistant designated to help me in the laboratory. The first person thus designated was E.K.Strong, who before long married Margaret Hart who had succeeded him in these duties.

As a third course one in advanced problems was given by me to a few students especially interested, and we began at once to conduct a series of minor studies, many of which before long were published in the journals, or were further developed by the students as their Master's Essays in the graduate school.

Ever since my initial appointment at Barnard College I have received the friendliest of encouragement from all the members of the faculty, from the administration, and especially from the most admirable and lovable of philosophers and chiefs,- William P. Montague, of whom there shall be more to say.

On consulting my chronological bibliography for those years, from 1909 to 1914, I find that I published five books and 30 articles in the journals. I was truly trying to "pull on my pants and get great". It may be instructive to see in brief what the nature of these studies was. Of three of the volumes, -"The Inaccuracy of Movement" (my Ph.D. thesis), "The Influence of Caffeine on Efficiency", and "Advertising and Selling", an account has already been given.

A fourth volume was "Outlines for Experimental Psychology" published to serve as the basis of the laboratory course. In this volume I for the first time began to take some systematic position in psychology; it was published in 1913. The movement that came to be known as 'Behaviorism' was getting under way and bitter disputes were being waged at professional meetings and in the journals between the 'introspectionists' and the behaviorists.

It seemed to me that there was justice on both sides. The importance of "conduct" as distinguished from "experience" was clear enough, and an 'applied psychologist' had to make much of this. At the same time it was clear to me that even the most subjective of experiences, such as a tooth-ache, or an after-image, exhibited what might well be called "behavior". Certainly such items, I argued, change with time, they respond to stimuli, they develop and retrogress. If visual-tactile objects such as guinea pigs exhibit "behavior", why not also algesic and affective objects, such as pains and regrets?

On this position I took my stand, and developed my courses accordingly. It was a position which I have since maintained, although in somewhat more sophisticated ways. The Experimental Manual began with topics listed under the heading "Externally Observable Behavior", passed next to items that were "Semi-Observable" and concluded with "Internally Observable Behavior." Thus the gap was bridged between the clamoring behaviorists and the sulking introspectionists, by showing that there was no gap between their respective phenomena, but only a continuum. Already, to those who know my work, this line of argument will have begun to have a familiar ring. The manual worked to my entire satisfaction as an aid to instruction, and only the rapid experimental and factual advances of the science in the quarter century since that day has made it out of date, so far as my own point of view is concerned.

The fifth volume also appeared in 1913, one of my favorites, "Experimental Studies in Judgment," which was No.29 in the Archives of Psychology. "Thinking" had been a topic of chief interest to me, perhaps because of the mixture of Logic and Psychology that my earlier training and my present teaching had presented. The earlier studies of "Judgment" had been chiefly introspective and logically analytic. I tried to put the behaviorist interest into this topic by inquiring, not into the <u>nature</u> of judgment, but into its <u>outcome</u>, and the way this outcome varied with numerous influences that could be experimentally introduced. I was especially interested in the influence of attitudinal factors, natural tendencies and habits, and the influence of instructions, and the way in which these operated along with peripheral or stimulus factors.

To some extent this interest grew from the "Law of Central Tendency" which I had earlier formulated, and called a "law of judgment". These experiments were repeated with new materials, so designed as to exclude so far as possible all <u>motor</u> contributions, and the law was again established. Using jokes and also abstract sales appeals various other problems of judgment had been studied, and some of these had been published among the 30 articles of those days. In this volume all these and certain new results from other investigations in the field, especially those dealing with <u>categories</u> and <u>direction</u> of judgment, were brought together. I have always been reasonably pleased with this volume on "Experimental Studies in Judgment", in part because topics were inquired into that opened up many new leads, later followed by myself or by others, but especially, perhaps, because it showed that even in the midst of my frantic activities as an applied psychologist I found the time and enthusiasm to carry on these studies of purely theoretical and more or less abstract character. In an advanced Seminar now in which the work of the department is surveyed, I find that I linger longest and most fondly over this monograph on <u>judgment</u>.

The strenuous life of these days resulted in periods of restless insomnia, in which curious formations were experienced that seemed to me to have psychological interest. L.S.H. and H.L.H. began joint records of their drowsiness experiences and the study of these records lead to one of the 1911 articles,— "The Psychology of Drowsiness." A further extension came in the article of the same year entitled "Vicarious Function of Irrelevant Imagery". This was the beginning of a general theory of the nature of thoughts and the process of thinking, which ultimately led to a volume on that subject, some years later.

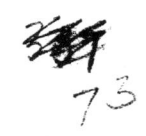

A non-experimental article on "The Obliviscence of the Disagreeable", really a literary rather than a very scientific effort, appeared as early as 1910, and this article was widely quoted in later studies of the affective factors in memory. Certainly two or three dozen investigations have since been made of such general conclusions as in that article had been lightly drawn on the basis of rather random results reported by other investigators and anecdotes and quotations collected from sources that had never dreamed of making contributions to science.

Except for a number of minor papers published here and there during those years, most of the other articles among the 30 are either partial reports of the caffeine study or represent the use of the data there gathered for the solution of other problems. Five of these dealt directly with the effects of caffeine. But using the caffeine records I was also able to make reports on " The Correlation of Abilities as Affected by Practise", on "Individual Differences as Influenced by Practise", and on "Variations in Efficiency During the Working Day." In later years I more than once went back to these carefully preserved records for data that would throw light on new topics, and many, many years later they were once more examined by E.L.Thorndike and made use of in his studies of adult learning.

Aside from the things thus enumerated, two other contributions from these early gasping years have continued to interest me, and also others who have followed them up more carefully. One of these is the article on "A New Experiment in Perception" in which the "law of the resting point" was formulated,—to the effect that in pictorial or plastic representation a moving object should be portrayed at a point of actual rest, in order to suggest motion, whereas if portrayed at a point of actual movement, it would suggest stilted arrest instead. There are many ramifications of this law, both practical and theoretical, and some of these I have followed up in later years, without ever having published the observations.

The other line of investigation had to do with the study of **recognition** memory, a topic that had clearly been neglected in favor of the myriad studies of **recall**. My students and I in those days conducted a series of studies of recognition, comparing it in various ways with recall, and these results were brought together in a paper entitled "Characteristic Differences between Recall and Recognition." One of these students further developed this topic in her Ph.D. dissertation, and others, especially E.K. Strong and Margaret (Hart) Strong, my earliest assistants became well known for their many contributions to this topic.

All in all, as I look back now upon those days and those achievements, I am quite satisfied with the record. For to have produced *in five years* five books and 30 articles, some of which at least have stood the test of time, was no mean job, while in the main wrestling with the $55 monthly deficit and also being "one of the pioneers" in the field of applied psychology.

PLATFORM ADVENTURES

Another somewhat exasperating feature of the gasping period here chronicled was my appearance in the role of more or less itinerant public lecturer. A good deal of interest had been aroused by the much heralded applications of the science of psychology to human affairs, and invitations to give addresses and speeches were frequent. I have no record at all of the considerable number of these opportunities that I siezed upon, these being chiefly those for which a modest honorarium was offered.

There were of course the more or less regular appearances before the clubs and round-tables of business men, and special lectures, or sometimes short series of talks, before the Institute of Arts and Sciences at the University. There were several salesman's conventions before which I appeared, with "pep talks" and "insights into human appeal and response". One of these that I now recall was before the salesmen of a large silk manufacturer; another was the annual get-together of all the sales force of a large publishing house. There were several trade associations and manufacturers' associations who were addressed. For several years I appeared regularly before the assembled employees of a large ####### public utility in the city, with psychological talks calculated to increase the efficiency and morale of the force.

I did not take to this sort of thing naturally, and never comfortably fitted into the receptions and entertainment provided for the visiting speaker by the program committees. If they had only forgotten me, left me immured in my hotel room until time for the banquet, and afterwards turned me loose, I could have been happier in my platform adventures.

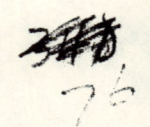

I acquired a certain stock set of little psychological tricks, "mind reading" demonstrations, and human nature stories which could be drawn on in the dull moments of these receptions and hospitalities, but was always a bit awkward and forced in my use of them. Since I never took kindly to formal dress, the frequent necessities of such apparel added to my discomfiture. I recall that a good many years later, on giving my presidential address before the American Psychological Association, I still suffered from these forms of misery. On that occasion I refused the prospect of talking for an hour in the choking wing collar then prescribed for the dinner jacket. I decided to strike an original note and wore instead my usual flat and lay-down collar, in which I could breathe and talk in comfort. But it was the only lay-down collar in the room, so that although nobody probably paid any attention to what I had on, I was throughout my address more or less conscious of my eccentricity. I was partially saved on this occasion by the knowledge that a close friend of mine, when he came to dress up for the banquet, found that he had forgotten to bring along his patent leather pumps. He saved his face by pulling on over his ordinary shoes his new and shiney rubbers; I had only to glance his way occasionally to get momentary relief from the embarassment of my flat collar. I am happy to note, moreover, that since that day or thereabouts flat collars with dinner coats have become quite the approved example of what the well dressed gentleman may wear.

Perhaps the most embarassing platform adventure I had in those days was before the Poor Richard Club, in Philadelphia.. This prosperous organization had invited me to address their annual banquet ~~of "America's foremost magazine-publishers,"~~ and I accepted the call. On the program with me #### were to be also Katherine B. Davis, then Commissioner of Correction of the City of New York, and William Jennings Bryan. They were formidable running mates, and I prepared the best possible talk, in a serious vein.

Reservations had been made for me in one of the most luxurious of the city's hotels. I arrived there and took mine ease until just time to dress for the banquet, which was to be held elsewhere in the city. What was my dismay, upon emptying out my suit case, to find that although my dinner coat and waistcoat and the terrible stiff shirt and choker collar were all on hand, the trousers had been forgotten. All I had with me ,aside from the upper half of the conventional speaker's uniform, was a pair of light gray pants, and these would never do. It was too late to do anything in the stores and the tailor shops were closed.

I finally arranged with ### one of the hotel waiters to borrow his pants,- several inches too long, to be sure, but still they were black and properly braided. Rolling them up at the bottom, and hitching my suspenders up to their limit, I decided that if I could just get into the banquet hall and behind the speaker's table , no one but me would be any the wiser, although I saw no way to eliminate my self-consciousness in the matter, even by applying psychology.

FROM COCA-COLA TO CHEWING GUM

If the speech had been a success, I might have forgotten all about this episode by this time. But even this consolation was to be denied. The banquet was held in an enormous ball room, and at each end was a vaudeville stage with performers cutting up throughout the meal. No sooner had these clowns disappeared, than, while the waiters were still rattling dishes, and the diners were still nibbling, half of them with their backs to the speaker's table, I was announced by the chairman for the first speech.

Giving my pants (temporarily mine) an extra hitch, I rose to my feet and began my didactic discussion of "Advertising and Progress",-this being the topic on which I had been asked to talk. It was a first class presentation of the theme, if I do say it, but no one paid any attention to my presence. No one even seemed to know that I was talking. Everyone continued to joke with his neighbor, the waiters continued to rattle the dishes, and all eyes were on the vaudeville stages, where it was apparently hoped another clown or strip-tease would appear.

In the balconies sat the wives and sweethearts of these revelling males, looking proudly down on the antics of their relatives, and paying no attention to the speaker's table . And why should they ? Even when I stood up I loomed no more conspicuously above the table than did William Jennings Bryan when he remained seated. Apparently no one even knew that I was on my feet, to say nothing of wondering whose pants those were I was wearing. I struggled on with sentence after sentence, making just no apparent impression on the din. Finally in despair I sat down abruptly, in the very middle of my speech, leaving Advertising and Progress to make their own way in the world. No one even knew I had stopped .

The Commissioner of Correction, being a lady, and the only one at the speaker's table, was accorded a certain respect when she was announced, and at least people began to turn their chairs around and to face the front. Dr. Davis, who sat alongside me, had whispered that the speech she had prepared had no place here, and that she was just going to "tell them some stories". This she did, mainly about Philadelphia politics, and by the time she was through the audience had quieted down to just about the level where it would be at all polite to introduce any speaker.

Thereupon the silver-tongued "orator of the Platte" was introduced, after we had done all the heavy barrage work for him,- although he was quite able to conduct his own barrage because of his picturesque stage presence, his far flung reputation as a speaker, and his sonorous tones. Every one of his references to "Old Glory" brought down the house, and I was a little ashamed, in the light of my own dismal failure, of having announced to him earlier in the evening that I also was born in Nebraska.

Just the same, when he was through, it was not easy to tell what it was he had said, and it seemed to me his remarks contrasted unfavorably enough with my sententious speech on the things that publicity has done for the march of civilization. I was not at all sorry that in the flambeaux parades in 1896 I had marched for McKinley, worn a McKinley button, and been a member of the "Republican Quartette".

But there was no denying that he was a better platform artist than I. The taste left in my mouth after this expedition to Philadelphia was unpleasant enough. It seemed to me to wise to avoid such public appearance so far as possible thereafter, so that instead I shortly began to accumulate material for an authoritatve book on "The Psychology of the Audience". And why not ?

LIFE IN THE CITY

Although we fitted ourselves as best we could into the life of New York City, we never took to it with full appreciation of whatever merits it may possess. It was on the whole more congenial to L.S.H. than to me, and she began to build up a small group of friends, many of whom she enjoyed for the rest of her life. She found great pleasure in the theatre, the opera, in concerts and other musical events, in spectator sports, in the Horse Show, when we could afford these things, and in the activities of literary and artistic people whose acquaintance she made.

But we were often hard pressed to insinuate these events into our schedule, even when we had incurred the expense of providing for them. We would relate with amusement, in later years, the story of the time we had carefully purchased good seats for a recital by Madame Melba, and one day discovered the tickets in my wallet and realized that the concert was already a week past,- we had been gasping for breath in the midst of one or another of our feverish projects.

For myself, I missed in the city the possibility of active exercise such as I had been accustomed to,-at the trade, at the University, at Fremont, and in the summers. Formal gym classes alone were available, except at week ends, and I much enjoyed the prowls and expeditions we could then make. But this was not enjoying the city,-to rejoice in leaving it!

Walks on park pavements were only exasperating. I tried gymnasium classes; tried solitary sprinting on Riverside Drive, much to the delight of small boys and others. I played handball with whomsoever might be available in the crowded gymnasium of Columbia, or with Gates in the somewhat cheerier courts at Teachers College; but this game proved hard on the arches. For some years we lived only a few doors from the Poffenbergers. This was a block from the faculty tennis court, alongside the president's house. We and the Poffenbergers often played there, but the court was in such demand that we had to get up before the milkman came in order to have priority. I chafed under the sedentary routine, loathed the jamming and crowding of fellow creatures in the subways and we both longed for the time to come when, for summers at least, we could have a place of our own in the country. It was not until eight years after our marriage that we finally achieved this.

In those days we first came to know Ed and Margaret Rice, with whom we became steadfast friends. Only Margaret and I are now left to review, when we occasionally meet, the early days when we lived across the street from them and they did many helpful things for us.

The two Montagues, William P. and Helen, we ran around with most of all in those days. They introduced us to the life of Greenwich village, to the Liberal Club, the Heretics, and similar groups that met here and there for dinners and for argument on social issues and causes. Helen Montague was interesting because of the determined way in which, although the mother of two children, she had persisted in her ambition to be a person in her own right, continued her medical studies and became an active practitioner in the fields of her choice. We both admired her for her courage and purposiveness and for her good cheer.

William P. was interesting to us for the same reasons that attract everybody to his whimsical and penetrating personality. Like the true philosopher that he is he "took all knowledge for his province". Everything and everybody he found interesting, and he had a particular penchant for "under dogs", for radical theories, for liberal and progressive movements. He aided and abetted his wife in her personal life plans and always took a venturesome hand in campaigns for any causes that seemed to him to have reason and justice on their side, even when to do so was dangerously unpopular.

Aside from enjoying his human charm, we found his insights and viewpoints and his range of scientific interests most stimulating. We counted it a rare privilege to have begun our professional apprenticeship in his department at Barnard College. I shall not undertake here to appraise the qualities of the most original and ingenious philosopher that America has produced, but wish only to record the deep satisfaction that L.S.H. and H.L.H. always felt to be numbered among his friends.

Often on Sundays or for whole week ends we would steal away with the Montague's, on foot, accompanied perhaps by Kasner the mathematician or some other crony of Monty's. We might walk along the Palisades, or find a New Jersey canal to follow, or make an excursion to Lake Hopatcong, or go up around Yonkers or Peekskill looking for agents with country places to sell cheap. Or we might just stay in town and play tennis on one of the clay courts maintained by private enterprise on some of the city's vacant lots. Both L.S.H. and Monty were especially fond of competitive games and of friendly sociability. Tennis and bridge filled the bill. Chess was easily available and it was one of Monty's favorite diversions. But another twenty-five years had to roll by before the Holly's found time to learn this beautiful game, to which they were thereafter devoted addicts, on a very humble level.

The aggregations of "rebels" in the dinner clubs of Greenwich Village were a new experience to both of the Nebraskans. We attended many of these with curiosity, and came to know in this way many such people as Henrietta Rodman, Rheta Childe Dorr, Florence Guy, Max Eastman, Henderson Deady, Adolph Elwin, Floyd Dell, Maurice Parmelee, Herman De Frem, J. George and Christine Frederick, Elizabeth Irwin, Katherine Anthony.

Occasionally we would particpate verbally in the debates, or present "issues" to the dinner clubs. We joined in the suffrage parades, along with the Montagues, John Dewey, and thousands more. L.S.H. was especially active in the movements calculated to give women greater professional and political freedom, and her earliest scientific investigations lay in the field of these interests.

On the whole we found that much of the talk at these places, though warmly motivated and kindly in intention, was likely to be "wild-eyed", and tended usually to overlook what we had both come to regard as the fundamental facts of individual differences. When Floyd Dell argued in the Liberal Club for the down-trodden bum, I would move, as a member of the audience, to include the much-abused and inarticulate dray horse on the list of beneficiaries. When "The Masses" was started with a great hurrah, I could not help, when opportunity offered, referring to it as "Them Asses". Perhaps this was a surprising attitude in one who had himself long known the goad of poverty and who had fainted by the roadside from hunger.

But any such surprise overlooks the fact that I had never complained of my lot. "Naked came I into the world" and I accepted the challenge to clothe myself with my own hands. All I ever wanted was a chance to earn my own way, and I never did acquire any sickly tolerance for those, no poorer than I, who felt that society owed them anything. Whatever may be the case in the present generation, at that date I had found that it was possible to achieve the life I most wanted, in due time at least, if I would only wait patiently and pay the price.

Perhaps it is wrong to expect such patience and such price from others. Perhaps there should be a machinery for finding every able and ambitious child and providing ample means to achieve, without anxiety, whatever good things he or she can attain. I am not here prescribing for social ills, but merely recording my recollections of what my own attitude has been.. It seems to me always to have been like the prayer of the tough old woodsman who found himself, unarmed, attacked by a ferocious bear. "Oh, Lord," he prayed. "I never done nothin' to make you want to help me. All I ask, Lord is, don't you do nothin' to help the bear ! And then Lord, if you want to see a good fight, just stick around !"

Of course, during those early years we learned more about New York City than we ever did in the years thereafter. We made frequent expeditions to all parts of the city,-East Side, West Side, Battery and Bronx, and for ourselves discovered Featherbed Lane. We ate at little red wine restaurants in the 40's and 50's, at Rector's, at Little Hungary, in China Town, at various cafes and hotels, and together we spent an evening investigating the goings on in the old Haymarket. We explored the museums and art galleries, rode on the ferries, visited West Point, and saw Coney Island.

Having agreed that there should be no children at least until we had both had a full chance to try out our personal interests and achieve a reasonable breathing spell, we were free to run about together with no domestic cares. The intimacies of our life and our close companionship in those days made for me the most beautiful thing I have ever known. I would gladly forfeit all our later years of professional achievement rather than lose the memory of the intense personal joy of those early years. Though gasping for breath, we were always together and completely "in with each other", with mutual faith and confidence, full of hope, and brimming over with energy. The tender relation we established in those days it was difficult to maintain in full depth when our separate professional careers came to pull us often in different directions, or to different places, or to entangle us separately with different groups of people.

Before the gasping period was wholly over we had a few visits from relatives in the West. Ruth's presence I have already referred to. My sister Gertrude came for a winter to stay with us and study music, and my folks paid us a brief visit, on a grand tour they were making just a few years before they both passed away.

FROM COCA-COLA TO CHEWING GUM

To the life in city apartments we never became reconciled, in spite of some of their labor-saving conveniences and coddling comforts. For several years we moved restlessly from one to another. Outside apartments gave all the noises of the city,—especially those of the garbage wagons, the street cars and trucks. Apartments on courts were likely to be dark, and exposed one to the even more offensive, because more personal, noises of close neighbors, who could often be heard even through the thin partitions.

For two or three years we continued to live uptown, on 136th Street. Then we moved closer to Columbia, to a fourth floor walk-up apartment on West 124th Street, and later to a cheap elevator apartment a few blocks farther down. In about 1914 we found a more comfortable place on West 118th Street, where we continued to live for ten or eleven years and during this period our summers were often spent in the city. When relative affluence came upon us with the inflation boom, we spread ourselves and moved into a large outside apartment on Morningside Drive. By this time we had built a place in the country for summer use, but we continued to hold this apartment and to occupy it with relative comfort until the Great Depression knocked the props out from under us and we moved to the country place as a year round home.

For me this was a welcome outcome for the country provided me with the sort of activity I craved, and gave me escape from the all too constant personal contacts of city life. But since L.S.H. had dug deeper roots in the city than I had, the change was not so convenient for her, and we had always to maintain a <u>pied a terre</u> in the city for occasional nights when she found it expedient or desirable to stay there.

With Father and Mother
on Columbia Campus.
Photo by L. S. H. who
appears as a Shadow.

OFF TO EUROPE AGAIN

In the summer of 1909, when our finances were still at their lowest ebb, I went to Europe again with my young friend. L.S.H. and I had spent a few weeks at Fort Defiance while waiting for his school to close, and we stayed at a near-by inn. In those days the simplest and cheapest plan was to change apartments each year, for since leases were not required for the apartments we patronized we could store our goods for four summer months for about the price of a month's rent. We decided that L.S.H. should stay for the summer at this hotel, where the Rice's, Breitwieser, and Henmon were also to be for certain periods, while they were assisting on Fort Defiance Hill. The food had not improved and this turned out to be in some ways a miserable summer for L.S.H. But she stuck it out until her man came back again in September, once more "bringing home the bacon."

This summer (or was it the next?) my young friend and I settled down in Zurich, which we had found congenial on our first trip. From there we made side-trips, such as to the Passion Play at Oberammergau, to Munich and to Dresden. But mostly we remained in Zurich, first at the comfortable Baur-au-Lac, then at a pension in the middle of a large park. The boy began systematic violin lessons, while I bought a guitar and instruction book and taught myself to get an elementary kind of pleasure out of this instrument. We also attended a Psychological Congress at Geneva, and I visited a bit with E.W. Scripture and his family, then living in Zurich.

CRESCENDO

On the Adriatic, 1910

87a

It was also on this trip, partly on the boat going over and partly at the hotel, that I dashed off the manuscript for "Advertising and Selling". It was truly "manuscript", all written with a lead pencil and on the most varied sorts of stationery. This is why some of the illustrations in that book are from foreign magazines and from a ship's news bulletin. It was for me a pleasant summer; we rowed much on the lake; played tennis in the park; took long walks in the woods; climbed hills. It was a less extrovert summer than the first one had been, but perhaps just as therapeutic for the young man and certainly less strain on the constitution of his companion. Just the same it was a great joy to get home to rescue L.S.H. from her ptomaine dangers.

In the second summer of our life together, in 1910, I went to Europe for the third time with my young charge. By this time Ruth, the youngest sister of L.S.H., whose health had failed, was found to require residence in a higher altitude. The Catskills were recommended and she was sent to Loomis Sanitarium, near Liberty, N.Y. Near by was the village of White Sulphur Springs, with a large and comfortable, well managed hotel, and cottages on the grounds.

One of these cottages was rented for the season and for the first few weeks of the summer we lived there together,- Ruth, L.S.H. and I. Then I had to go galloping over Europe again, and left the girls to their own devices. But they had arranged for company for most of the summer, and Mrs. Rice, two cousins of L.S.H., and also a McCook High School colleague, Martha Abel, were there in turn, or sometimes many together. This was a benign arrangement compared to that of the previous summer.

When the season was over and the wanderer returned with exchequer again replenished, he was met at the pier by L.S.H. Since we had, as usual, no apartment to go to, we were taken in by the Rice's who by this time had moved to a house in Brooklyn where Ed had become associated with Pratt Institute of Technology.

In 1911 another therapeutic European trip was contemplated, after which the young friend would apparently complete with good success his college course. But by this time we had become able to meet our monthly deficit, thanks to the bondage to applied psychology . We had resolved that never again, if we could help it, should we be separated for a summer.

So it was arranged that a party of five should go,- the young friend (whom we secretly called Pan, from the panoramic nature of our travels), his father and aunt, along with L.S.H. and myself. I was to be recompensed as usual and L.S.H. was to pay her own way with the proceeds. Nothing would accrue to the exchequer, but we would be together, and in Europe.

Again we made headquarters at the Baur au Lac, in Zurich, one of the most seductive hotels man ever made. "e had on the whole what I should call a fairly good time. But since all plans had to be adapted to the two quite elderly people, we came far from seeing Europe the way we wanted to,-just we two. We did however have the advantage of many luxurious side-trips that we should have never been able to finance by ourselves. But again we made a firm resolve. It was that our next trip to Europe must be entirely on our own, and in our own way. It was to be over fifteen years before we undertook to make this dream come true, but when it did we had a perfectly wonderful time.

In spite of the suggestions of tourist frivolity in the references to these trips, it is to be emphasized that their aim was primarily psychotherapeutic. The rehabilitation of my finances was wholly incidental and subordinate to the reconstruction of my companion's attitudes and outlook. The clinical picture was recessive and hebephrenic; the therapeutic goal was extravert activity and reorientation through frank confession, sympathetic discussion, and the promotion of insight. This was before the vogue of "deep analysis" and the cult of erotic symbolism. Perhaps it is well that this was so. The less bizarre procedures adopted brought effectual personal, academic and social adjustment on an enduring basis to a personality type with which conventional psychoanalysis makes little or no progress. Perhaps the early and successful experience with a mental pattern for which the current prognosis was wholly unfavorable was one of the things that inclined me to see only a poetic value in the Freudian webs that were to be spun in the literature and in the clinics in the succeeding quarter century. It would be in many ways valuable to put on record the details of this instructive initiation into the field of psychotherapy. Its lessons have been made use of frequently enough, both in practice and in theory, but there are purely personal reasons for not elaborating the record more fully. These considerations might in fact be construed as an important part of the ultimate therapeutic plan.

THE PROGRESS OF L.S.H.

During these first five years L.S.H. was not only trying her hand at writing short stories, when the cares of the household would give her a few moments of leisure. She was also able to begin graduate work, by taking here and there a course that seemed to appeal to her. One of the first of these was a course in German Poetry, by Rudolph Tombo. Since she was proficient in German and fond of poetry this course was enjoyable enough, but it did not appear to be leading in any special direction.

She decided to go in for serious work in Education and in Sociology. An endeavor was made to secure a scholarship or fellowship, on the basis of her academic record at Nebraska, which had been excellent, and favorable letters were written by all of her professors, as had earlier been the case with H.L.H. Similar also was the outcome. Since I have by this time had long experience myself in trying to select scholars and fellows from long lists of applicants, all of whom present a good appearance, I realize how inadequate and undiscriminating is our academic machinery for doing this. How often we pass by those with the inner spark and choose instead someone with only the outer trappings. I believe it is not too personal to record my memory that the man who, instead of me, received the fellowship at Columbia in the year of my graduation from Nebraska shortly abandoned his quest and spent his life raising apples in Montana.

We can now fairly well measure the ability level of our candidates, and to some degree appraise the quality of work they might do, *if they wish*. But we have no technique for diagnosing the validity and strength of wishes. Until that is possible, there will be

FROM COCA-COLA TO CHEWING GUM

Ruth and W.S.H.

91a

strong likelihood that our elected fellows will rest content with their first and easily won laurels, while the work of science is being done by those who were appointed their alternates.

At any rate, applied psychology came to the rescue, and enabled L.S.H. to pay her tuition charges, her diploma fees, and the expenses of printing a dissertation. She took first an M.A. degree in 1913, because it was still uncertain how long we might be in New York City. But she went straight forward with an experimental research, working chiefly with Thorndike, Giddings and Monroe. In 1916 at the end of this initial period of five years gasping for breath, she received the degree of Ph.D. from Columbia University. She was excused from the preliminary written examinations because of the quality of her work, and had to face only the oral examination, chiefly on the field in which her research topic lay.

L.S.H. had long been strongly interested in the social and educational barrier encountered by women, and especially by married women, who wanted to depart from the conventional domestic mode of life and exercise their gifts and talents in professional ways. Examining the literature concerning the achievement of women she had been impressed especially by the dogmatic and unsupported character of the statements there found. It was clear enough that the historical achievements, in the arts, sciences, and professions, were mainly accredited to men. But why?

Two dogmas cropped up constantly among the arm-chair observations about women (chiefly written by men) that, it seemed to L.S.H., could be put to experimental test. One was the handicap that women were supposed to suffer because of their menstrual rhythm. The other was the assertion that women as a species were less variable, among themselves, than were males. She immediately set about investigating these two dogmas by the techniques of the laboratory, and during the next few years numerous studies by her on these two topics appeared in the technical journals. A study of the first, which was her Ph.D. dissertation, appeared under the title "Functional Periodicity" as No. 69 of Teachers College Contributions to Education, in 1914

Already the caffeine investigation, of which it will be remembered she had been Assistant Director, and which she had known in all its details, had begun to bear scientific fruit. For the study of periodicity in women represented a direct carrying over to this question of the techniques elaborated in the drug experiment.

During the two years or so before receiving her Doctor's degree, she had been active in a part time position as a clinical psychologist, giving intelligence tests, which were then just coming into use, in the Clearing House for Mental Defectives, and later in Bellevue Hospital. She had begun this work as a temporary substitute during the absence of the first appointee. Shortly all of this work was put on a Civil Service basis and new jobs were created. L.S.H. took the civil service examinations, headed the list, and was the first psychologist appointed on this systematic basis to clinical work in New York City, or probably any where else.

An incident that occurred in the middle of her graduate career throws some light on the difficulties encountered in those days by married women in professional fields. An instructor in education was wanted in a New Jersey normal school and a woman would be considered. One of the most distinguished professors and executives at Teachers College suggested "Miss Leta Hollingworth" as a suitable candidate. Subsequently he discovered that she was a married woman, was in fact the wife of one of his former students, now a colleague in the university. He sought me out and apologized, expressing his great embarrassment at what he had done. "I did not know that she was your wife", he pleaded. There seemed to be no way to let the kindly gentleman know that far from being offended by his recommendation, we were grateful to him for it and that we considered marriage no necessary barrier to professional activity, even in the case of women.

Toward the end of the first five years at Barnard, she was gasping for breath as vigorously as her mate. For she was running our apartment, doing our housework, helping me ever and anon in some project in applied psychology, hastily travelling down town (our word for it was "pattering") to her duties as clinical psychologist for half of each day, and also carrying her load as a graduate student and candidate for the doctor's degree in Education and Sociology. All this with an ill sister on her hands, who required attention from time to time.

Upon receiving her Ph.D. degree L.S.H. had to choose between two opportunities that opened for her. One was a full time position as psychologist in the Psychiatric Division of Bellevue Hospital, where her work had been so favorably received that it was to be expanded. The other was an appointment at Teachers College, Columbia University, which, as at first conceived, would involve the principalship of a school for mental defectives of school age , but which shortly appeared more likely to involve teaching ,in connection with such topics as exceptional children, adolescence and mental adjustments.

I recall that she hesitated long between these alternatives, and frequently asked me to help her decide the matter. My own view was that the two things were so different in character that no outsider should contribute toward such a decision,-it should be made in terms of the individual's deeper interests, with the future always in mind. Just the same, I was mighty glad when at last she convinced herself that it was the University connection that she most wanted, in spite of her enthusiasm for the new field of work in which she had had such an effective pioneer hand.

Now that L.S.H. had chosen work that would conform to the same schedule as mine, the University calendar would determine our coming and going. We would have our vacations together, whereas under the Civil Service appointment there would have been for her but a short annual period of rest. Not that we were going to use our vacation periods resting, for this we almost never did. But we could be together, and that was what we had been struggling for ever since our Senior year in college. To be sure we had no certainty as to the future. Neither of our appointments carried any assurance of tenure, beyond the specific year of appointment. Had we known in those years how our fields of interest were going to develop and how rapidly the work in psychology and education at Columbia was going to expand, we should have had no uncertainties.

Even as it was we were quite content. For the time being the budget was breaking even, we had both received our professional training, and now there were two Ph.D.'s in our small family Now that the worst of the gasping was over, we could afford to take a deep breath and look about us. We were both deeply absorbed in the fundamental features of our respective occupations, and could now begin more calmly to follow up the lines of our chief enthusiasms. Perhaps by keeping on we might achieve worth while results, and permanent appointments. Who knew ? But we could by no means afford to 'let down' at this point. It was still as urgent as ever that we waken at an early hour, "pull on our pants and get great .

I have already sketched my own busy endeavors during this period to add to knowledge in the field of my specialty. L.S.H. was no less active. Even before the publication of her Ph.D. dissertation she had published several articles bearing on the general question of the achievement of women. In Oct.1913 appeared from her hand a paper on "The Frequency of Amentia as Related to Sex" in which she showed that the greater frequency of feeble minded men in institutions (long advanced as an argument for greater male variability) was matched by a greater frequency of feeble-minded women, outside such institutions. The difference was due only to different standards of "feebleness" in the two cases, and to greater solicitude if the individual should turn out to be a male.

During 1914 two articles on "Variability" appeared. One was a survey of the available data and a critical discussion of the fallacious conclusions that had been based on them, with suggestions for better explanations of the failure of women to get into the biographical dictionaries. The other was a joint paper with Helen Montague, in which it was shown that measurements of 1,000 infants at birth, in a great many physical and anatomical respects, disclosed no difference in variability in these respects as between the sexes.

Also in 1914 appeared an article on the economic and social relations of feeble-minded women, showing again, from analysis of the cases appearing in the clinic, that it was social devices and factors, not psychological differences, that underlay the dogma of greater male variability.

CRESCENDO

LSH at
417 West 118th St.

At this time L.S.H. also conceived a plan for a book that she hoped ultimately to write on the status of women in our social and economic life. She began to collect materials for this volume, and did so throughout the remaining years of her life, but never did find time to settle down to the writing of the book. It was to have been entitled "Mrs. Pilgrim's Progress".

She never did lose interest in the problem of the psychological, social and economic dilemma of women. "Mrs.Pilgrim's Progress" was mapped out as a life long project, to be completed in the leisure of retirement. But occasional articles continued to appear from her hand on the topic. In the same year that she contributed the chapter on "Vocational Aptitudes of Women" to "Vocational Psychology", appeared also an article in the American Journal of Sociology in which she discussed "Social Devices for Impelling Women to Bear and Rear Children", a topic not unrelated to her own decision to postpone procreation until other urges had been given their due opportunity.

Within another year four other articles were published dealing with the psychological characteristics of women. As late as 1927 she contributed to Current History Magazine an article on "The New Woman in the Making", and two years later she wrote for the Encyclopedia Brittanica the article on "Psychology of the Family."

But in the main, after her appointment to the staff of Teachers College, Columbia University, in 1916, the contributions of L.S.H. were on educational topics and their social bearings. Her bibliography, compiled after her death in 1939, listed six books and 85 articles, besides numerous reviews, summaries, and memoranda, reports and curriculum bulletins. In addition some two dozen monographs were published by graduate students working under her general sponsorship and guidance.

97

The "Biography of Leta S. Hollingworth" was published in 1943 by the University of Nebraska Press. In that volume chapters are given to the various projects and activities with which she was associated during her 23 years at Teachers College. Her publications in her chief fields of interest are also briefly reviewed there. A volume entitled "Education and the Individual" (In Honor of Leta S. Hollingworth) was published by Teachers College a year after her death, in connection with a Memorial Conference held at the University. In this volume chapters are given to the summary of her work in the chief fields of activity during her career at the college. Both these volumes contain her complete bibliography. Since these detailed accounts are now available and a full endeavor was made in the Biography to describe her life and work, her outstanding characteristics and interests, no further summary of her achievements need be undertaken in this volume.

THE AFTERMATH

The year 1914-15 represented an important upturn in our affairs. L.S.H. was launched in professional activity and was earning an income on her own. That year I was made assistant professor in Barnard College and my salary was nearly doubled. Since I still carried the Extension courses and had developed certain consulting connections with several business firms, we breathed more easily. In fact, we moved to an elevator apartment, with an extra bedroom, and engaged Francie, our first working housekeeper.

Francie was a slow and illiterate Porto Rican girl who spoke only pigeon English. But she was neat, clean and faithful, and knew how to make good things to eat if given time and due warning. She was also a fine laundress, but she could not do the marketing, plan the menu, or read the cook book. L.S.H. therefore retained numerous responsibilities in our home. Nevertheless Francie served us for the next eleven years, whereupon, for the time being at least, she retired to a farm in Porto Rico that she had bought with her savings, long before her employers were ready to retire.

The next two or three years were busy ones for me, in strictly professional ways. At Barnard, upon my advancement to a seat on the faculty, Montague generously recommended the formation of a separate department of psychology, and I was it. Students increased in number; I dropped my teaching of Logic and devoted full time to the department. We were given then the suite of six rooms in the main building (Brinckerhoff, but usually called Milbank since the main entrance was in that wing) which remained ever after the Psychological Laboratory.

In 1915 the "four horsemen" already referred to (Tipper, Hotchkiss, Parsons and myself) published our standard book on "Advertising, Its Principles and Practise." Tipper was an economist and practical business manager, Hotchkiss was a professor of English, Parsons was principal of a school of design, and I was the human nature expert. Between us we believed that we could tell everything then known about marketing by the printed word.

"Vocational guidance" and "employee selection" came into vogue and it was suggested vaguely that psychological tests of aptitude, interest and fitness might be put to good use. Hugo Muensterberg of Harvard had advocated such tests and had popularized the idea in magazine articles and in books for the general reader. Professor Bonser, at Teachers College, proposed that I offer there a course of lectures on these possibilities, in a summer session.

In the laboratory at Barnard we instituted experiments with such tests, and we studied interviews, letters of application, recommendations, self analysis of traits, judgments of photographs. In general we sought to appraise the current procedures of personnel selection, to improve them, and to introduce new techniques. Some of these results we published in the technical journals in 1915, and the next year appeared the book "Vocational Psychology". To this volume L.S.H. contributed a succinct and characteristic chapter on "The Vocational Aptitudes of Women."

This volume presented the material developed in the initial course in Teachers College and subsequently expanded into a more extensive course in Extension Teaching. The brief foray into the field of vocational psychology led to a number of interesting experiences. The manuscript of the book itself was declined by one publisher on the grounds that it was too critical and conservative. This was as a matter of fact my attitude toward these widely heralded new developments. I thought they should be carefully validated before being so loudly exploited. But such lack of faith was not always welcomed,- perhaps it was only my boyish "cynicism" cropping out again.

A conference of traction representatives, interested in the elimination of accidents from street car traffic, was called in the city. A physiologist, a popularizing psychologist and H.L.H were among the specialists invited to throw light on the topic. The physiologist (F.S.Lee) spoke of the possible importance of fatigue. I proposed a long-time investigation by empirical methods, in which men with known accident records were examined in a long array of tentative tests to learn whether perhaps some tests might discovered which would aid in selecting new men who were less accident prone. This proposal received only luke-warm interest.

Then Muensterberg arose, with his imposing stage presence and his quaint German accent." You do not need zee long investigation", he declared. "You need only go to zee qualified psychologist and he will give you zee tests!""In fact ", he continued," I have eet in my pockeet." Whereupon he produced a pack of cards bearing designs to be sorted into appropriate categories. When he later published a description of this test he announced instead that it was for the selection of ship captains.

But the point of the story is yet to come. Going down in the elevator after the meeting adjourned the typical comment heard was-"That's the boy. We don't want any of these long investigations. We want action." This satisfaction of the business man with thin results was one of the discouraging things about applied psychology. Two of the things of mine that have been most widely quoted around the world, and from which I still get echoes, were trivial and intended to be only suggestive. One was a tentative description of the mental characteristics of the average man . The other was a brief analysis, using 25 Barnard students, of the buying habits of their respective fathers and mothers. These tentative results have been widely quoted and important deliberations have hinged on them, but so far as I know they have never been extended nor even repeated. Certainly even if the results were of any wide meaning at the time they were secured, they need not be expected to apply a quarter century later. But I still get communications about "this important study" of the buying habits of men and women.

Walter Dill Scott was active in trying out and advocating the newer procedures in employee selection, and he was very successful in winning the cooperation of large industries in such try-outs. He came to New York on one occasion and I helped him stage an all day experiment in Schermerhorn Hall. Prospective salesmen were interviewed in relays by experienced sales managers and employment experts. On the interview basis they were ranked by each manager for probable success as salesmen. Tests arranged by Scott were also given, and all these results could be compared with one another, with the men's occupational history, and their subsequent production records.

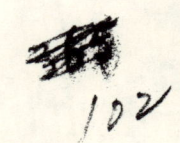

In 1916 I staged a somewhat similar demonstration before a large assembly of salesmen and managers in Detroit and a report of some of the results was published in Salesmanship Magazine.

An instructive incident occurred during the early Teachers College course on vocational tests. The two Fowler sisters, pracising phrenologists with an office on the Avenue, attended the lectures to see what was going on in competition with them. Unaware of their presence and of the fact that they were the daughters of the original Fowler of Fowler and Wells, famous American phrenologists, I soundly trounced the pseudo-science as nonsense.

One of the sisters departed, deeply offended. The other presented me with a handsome china phrenological bust which is still around the laboratory and she offered to pit her powers against ours in any scientific test we might devise. I jumped at this opportunity to convey an impressive lesson to my students. We had just measured a group of Barnard College girls in intelligence and musical ability, using such tests as were then available. Some of these girls appeared before the class; the phrenologist appraised their bumps and ranked them in order for the two traits. Then we removed a screen, disclosing our own rank order.

There was just a zero correlation, a chance relationship, between the sets of results and Miss Fowler promptly contended that this showed that ours were of no value. Perhaps she was right. Next we were to bring before the class, wearing a mask, a man whose characteristics would be well known to all when the mask was removed. The phrenologist was to give a complete "reading" of his traits and aptitudes, whereupon we were to remove the mask.

The victim was Prof. Walter Dill Scott, well known for his astute and practical business sense, and for his exceptional executive ability, and one of the leaders in the field of business psychology and personnel relations. He subsequently became chief of the personnel division during the World War and has now closed a long and conspicuously effective period of service as president of Northwestern University.

The phrenologist declared that the man before her, whose face she could not see, was financially irresponsible, a dreamer, with the artistic temperament, whose wife had to hold the purse strings, and who would never get the best of a bargain . These and other things she said about the canny Scott were so out of keeping with his acknowledged characteristics that the class roared with laughter. But Miss Fowler was not dismayed. She had been correct, she declared, and the man had simply missed his calling. Again we could not disprove her claim.

But once more the best point is to come. Before the summer was over a considerable number of the students in that course had visited the phrenological studio and paid $25 for a reading,- more than they had paid to attend my critical and obstructionist lectures ! Never again did I confer upon any pretender the prestige of trying to expose him before a class of students.

Aside from "Vocational Psychology" and the "Advertising" book my publications in 1915 and 1916 fell into two distinct groups. On the one hand were several articles on applications of psychology with special reference to advertising and vocational or employee selection. These represented no new advances but merely reflected the frequent requests coming in for addresses, papers, and consulting services.

But "pure science" was still being tentatively entertained. A paper on the "Logic of Intermediate Steps" appeared *in abstract* in the Journal of Philosophy in 1915, and in 1916 in the same Journal "The Psychophhsical Continuum" first appeared in print, after being read as a paper before the American Philosophical Association.

My ambivalent interests were still clearly in evidence and in those days I attended the meetings of the Philosophical Association as well as those of the Psychological Association. The last paper mentioned represented some of my last flounderings in the endeavor to establish some kind of rapport between my inner epistemological or metaphysical predelictions and my more overt psychological activities. The point of view there crudely enough formulated continued to infect my thinking, and , combined with later observations, developed into a systematic weltanschauung that for me at least has stood the test of time. But more of this may appear in due season.

By the end of 1916 my sadly dissociated intellectual personality had become noticeably trifurcated. Worse than Jekyll and Hyde, I was living three professional lives at once. Under the urge of necessity I was being a busy psychotechnician, with consulting connections with factories, agencies and stores. My professional duties and my real subjective drives kept me occupied with pure psychology, especially in its laboratory aspects. At the same time my earlier abstract and theoretical leanings kept cropping out and one third of the time I was acting like a half-baked philosopher.

Way back in Nebraska the doctrines of Bolton and Hinman had warred in me, always under the press of economic emergency. Ten years had now passed and I continued to present the same unstable picture,- a speculative system maker debating with an empirical scientist, both meanwhile harassed by the collector who demanded immediate payment of the laundry bill.

Reference to my bibliography shows that except for two books published jointly with Poffenberger in 1917, there was an empty gap of some three years before prolific contribution to the literature began again, in 1920. This hiatus was of course occasioned by the exigencies of the World War, which must come in for a section of its own.

The two joint-author books were lightly enough tossed off. One, "The Sense of Taste" had been requested by the editor of a series on "The Life of the Senses". Since Poffenberger and I were already collaborating on a "Text Book of Applied Psychology", we decided to take on "The Sense of Taste " also, more or less for the fun of the thing since neither of us had done any special work in the psychology of the senses.

FROM COCA-COLA TO CHEWING GUM

A Tri-furcated Personality

"The Sense of Taste" succumbed to a perhaps well-deserved fate. It was soon forgotten and the publisher went out of business, although neither of these events had any direct influence on the other. The "Applied Psychology" on the other hand met with a kind enough reception, since it was the first book of its kind. It was enlarged after three years, and after a similar period again enlarged and revised. By that time I had wholly worked myself out of applied psychology and Poffenberger alone assumed responsibility for its subsequent honorable career.

LABORS OF A PSYCHO-TECHNICIAN

Once I had become known as engaged in the solution of practical psychological problems, it was most astonishing to see the number and variety of requests for such services. I have an old collection of such requests, from the earlier days, that is by no means complete, but it illustrates the versatility and nimbleness expected of workers in psychotechnology. The nature of these requests may be shown by citing a few of these examples.

Of course many of these are requests for help in problems of personal adjustment, the problems ranging all the way from how to remove hair on the face, or how to prevent blushing, to desires to be given intelligence tests, aptitude measurements, or to be guided in the choice of a school or a job. This is the field in which applied psychology in its modern form has experienced the most rapid and useful development. But the requests range still further afield.

One man wants to know how to become reconciled to the peculiarities of his wife; another wants to know how to overcome stage fright; another suffers from a chronic fear; another wishes to be cured of stuttering; a federal department wants advice on how to interview farmers; a newspaper wants an explanation of contagious yawning; a teacher desires aid in correcting mirror writing; a perfume manufacturer wants psycho-galvanic studies of the effect of his products; a silk manufacturer wants studies of the appeal of his fabrics; an evening newspaper wants to support its advertising columns by evidence that suggestibility is greater in the the late hours of the day.

A famous railroad wants advice and perhaps experiments to guide it in deciding what color to paint its box cars; a city planning commission requires data on the legibility of traffic signs; a manual trainer wants to know the psychological height for work benches; a maker of rosaries wants to know how to link up his product with jewelry so that jewellers will stock up on rosaries as well as diamonds; an advertiser wants to know where on the page his return coupon should appear; several people want to know what differences in buying habits men and women exhibit; more than one request concerns the question whether appeal to the eye is or is not better than appeal to the ear; another correspondent wants to know why he cannot spell; a copy writer wants his advertisements criticised; a business firm wants tests made to determine whether or not a competing product uses an infringing trade-mark; a club director wants to know how to pick the prospective leaders among his boys; a statistical organization wants studies made of the most effective way of graphically presenting data; a rubber company wants tests for the better selection of clerks and other employees; so also does a large department store.

Somebody wants to have measured the relative value of moving and stationary window displays; a type foundry wants studies of the legibility of different type faces; a paper company wants to know how the color of paper influences the legibility of print or writing on its products; another firm wants to know what the effects may be of different kinds of music; coffee roasters need to have studies of the effects of various methods of brewing their favorite drink; a lawyer wants a client examined for his mental responsibility, the psychologist to take the stand in his defence; a manufacturer wants comparative studies made of the pulling power of various women's magazines.

To continue just a bit further, a child health organization asks for recommendations concerning the best incentives to feature in their work; a sales managers' group wants a demonstration of the new tests for selecting salesmen; a doctor wants help in the management of a functional blepharospasm; numerous clubs want some one to give them a speech; assorted papers and journals would like to have a popular article on this and that; and one enterprising public relations counsel offers me 2.5 % commission on any business that I am able to secure for him.

This, be it remembered, is not an exhaustive list, but only an array of random samples of hundreds of requests that poured in upon the young assistant professor of psychology who was doing his best, meanwhile, to advance the knowledge of human nature and to instruct the American Philosophical Association concerning the "Logic of Intermediate Steps" and the "Psycho-physical Continuum."

Buried in one of my files are some forty reports of more or less detailed investigations, "not intended for publication", made in my capacity as consultant for manufacturers and agencies. They are all dated between Jan.1914 and Dec.1917. They have to do for the most part with consumer-studies and marketing problems. There are tests for the name, the package, and the slogan, for a new breakfast drink; a series of studies of the most effective appeals for food products; comparisons of colored advertisements with black-and-white pages; reports on attention and distraction; on trademarks; on the value of small and large space; and so on.

It will surely reveal no trade secrets if I list a few of the familiar names of products or commodities in the interest of which these studies were made. Among these were such as Jaffee, Jonteel, Beech-Nut products, Shaw Walker Filing Cabinets, Bullard Lathes, Klever Kraft table ware, Tokyo Bond paper, Savage Arms, Auto-strop Safety Razor, Virtuola Player Piano, Ladies World, Dictaphone, Ediphone, Postal Life Insurance. These studies were made sometimes for the companies themselves, sometimes for one or another advertising agency that had or wished to secure the account, sometimes simply for free lances who wanted to do something startling and new and thus land a soft berth somewhere.

It was into such activities, in part, that our gasping period led us. These studies never succeeded in throwing much new light on human nature. Sometimes they did demonstrably increase the business of their sponsors; more often no one ever knew whether they did or not. But it was with a great personal relief that, when I was called on for war services, it was possible to turn all these consulting and consumer-study services over to Franken, a former student who had also succeeded to my courses in New York University. Although it was not widely known at the time, the main purpose of the World War was to put an end to my activities as an applied psychologist.

It may be in place here to balance this somewhat dreary portrayal of academic penury with the rosier picture of ensuing years. It would be too bad if this financial recital should have the effect of driving prospective ambitious scholars into other fields. It is still possible in American universities for a young and untried instructor to secure comfort and security for his family and still lead a fairly decent scholarly life. All that is necessary to this end is that he be willing to prostitute some share of his energy and his wits to technological activities that may not at the time be wholly congenial.

In the present case the severe measures taken in the earlier years to balance the budget were effective enough, so far as bookkeeping is concerned. They continued, moreover, to yield returns long after the original emergency had passed. There is in the files a joint income record, running from 1909 to a quarter century later. Perhaps a reproduction of this curve of prosperity in relative terms rather than in actual dollars and cents will serve the present purpose; such a graph is here presented.

When the annual figures for the twenty five years are graphed the regression line of income on years is direct and linear. Ten years after the date of beginning the original annual income figure had been multiplied by 10; after a quarter century it had been multiplied by 25. Thereafter there were numerous vicissitudes and little evidence of a definite trend. Sometimes, indeed, annual income was wholly cancelled by capital losses. Sometimes there were appreciable capital gains. But on the whole the curve need not discourage any one from undertaking the academic life without patrimony.

CRESCENDO

110B

A Forgotten Page in Applied Psychology

In the middle nineteen-forties, when some of these sections are being written, applied psychology is rampant. A national organization in this field has practically taken over the august American Psychological Association as a minor sub-division. It is electing to office dapper young clinicians and statisticians quite unknown to the old guard. A vigorous Psychological Corporation, with annual business of a million dollars, employs an astonishingly large group of experts and assistants, some of them drawing stipends hitherto known only to college presidents. Thriving lay organizations in the fields of personnel and management, opinion survey and market investigation, tempt young Ph.D.'s in psychology with an economic status they could not hope to achieve in years of academic service.

Safely by-passed by this maelstrom of technology I can now view it with comparative tolerance because of certain symptomatic developments in which I had a hand some thirty years ago, back in 1916 or thereabouts. I refer to The Economic Psychology Association and to The Morningside Press. Most present day psychologists never heard of these activities and most of those who knew about them are gone. It may be of some interest to record here these forgotten episodes as part of the early history of psychology in America.

The Economic Psychology Association was really energized by two business men who had been active members of the extra-mural classes already reviewed in earlier sections dealing with my outside #### lectures and researches in applied psychology. One of these men was a vigorous business engineer, interested in problems of organization, management, marketing, business efficiency, salesmanship and advertising. He had experience as an editor and writer, as a business counsellor, and one of his chief interests was the human factor in business. The other man was a lively young salesman and an ambitious promoter, full of enterprise and thoroughly on the make.

Both of these men saw large commercial possibilities in the organized use of the things that came up in connection with our round-tables and lecture courses. They were confident that if I would come in with them to provide the scientific methods and research they could persuade business firms to contribute funds to underwrite the cooperation of science and industry in unprecedented ways. So we three established the Economic Psychology Association; one of us president, one treasurer, and the young promoter as executive secretary. The executive secretary was to do the work while we lent him our moral support, business contacts, and scientific ammunition.

Circulars were printed outlining our aims, citing examples, indicating future activities. Firms were invited to become sustaining members on payment of $100, and scientists paying $5 could become associates. A symposium on the human factor in industry was organized and brought together a gratifying number of business leaders. A half dozen firms and a dozen individuals sent in their checks. More circulars were printed; the executive secretary gaveup what he said was a $3,000 job to devote his whole time to solicitation and publicity. He drew up and submitted, to an impressive list of directors who had allowed us to use their names on our letter heads, a budget for the year, in which first of all he was to receive $3,000 and expenses. After that the purposes of the organization would come in for such support as might be available.

I tried to dampen this ardor by insisting that we first do some research on "the human factor" and let individual salaries come later, if at all. Only in this way could we keep faith with our membership and avoid becoming a mere exploiting organization. I cut off the supply of data and ideas that had been the promoter's chief ammunition up to that time. He sent to other universities asking to be provided with their master's and doctor's dissertations in applied psychology, but received only luke-warm cooperation.

Soon criticisms came in from others. Muensterberg, who had agreed to be an honorary vice-president, wrote objecting to the proposed budget. Angell wrote from Chicago questioning the propriety of the whole enterprise. Willetts, of the Wharton School, complained that he had been misled and exploited. It seemed evident that an Economic Psychology Association managed by live wire salesmen would be of doubtful credit to the science. So I resigned from the board of directors and sent copies of the letter stating my reasons to the other directors, who in turn also promptly resigned. Thus ended The Economic Psychology Association.

Poffenberger and I founded The Morningside Press as a name under which to print and sell test blanks and outlines or manuals, for which Columbia had come to be a well known source. We believed that the few commercial firms handling tests and manuals were profiteering on them and that such materials could be provided more cheaply, to the general advantage. We circularized a few psychologists to this effect. Prompt reactions came only from the chief commercial firm then handling test materials and from individuals more or less directly connected therewith. They were bitterly enraged at our assertions and resented our prospective activities. These letters have been preserved for a thirty year period and it is amusing to read them now that there are dozens of concerns engaged in the printing and sale of the things we intended to handle.

We went far enough to print a few test forms and laboratory outlines, and listed them for sale. But practical difficulties soon arose. We had no place for private business except our apartments which made poor store houses for our supplies. Our families were visited from time to time by inquisitive tax agents and representatives of city bureaus, seeking to locate our alleged place of business. We had no clerical force to do the packaging and mailing unless we should first invest rather heavily in the uncertain business. And so thus ended The Morningside Press.

It was years later, after World War I and after J.McK.Cattell had been dismissed from Columbia that he establishd the Psychological Corporation, and once again I sat on a board of directors of an organization to study the human factor. Year after year we met and listened to ininspired predictions of what we might some day accomplish, for industry, for science, for humanity; but we did nothing. Since we met always in Cattell's private offices down town and were all interested in helping him keep up such activities as might interest him after his dismissal from academic life, we came faithfully to board meetings and sat sleepily through the hours of reminiscence and prophecy.

As years went by it became clear enough that the Corporation was just another paper organization, of which there were so many. Nothing would happen unless some individual should appear and throw himself heart and soul into the enterprise. This Cattell was obviously not going to do. The contrast with the earlier Economic

Psychology Association was curious enough. Both were organized for much the same ostensible purpose. The latter had the devoted individual, but he was a sales promoter and wanted first of all his own salary. The Corporation instead had a top heavy scientific frame work and an imposing list of inactive directors, but no one to blow the breath of life into it. Both organizations were useless. So I resigned again from a board of directors and had no longer to endure the tedious half day sessions of the directors of an organization whose existence was solely in its articles of incorporation.

As time went on the unbelievable but necessary really did happen. A young psychologist with a taste for the non-academic and with private means which made immediate returns unimportant, adopted the Corporation more or less as a hobby. Devoting his young energy to the psychological corpse, he enlisted the aid of other young men outside of academic walls, and built the paper organization into a thriving concern. It does now effectively all the things the Morningside Press and The Economic Psychology Association once dreamed of, and many additional and newer things, on an impressive scale. It has become a prosperous business enterprise; what contributions it will make to the advancement of psychology remains to be seen.

WE JOIN THE MONTROSE COLONY

After the favorable turn of events in 1914-15 we began to give some thought to improving the general conditions of our own living. As already described, we had found a more comfortable apartment for our winter months. We no longer galloped through Europe in the summer and for some years spent these hot months in the city. One thing about city life was that it was conducive to intellectual work. In the absence of active diversion and exercise, we worked on our data and wrote. In fact a good deal of my scribbling in later years could be explained in part by the need for something to do in the city. But we both wanted some place in the country where we could live more informally and in a more secluded way than the city crowds made possible.

For several years we tramped up and down the valleys in all directions from the city, looking for available spots. We went to Long Island and surveyed its possibilities; surveyed near by sections of New Jersey; went out into Connecticut, up into Westchester County; all with little success. Since we were forced to take trains to distant points and then explore on foot, we found little that was real country, and the typical suburban life had just no appeal for us at all.

The Montagues told us of periods they had spent at a boarding house at Montrose-on-Hudson. While I was at Fort Defiance Cattell had one day driven over to a "colony" of Columbia people, just then getting well under way, in the woods across the railroad from this village of Montrose. There or near there Dean Russell had a real farm where he raised pure-bred cattle. Bigelow also had a large acreage close by. In the colony itself a small group of profes-

FROM COCA-COLA TO CHEWING GUM

5 x 7 landscape
glossy
chos i

C133r
Hollingworth

July 1924

The Colony Assembles for a Tournament

111a

sors, headed by Thorndike, had bought up some old farm and nursery land, and each had taken a few acres with a good building site. Woodbridge, Thorndike, Keppel, Bagster-Collins, had already built places, and Woodworth then had a house under construction. At that time this set-up looked interesting, but it was then far beyond the resources of people in the "gasping period.

But in about 1913 the Montagues persuaded us to go up to Montrose with them and occupy for part of the summer the parsonage in the village, square on the Albany Post Road, which they had learned could be rented. We did this, commuting daily to work in the summer session, and came to know the territory, and visited often with the people in the colony. The next summer Woodworth invited us to occupy his place while he and his family were away on a "sabbatical". The Montagues came in with us, as did also the Strongs, and that summer the virus got us that gets everyone who has the good fortune to spend a summer at the colony.

The colony was located in deep woods, on its own private road, not more than a ten minute walk from the railroad station. Still it was so remote from other places, and so surrounded by woods that deer used to come up to our porch to be photographed. In the colony there was sociability with privacy. People saw one another when they wanted to, and at other times lived the lives of hermits if they wished to. And travel back and forth to the city was not bad even if the train time did run over an hour. It took almost that time for people living in Brooklyn to get to the University campus.

FROM COCA-COLA TO CHEWING GUM

112a

A Corner of the
"Colony Lake"

Sufficient land had been bought up, large areas of it by Thorndike, so that encroachments from any side were unlikely. There was a lake in which the colony members had, or at least exercised, rights to swim and skate and boat. Much of the timber was second growth but there were many large trees that had never been molested,- oaks, elms, hemlocks, spruces, pines, black birches, dog - wood,-in fact we later counted some thirty five varieties of trees and shrubs on our own place when we had acquired one.

We prowled all over this acreage, and also over adjoining and more or less remote sections, looking for a place that would be ours. No where could we find a more likely spot than a piece of about 2.5 acres adjacent to Keppel and Woodbridge, and this Thorndike was willing to let us take. In later years we added to it on several sides until we had an area of some five or six acres. Here in the woods we decided to pitch our more permanent "tent", along with the group of congenial colleagues and their families. We were in a sense the first immigrants to the colony, since the others living there had been members of the original group of settlers.

The first problem was to drill a well, for geologists had warned that in this geological formation, which was volcanic, the fissures ran practically up and down and there would be little chance of finding water bearing seams. Some of those who had already drilled their wells were on scant rations, and the well was in any event a great gamble, for drilling, through solid rock, was several dollars a foot, and the depth might run up to 250 feet before complete discouragement, or an adequate flow, as the case might be, set in.

The drillers could give no advice except to decide where we would like to have our pump house , and there to drill. So we started in and about 125 feet down found a trickle; we went on for another 25 feet, found a little more, and since drilling had by that time become difficult, we stopped. The next morning I made a trip up from the city and eagerly let a stone, tied to a string, down the bore to see how far up the water had come over night. I could not find string enough to reach it.. Still there was water there, and the drillers surmised that if we pumped it out more would flow in.

So we started on our house. We had decided on a place with no cellar excavation, and no lining,- just an outer wall and simple partitions, that would cover us during summer months, and yet give us lots of room. Falling back on my carpenter experience, I drew up detail plans, and secured a young man in the neighborhood who was just getting under way as a builder to take main control. This was Clarence Valentine, who subsequently became the mainstay of nearly everyone who built in the colony .Men in the vicinity were hired to help, and as much of the work as I could find time to do I did with my own tools. We ran up the frame and shell, got the roof on, and before the place had been either painted in any way or furnished, we moved in, in the summer of 1916.

The neighbors gave us a "house warming" that contributed largely to our needed stock of minor utensils. Home made furniture ,dry goods boxes, and wooden shelves, constituted our major equipment, with a few chairs and iron beds that we had to buy. Having moved in, we then at our own leisure began to stain and to paint, and gradually, as the years went on, added to our equipment until all we had to bring from town when we moved to the country for a summer would be rugs, blankets, and our clothing.

The water problem, which was in some ways the severest one confronting people who built in the colony, was not solved by our first well. It would have contented the villagers, who still carried water by the bucket, as we had done in my childhood. But it failed to serve even so modest a plumbing system as the one we had installed. For a time we staggered along, having water hauled to us in vinegar barrels, but even this did not solve the plumbing problem.

Then we blasted out of solid emery a cistern twelve feet across, lined and covered it, and sat down to wait for rain. No rain came. In despair we had water hauled in barrels from the lake and poured into the cistern. When we inspected the matter after a few loads, we found the water gone. There had been a crack in the lining and the water had probably trickled out and gone back to the lake.

Before long, dissatisfied with cistern water for general use anyway, we got together the cash to drill another well. This time, ignoring the drillers, we used our own common sense, went down into the valley instead of starting on top of the hill, and after 75 feet of drilling found an abundant flow of water, which would easily have served us for the rest of our lives.

Characteristically, just as we had solved the water problem in these devious ways, a water district was formed, the Catskill Aqueduct was tapped, and running water was laid right to the edge of our land, the same supply that keeps New York City going. Not to be outdone, when we rebuilt in later years for year round residence, we tapped in also on this water system, and after that we had four sources of water supply,—two artesian wells, a twelve foot cistern, and the water shed of the Catskill Mountains.

Before long we bought a Chevrolet touring car, and then we could come out for week ends as well, with a hamper full of food, and Francie in the back seat to take care of us when we got there. Summers we would commute to the University for our summer session duties, which both of us continued for many years. During the real vacation weeks we basked in real life. I could dig up trees, saw wood, make garden, crack rocks, work on the road, chop away at chestnut stumps, and never yawned for lack of vigorous exercise. L.S.H. was in those days as energetic as I and she often took charge of one end of a big cross cut saw after I had felled a huge dead chestnut tree; together we would transform such logs into posts, or wood for the huge fireplace . So jealous was L.S.H. of all the branches and twigs, after her long years in the sand hills of Nebraska, that she could not see them burned as brush. I made a little "altar" and with a shingle hatchet she would chop up these faggots and bind them into bundles for use as kindling.

On road days the whole colony would turn out and work on the colony road which, since it was privately owned, we had to care for ourselves. Then we would in turn work on our individual roads. In the early days these road day festivals were a very distinctive feature of life in the colony.

We worked and worked trying to clear trees and rocks from a patch that would grow vegetables, but with little success. We were so enamored of trees that we refused to cut down enough to let in sunshine for the garden to thrive on . As time went on we cleared another area, a saddle-back patch, raised either end by filling in with stone, and thus made for ourselves a tennis court. There were already two such courts in the colony, and we had from time to time tournaments for the colony championships.

Our Original Home at Montrose

Most of the younger members of the families played tennis and swam (the children ran chiefly to boys in the ratio of about six to one). At swimming time the whole colony would adjourn to the lake. Then we would go back to our individual homes and live the life of hermits, deep in our writing or studying or whatever else we found to do. On rare occasions we would all assemble for a tea, or for another "house warming" as new people joined us, and with a few families there were occasional interchanges of plans for an evening of bridge. The Thorndikes and the Keppels were most interested in bridge, and we have had many, many pleasant sessions with them thus engaged, *and later with the Gates's and the Jersilds.*

In later years the colony just about doubled in size. New "immigrants" would occupy some house for a summer, as we had done, and they would be lost forever to any other place. Shortly they would find a likely site and arrange with Thorndike to take it off his hands; he would then in turn reach out in various directions and buy up adjacent acres so as to extend the bounds a bit and thus still further protect us all from foreign encroachment.

In this way the Poffenberger's soon came, to occupy a place next to ours; the Gates's came and took up "millionaire hill" which we had all thought nearly inaccessible, but which they speedily and beautifully transformed into a habitable spot; the Reisner's followed, taking a hill overlooking the village and the far country across the river; Hull and Robinson, Ruth Strang, and the Jersild's joined the group, and every house built differed from every other. The younger generation had already begun to add their own abodes, as in the case of the younger Bagster-Collins's *and Thorndikes,* and still later the MacCurdy's arrived. The Evans's took over the Woodworth place and further developed it.

Everyone who has come has shortly endeavored to add bits of land to his original domain, and the houses of most of us have undergone frequent alteration. Our own place has been one of the most mobile in this respect, and we are sometimes accused of not really fastening our staircase down but only "buttoning" it up for the time being. We added a room on one corner; then we extended another corner and added a house keeping wing ;then we revised the interior and moved a few partitions. Since it was only a frame structure with no plaster to be disturbed, we made and remade the place to our heart's content until we had things just the way we wanted them for our own psychological comfort, quite regardless of design or architectural traditions. One of the colony sons became in time an architect and when asked to state what 'style' our house represented declared that it was "Swiss Family Robinson, Modified".

The time came when we completely turned the place inside out, mined and sledged a cellar under it, and turned it into a year-round home, which we christened "Hollywyck". But all this belongs to a later era. For the time being we called the place by names that were almost as mobile as the architecture,- it had been *Incubus*, Rock Ledge, Hermit Rock, Hob Knob in turn before it became Hollywyck, but to most of the people who came to know it, it was just "The Holly's place". We had the good fortune, as things turned out, to be near the center of the colony, as it subsequently developed, and much of the traffic from one place to another, on foot, came in sight of us, so that we have also been jocularly known as "Central Tendency" or "Civic Center".

This place speedily became for us the nearest thing to home that either of us had ever known. As has already appeared, I was never quite sure that I "belonged" in our family. L.S.H. had lived, after losing her mother also at an early age, with her grandparents,then either with an uncle's family or with an uncongenial step-mother, and for years we had both simply boarded and roomed about,as while in college or teaching, and in New York we could never dignify the apartments we lived in by such a term as "home". But here was a place truly our own, made to suit our own idiosyncrasies, and largely by our own hands. Trees became towering things that we had originally identified as just promising shoots,much as did the cotton wood tree that my father had planted alongside the well at home. In time we had touched every spot and left it as it was or shaped it to our heart's desire.

To this place came the friends we most cherished, many of them being or coming in time to be members of the colony itself. Not far away was Fort Defiance,of which we had pleasant memories. In the other direction,and not far away, lived many of the people L.S.H. had come to know and like,in her professional or social relations in the city,like the Seabury's in Ossining or Margaret Lane and her sister Enid Johnson in Croton. Close at hand were the highlands of the Hudson,and in time the wonderful place for hikes,the Blue Mountain Reservation in which I now spend many pondering hours,wandering usually alone. In near-by Peekskill were the Donald's, life long friends of L.S.H.,from one of her early home towns. And we made many new acquaintances in the general neighborhood,and brought many,many of our city friends out to our place for visits and good times together with us.

CRESCENDO

119a

*Our Tennis Court,
L. S. H. Serving.*

So far as I am concerned the place at Montrose has been my physical salvation. It has afforded me not only relaxation and rest and friendships of the best kind I have ever known, - it has also allowed my organism to continue its accustomed familiarity with manual activity and given the larger musculature every needed opportunity to share with the scribbling and lecturing and reading mechanisms a wholesome life. The place came to mean for me always some form of physical work, usually constructive in characacter, and except for the long confining periods in the city in the winter, it might have ruined my scholarly propensities. For I have never been able to do mental work here in any organized way, - every glance out of the window suggested some physical activity to be started or continued . Of all the books and articles I have written, none so far as I can recall were accomplished here, until the occasion of writing these Memoirs, and most of this is being done at Montrose, in the place that has now been our home for more than twenty three years.

Usually as I did a few desultory things at this desk or wrote a few letters on this typewriter, I could hear in the adjoining room the steady click of another machine in the hands of L.S.H. who easily and comfortably did a great deal of her intellectual work in this house. Tonight no sounds at all come from that machine , and when I look into the room it is strangely and unbelievably empty. Sometimes I can scarcely bear to leave the door open into that room, and yet I cannot bear to close it. Empty though the house now is, it is the place where Leta Statter and I spent the greater number of our joyous hours together, and it will always remain for me the nearest thing to "home" that I shall ever know.

A Glimpse of "Road Day"

Down-stairs in a "visitor's book" beautifully bound in leather for "The Holly's" by "The Boltons" are the names of some, but far from all, of the many friends and acquaintances who have visited us, some of them recorded as "regular visitors since 1916." Many of these names will be familiar enough to some who glance at these pages. I am going to list here, chiefly to aid my own recollections and refresh my memories, some of those inscribed or otherwise recorded :

Thaddeus L. Bolton
Martha Busse Bolton
Joseph Jastrow
J. McKeen Cattell
Arthur T. Jersild
Catherine Jersild
Mabel L. Robinson
Helen R. Hull
Margaret G. Rice
Robert E. Young
Aurel D. Young
John Poffenberger
Helen Poffenberger
Georgina S. Gates
Arthur I. Gates
Ruth E. Denio
Mary Ben Fuller
Karl M. Dallenbach
Peggy Dallenbach
Albert T. Poffenberger
Theodore A. Jackson
John P. Foley
Anne Anastasi
Margaret Hart Strong
Edward K. Strong
Sara Birchall
John H. Johnson
Thomas A. McKay
Alice Rohe
Winifred Starbuck Scott
Guy L. Bond
Cleo Scott Findley
Margaret L. Chase
Eranest A. Hollingworth
Louise Hollingworth
Louise Pound
Irving Lorge
Charlotte Bühler
Katherine Anthony
Elizabeth Irwin
Florence Guy Seabury
David Seabury
Metta Maund Rust
Y. Shen
E. Hall Downs
Godfrey Thompson
L. M. Terman

H. W. Puckett
Mary D. Puckett
Donald MacMurray
Alan MacMurray
Frank Jones Clark
Henry W. Nissen
Ruth Quigley
Carl J. Warden
Gardner Murphy
Ray H. Simpson
Dwight W. Chapman
Henry E. Garrett
John Volkmann
Richard E. P. Youtz
S. D. Shirley Spragg
Carney Landis
Robert S. Woodworth
Jane T. Spragg
Adella Youtz
Kathryn Murray Bates
James M. Dunlap
Rose Young
Edward H. Reisner
Betty Reisner
Gelolo Mc Hugh
David Murphy
Susi Engelbrecht
Frederick H. Lund
Nellie B. Pickup
Muriel Evans
Frederick A. Stuff
S. H. Martin
A. T. Watson
Grace H. Watson
Jean Mills
Anne Leigh Goodman
Grace Stuff
Gertrude Moore
    and many others who
    forgot to sign the
    book. But they are
    not forgotten.

COLONY CHARACTERS

During twenty five or thirty years of life in the colony many people appeared with idiosyncrasies and eccentricities that made them memorable. As is to likely to be the case with memories, these characters were not ~~[illegible]~~ the more substantial members of the community, who exercised some control over whatever peculiarities they might have harbored, but in the main the more transient and less consequential individuals. The fact that these stand out in memory does not mean that we were a group of deviates, but only that memory chooses the bizarre and the recalcitrant perhaps just because of their temporary vividness.

Of course there was an oft asserted impression in the village across the tracks that we were all peculiar, and perhaps a bit daffy. One workman expressed this view when he wondered why we people came way up here in the woods to build our houses, when there was still plenty of room along the Post Road "where you can see the automobiles going past all day". But it was also rumored that we "drank", that we were "in favor of free love", that we were irreligious and did most of our hammering, wood cutting and grass cutting on Sundays, and never went to church. It was also asserted that we were all millionaires, presumably because there was usually employment to be found in the colony for the occasional casual villagers who wanted work to do, and because some of us had more than one car, and one of us a station wagon. At least one woman expressed a sense of injustice because none of us gave her boy money with which to go to college.

There were many old families in the neighborhood when the colony began. Such names as Lent, Travis, Lounsbury, Peterson, Hunt, Cole, Reynolds were borne by many. Coles and Hunts had stores; Lounsburys and Lents did teaming; Travis did mason work; farm lands belonged to Reynolds, Peterson, Anderson. We nearly bought a hill from the Reynolds patriarch who assured us that his wife would sign the deed for if she did not he would "cut her off without a shilling". Of his son, in time, we bought ice and coal; of his grandson, coal and cement; now we travel on the train with his great-grand-daughter. Although the old industries have largely gone,-the nurseries, the farms, the ice house, the brick yards, and horses when they rarely appear rouse all the dogs to high excitement,-these old family names continue to cling to large sections of the population,who have not by any means all been drained off by the nearby cities. At this day, in the territory from Ossining to Garrison, on this side of the river, there are 45 telephones listed in the name of Lent and 42 in the name of Travis, as compared with 20 and 18 such listings in the directory for Manhattan. For others of these old names there are listed telephones for 15 Coles, 25 Peterso(e)ns, 15 Hunts, 12 Lounsburys and 18 Reynolds in the regional directory.

In spite of the commonplace lives led by the members of our little university group and their children, and in spite of the length of time, over a third of a century, that the colony has been in existence, the place remains an object of curiosity and conjecture to many. Only yesterday, in February, 1944, the Peekskill daily paper ran a two-column article describing the enterprise, with the head line "COLLEGE HILL NO MYSTERY".

Old Lady Bloomer

One of the familiar local characters in the early days of the colony was an impoverished woman who lived alone in an old house up in the woods beyond our territory. It was said that her only source of income was the baking of communion wafers for Trinity parish, in the heart of the Wall Street section of the city. If this was true it was well that her shack was remotely located from the communicants for the impression she made was unappetizing. There was a story that her family, once well circumstanced, had made donations to the famous parish so that at least to the extent of buying her wafers she was regarded as a pensioner of the church.

When I say she lived alone, this is forgetting her horse. He was a superannuated, bony wreck, whose hooves were never trimmed but grew long and curved, bending back and under so that eventually the beast walked on the tops rather than the bottoms of his feet. This handicap seriously impeded his gait when the old lady occasionally drove him through the woods and down the colony road to the village. The wretched animal often fell down on these trips and then his rounded hooves gave him no grip so that he could not get up unaided. Mrs. Bloomer would then go on foot to the nearest house. "Old lady Bloomer's horse is down again", - the word would go round, and the available able bodied boys and men would follow the distressed woman to the spot and by their united efforts hoist the animal upright. As time went on the horse went down more than once on a trip. Finally he fell in sight of the Keppel house, never to rise again. He was interred by the Keppel males almost where he fell, which was only a few feet from the dug well on the old Bell place. The well was never used again and this inadvertent bit of sabotage almost runied the immediate sales value of that piece of property.

Culligan and Moran

Just across the railroad tracks and close to the Reynolds coal yard there once stood a floorless tar-paper shack, snug under the brow of a small hill. Casual laborers were allowed to live here, especially those who helped unload the coal cars. When not thus employed they would often work for us by the day. Jim Culligan lived there when we first came to the colony in 1916. An old and withered Irishman, he smoked a stubby pipe and would put in a good day of work for $2. But he nearly ruined our place one dry summer day when he put off his coat with the burning pipe in the pocket and went off to another corner of the grounds. He was recalled by a raging grass and brush fire that swept through the trees and which he managed eventually to control. The devastated area centered in the spot where he had laid his coat on the ground, a coat that he never saw again. It went up in flames along with some of our young evergreens.

In those days brush fires were always a menace. On a Sunday I discovered one coming over our front hill and found it sweeping in all directions. Sending word to the neighbors I rushed down to attack it, ruining my best summer clothes in the process. Another fire got away from control on the Poffenberger place and we just managed to get it surrounded when the fire department rushed up on foot with chemical extinguishers in hand. A neighbor had telephoned that the Poffenberger house was going up in flames. This was many years ago but traces of that conflagration, which might very well have taken not only that house but others as well, may still be seen in the landscape.

Culligan was found dead in his shack one day and the place was shortly occupied by another man who said he was Tom Moran. Tom was large framed and heavy footed; he could roll the heaviest rocks and push loaded wheelbarrows up hill. But he was poor at gardening because his feet took up so much area, and at trimming because he "couldn't see so good". Tom never started conflagrations for he did not smoke; but he used snuff incessantly and his hearty sneeze could be heard at astounding distances. Here and there through the woods he cached tin snuff boxes, usually in the crotches of trees, so that he was never far from a supply. Long after he was gone we continued to find these half ##### empty boxes. Tom had lost a thumb and finger from one hand. He said another fellow once boasted that he could hit a dollar at thirty paces and Tom, holding up such a coin, dared him to prove it. The man fired and Tom was thereafter fit for only the heavier jobs in the brickyard. That was why he preferred to work in the woods for us and shovel coal for Reynolds.

Despite various shortcomings, such as a fondness for whiskey, Moran was a devoted employee and he sedulously stayed away when drink had been too much for him. He seldom appeared on Mondays, his excuse being always that he "didn't feel so good". There is still in use in the shop at "Hollywyck" an 18-inch length of steel rail, cut from a N.Y. Central express track rail by the repair gang. Tom had found it, managed to get it on his back, and carried it up the hill a half-mile when he came to work one day. "I tho't ye'd like it fer an anvil", he said. And that is just how we have used it for a quarter century. Tom too was found dead one Monday morning on the packed dirt that was the floor of his shack. It had been bootleg whiskey and too much even for his stalwart frame. It had been a cold winter night; his chickens and stray dog were sheltered with him in the shack, but the fire had been out for many hours.

Wait, and Others

Moran's place as man of all work in the colony was in part taken by William Wait, a retired farmer, with a family, his own home, and other property. Such income as he may have had he supplemented by work in the woods. Small but astonishingly wiry and strong, he especially loved a hard job such as a tough stump, a big boulder to crack, or a rocky ledge to dig through. He had no vices but a proclivity for conversation. His work was sometimes interrupted by calls to jury duty in the county seat, for he was a substantial citizen. He is older than I, perhaps, but still going strong and only this morning, a cold day in February, as I went to the station on foot, I met Wait trudging up the hill with his lunch basket in hand and a warm cap over his ears. "What you doing now, Wait?" I asked. "Oh, chopping down trees,-cleaning up the woods." This he has been doing now for a good twenty years, for one or another member of the colony. Without his dogged patience and sledge hammer blows many a local project would have been abandoned. He has steadily refused to learn to drive a car, apparently feeling that gasoline engines are just his competitors. In this as in many of his more explicit judgments there is some solid wisdom. I have a secret ambition to be in years to come as erect and sinewy a man.

As years went by and places were expanded, each house was likely to acquire a resident handy man of its own. But there has always been work for Wait, in one place or another. These resident handy men have been numerous and usually transient. One of our own stayed five years and said that this was longer than he had ever before remained in one place. Perhaps because of the greater regimentation of living in, these handy men,-gardeners, butlers, chauffeurs, or what not,- have lacked the idiosyncrasy of the more casual workmen, such as Culligan, Moran and Wait, although they all had vulnerable points .

Old Man Anderson

The local patriarch of the immediate territory that the colony came to occupy was a man who had been born thereabouts and lived in a small cottage said to be a hundred years or more old. There were in fact at least three different spots where his birth was claimed by him to have occurred. One was his little cottage of clapboard on hand hewn beams. This stood right on the extension of colony road, said to have been in early years part of the Kings Ferry Post Road, the chief route into Pennsylvania from Connecticut. There is still a Kings Ferry Road across the tracks, running from the village post office to Verplanck, once an important Dutch shipping point on the river. When we first joined the colony the ruins of old piers could still be seen there along the Hudson. Washington's army is of course said to have come down Kings Ferry Road, and hence through the colony territory, on the way to Philadelphia.

But Anderson also declared he had been born at the edge of our own acreage where there stood an old apple tree (planted by his father) and where there was an abandoned dug well, solidly walled, and a hillside excavation that might have been a basement, close to Keppel's study. There was at least one other spot where the venerable man told me he had been born, and how many birth places he had pointed out to others I do not know.

At any rate, however often born, he was old when we came there and twenty years later he was still walking to Peekskill and back, six miles, carrying provisions. But he easily lost his way by this time. Not many months before he died, surely nearly 90, we found him wandering near our house one dark night, crying "I'm lost, I'm lost." I steered him down the road and up a different hill to his own cottage. He was then living alone, in one room, with bed, table, trunks, piled close to the kitchen stove, the matches and kerosene light stowed away under the bed.

Many stories circulated about this man's irascible temper, his long standing feuds over roads and boundaries, his eloquence when he was a member of the school board. He owned about 70 acres, patches of which he once farmed, but the cultivated pieces gradually shrunk to a vegetable garden and second growth timber covered the old farm. Now and then he would sell a small piece, but most of the land he clung to, demanding a price that no one would pay for it. There were two swamps which he called "the upper and lower basins" and his dream for a life time was of the day when these would be transformed into lakes, perhaps accomodating steamboats.

He had a family, but in later years the wife and children lived elsewhere. When one of the girls married a house was built for her above the knoll where stood the alleged Revolutionary cottage of her father. There she lives now, with husband and children. These youngsters, lively and friendly, trot up and down the colony road on their way to school and back, the same road along which their grandfather plodded for a lifetime, and across which he repeatedly built barriers to traffic on foot or by vehicle in order to keep a firm hold on certain boundaries and disputed rights of way.

The Lost Half Acre

On the Bell place, an abandoned farm just beyond the Anderson house, was a "lost half acre". The title was in some way clouded and the taxes unpaid. Every week end in summer a stocky stranger, in leather coat and puttees, was seen going up the colony road, with a pack of provisions. He disappeared over the hill on the Bell place and in time we discovered that he had gathered old lumber and built a well hidden shack under the steep far side of the hill and hollowed out a swamp hole for a water supply. In time we learned this squatter's name and that he had once worked in one of the county offices. Apparently he had discovered the "lost half acre" and was intent on homesteading it. Whatever his intent, he meant business, for one Sunday when four of us were looking for cherries on the old trees of the Bell place the lone squatter dashed out from behind a rock flourishing a huge pistol and easily persuaded us to leave the premises. Before long Thorndike purchased the whole Bell tract and took the necessary legal steps to have the lost half acre included. Whereupon the hostile squatter appeared no more and we lost our most vivid reminder of old days on the frontier.

Clarence Valentine

The phenomenal artisan of our community is a man who throughout the Great Depression never lacked all the work he could manage. When he supervised our first building in 1916 he was just starting on his own as a young carpenter. His wiry agility, versatility and quick intelligence, and his friendly ways, soon made him indispensable in the territory. He seemed to pick up the essentials of every skilled trade and whenever the statutes and trade rules made it possible, or when emergency arose, he could be counted on for effective service as carpenter, painter, plumber, electrician, dynamiter, cabinet maker, stone mason, tin smith, auto repair man . He grew to be a man of known integrity and influence, was a perennial member of the school board, of which he was president, and was given other civic responsibilities. He could provide steady employment for any number of relatives as well as for a varied group of workers, including such specialists as electricians, plumbers, masons. As a contractor he escaped many restrictions of the trade unions when he worked in the country, and he could employ union men in the towns where walking delegates abounded.

When wars came, and I have observed him through two World Wars, local work would subside but Clarence was always in demand then (as at any other time) in nearby factories or ship building yards. Starting from scratch in the region where he grew up as a boy, he became one of that region's most dependable citizens. Whenever a neighbor came over with a worried look, as if something had gone wrong with the world, you knew that his first question would be, "Do you know where Valentine is working today ?"

Because of such importunities and dependencies Clarence was led to develop idiosyncrasies which were often enough annoying, yet in a way endeared him to everyone. He would always leave a job to help in some emergency; often enough, emergencies elsewhere followed. It came to be said that he never did get to finish a job. And it is true that the urgencies of starting a new building had such attraction for him that he could easily forget to put finishing touches on the one before it. Sometimes he would dash back on holidays, on a Sunday, or after working hours, but often the house was remodelled, and likely enough by Clarence himself, before he got around to these neglected details. For fundamentals and for emergencies, however, you could always count on Clarence. So when The Great Depression came and men sat along the curb waiting for P W A jobs, for hand outs, or applied for chronic relief, Clarence reduced the size of his construction gang but so far as he was himself concerned he was never unemployed. The reason, for one thing, was that he was so manifestly employable. There must be some socio-economic significance to this fact.

"Ask Mr. Foster!"

Beyond the Anderson and Bell farms ran Washington Street and bordering this road were the places of certain celebrities. The Dean of Columbia's Teachers College had a farm on a corner where he raised fancy cattle; near by was the Treasurer of the same institution, with stone battlements around his garden. Above him, half way up Spitzenberg Mountain, was a retired judge; near him was the home of an actor. But the man we saw most of was Mr. Foster.

He drove a white horse to the station, coming across the Anderson farm on a road long since engulfed by that acreage, then down the colony road. Many railway stations and hotels contained offices or booths over which hung the sign "Ask Mr. Foster." And here he was in person. We saw him every day but never asked him anything. Seeing him amble by with his old white horse and farm buggy it would not have occurred to you that he knew the answers to questions.

All of these celebrities moved away. The thoroughbred cattle were transported to a New Jersey farm. The Treasurer set himself up with a partner in Wall Street. A theatrical producer who was famous for his herb garden came instead. The Foster place was taken over by a Washington lawyer whose wife, a Ph.D. in anthropology, started an independent dairy and organized a milk route. By this time no doubt all the places have changed hands again. When a good opportunity next presents itself I intend to ask Mr. Foster.

Folk Lore

The neighbors in the colony were able and congenial people whose ways and tastes, as much as anything else, attracted us to the place originally. Most of their idiosyncrasies were swamped by their evident virtues or were subdued by their own sense of propriety. As I look back upon them now however there are certain memories at which I chuckle or groan. Many of these memories are of events which at the time were anything but amusing; the obliviscence of the disagreeable has taken care of that.

A large collection of stories became the common lore of the colony and some of them were often recited, to new comers, at parties, or in casual conversation. Many of them derived their flavor from the context from which they sprang and the cumulative background of related episodes. Sometimes they neatly reflected the personal characteristics of the individuals concerned in them. A bare recital of their topics is all that need be given here.

There was for example the house that was built of field stone with walls two feet thick. But the workmen took the architect's floor plans to refer to outside dimensions, and built accordingly. When the owner returned from abroad to occupy his new home all the rooms were found to be several feet short of expectation, in all directions.

Another man, with a penchant for retired fire horses, superannuated collies, and other assorted barnyard creatures, acquired two gorgeous peacocks. So fetching to the eye, these animals turned out to be both filthy and raucous and they perched by day and night always on the premises of neighbors.

Another neighbor, hard pushed for time because of commuting daily to his work in the city, always mowed his lawn after dark, with a kerosene lantern dangling from the push bar of his mower. The family across the road from him had a little mountain burrow that patiently bore one of the boys to the village school and waited there to bring up the hill at noon for a warm lunch.

Two or three astute husbands throughout the years refused to acquire mastery of automobilre and eschewed practical domestic chores save occasional bits of landscaping. They thus achieved maximal freedom for cultural pursuits and educated their wives in resourcefulness.

There was a native who sold a colonist evergreen trees which he thereupon collected from the purchaser's own land. And there was a well known workman who, having earned $14 a day in the inflation days refused to work for ordinary wages thereafter and lapsed into a shiftless state of fatal deterioration.

There was a distant relative of a famous American orator. He worked as a semi-dependent day laborer but family tradition prompted him to long and diffuse vocalization which seriously interfered with his work. It was "just bad luck" that kept him also from being a distinguished man.

Collisions were constantly expected when automobiles were introduced on the narrow and winding colony road. In the only one that ever occurred I was one of the awkward victims.

There was a boisterous Gaelic estate, full of dogs, horses, chickens, goats, geese, motor cycles, buzz saws and boys, the master of which expostulated at the occasional whistling of a neighbor.

Frequent surveys of boundary lines, each survey appearing to push farther out the lines of whichever proprietor engaged the surveyor.

Recurrent strokes of lightening that one after another blasted the imposing hammock trees that had been trimmed and cleared in order to perpetuate them.

The aspiring troubador who sang airs from Gilbert and Sullivan to any girl who would listen until by midnight or later she might fall asleep or be attacked by sudden illness.

The children who loved to dig in the dirt with spoons and table knives when the adults had tennis tournaments but who always insisted on digging in front of the spectators, never behind them.

The hired man who sat patiently near a misconducted garbage hole until he had sighted and shot with a rifle Thirty one rats, and who was finally prompted to resign because of his conviction that his meals, served directly from the family table, were "pizening him".

The hound dog who secured his own food, two pounds of salami, by burglarizing the larder of his master who was away at work.

The man who crawled on hands and knees the length of his shallow attic to extinguish the flames from a sulphur candle that had melted and overflowed its container. He was barely able to get back to the manhole before he had to take another breath.

The stray police dog who bit guests and refused to be driven away, and who when finally transported by automobile to a remote spot succeeded in driving the car down a steep grade, off the road, through two fences and into a swamp, and came back again the very next day.

The young oracle who never achieved any special distinction himself except his eagerness to advise others how to do whatever they were doing. In time it became good form for anyone volunteering suggestions to another to preface his remarks with "Delbert says .....". The edge of the joke was a little dulled by the fact that Delbert was so often right.

The band of gypsies that ventured up colony road one day and failing to tell any adult fortunes contented themselves with holding up a small boy on the road and robbing him of fifteen cents that he had in his pocket.

Tame enough, these little episodes of colony life, but to the grown ups they sufficed to lend bits of color to otherwise gray stretches of memory. The younger generation is less satisfied with life in the woods and inclined to more sophisticated diversions like golf, movies, night clubs, and motor expeditions, all of which have in common the elementary fact that they are enjoyed away from home.

THE PLATTSBURG EPISODE

By 1916 then we were all set for a breathing spell, but still definitely pulling up stream. Thanks to the revenue derived from activities in the field of applied psychology, L.S.H. had completed her professional training, received her doctor's degree, and been appointed to an instructorship in Columbia University. We had found a place in the country for our summer months, and were living in reasonable comfort. I was in my second year as assistant professor at Barnard, and the salary was $2,500 .

But psychotechnology had been stirred up and would not rest. At Carnegie Institute of Technology in Pittsburg a new Division of Applied Psychology had been established, with W.V.Bingham responsible for the organization. I was invited to come there as full professor at just twice my Barnard salary. Even assuming that I wished to commit myself for life to psychotechnology, there was still a dilemma, and one that more than once confronted us in later years also. This was the problem of our joint professional lives. If we moved to Pittsburg to accept what seemed like a fine opportunity, the work of L.S.H. , just getting under way at Teachers College, would be interrupted. I then and there decided that our joint interests were to be primary; whatever opportunities came along, they had to be joint opportunities, or else we should simply stay together where we could, regardless of financial considerations, prestige, or anything else. It was on these grounds that, in later years, I was led to decline the Chairmanship of our Section of the National Research Council.

I had informed the authorities at Barnard of the call to Carnegie, and while it was still being toyed with and we were in attendance upon a Psychological Association meeting in the West and in conference with the Carnegie people, a wire came reporting that Barnard College had advanced me to be Associate Professor, with a 50 % percent increase of salary. All conferences were promptly called off.

FROM COCA-COLA TO CHEWING GUM

Some of Our Dogwoods
Photo by L.S.H.

During the next year, on our new status, and breathing freely enough, it seemed that we might almost begin to plan the sort of life we *wanted* rather than conform always to the demands of exigency. But we forgot to reckon with the World War, with which the rest of the planet was already shaking, and which soon broke upon us in this country. Psychologists organized to put their services at the disposal of the army. Committees on tests and personnel were formed and psychologists in great number entered enthusiastically into the service, especially in devising tests for enlisted men, trade tests, aviation tests, and so on.

My enthusiasm for applied psychology was always weak enough, and my military apathy has already been recorded in these pages. I was negativistic toward these enterprises, although by this time I had been elected to the Council of the American Psychological Association and was expected to play an active role. Moreover it began to look to me as if the trend of developments was going to select for destruction the best young men in our population, while those who could socially be more easily spared might be rejected as unfit. I was averse to such an outcome.

The war went on and in time our men began to be sent home from the front, many of them with war neuroses which appeared to be functional or psychological in character,— "shell shock" was the term in common use. A special hospital for such cases was established at Plattsburg Barracks, New York. In connection with it there was planned a Reconstruction Service. There was to be educational endeavor to make these men better fits, occupationally and mentally. There were to be curative work-shops for the immediate occupation of the men in forms of exercise conceived to be of therapeutic value for their special difficulties. There could be developed psychological services for the examination of these psychoneurotics, for such aid as psychology might give to their restoration to health, and for such study of these clinical pictures as the circumstances would permit. The Surgeon General's office asked me to go to Plattsburg to take on these duties. It appeared likely that a civilian might better enlist the cooperation of the military patients, so that I was to go under the civil service as a curative work shop appointee. Many of the men who had gone from professional work into army services received larger salaries than they had been earning in times of peace, but I was asked to sacrifice some $2,000 a year thus to serve my country.

Although we had firmly resolved not to be separated again for long periods of time, we decided that I should take on these duties. In August, after the summer session was over, L.S.H. and I walked glumly down the colony road toward the railroad station. At what is now Reisner's drive we parted, she to return to the house to carry on alone again. She later told me that after I had disappeared down the hill she ran up into the woods and cried her heart out.

Reporting at Plattsburg I found that as a civilian I could not be accomodated on the grounds of the Camp, but must put up at a dismal hotel near the railroad. Men for the Reconstruction Service had already been detailed there and were in charge of a non-commissioned officer. I tried to join in, in my civilian status and found that I could make no headway, either with the authorities or with the men. As a civilian I had no "powers"; people, including the patients, might listen politely, then grin and go their way. So I accepted a Captain's commission, which was all that the Surgeon General's Office saw fit to tender me. As head of a division of the hospital I had then to negotiate with the Majors and Lieutenant Colonels who not only headed up the other services but also occupied many of the subordinate positions in them.

Furthermore, no psychological workers had been detailed to the service here, and only one teacher. The other men on our staff were plain workmen, wood workers, metal workers, gardeners, automobile mechanics, a printer, and a few non-descripts. They were supposed to teach the various trades in therapeutic fashion.

Meanwhile as the Hospital got under way we were treated to a series of lectures by specialists imported to tell us what was the trouble with our patients, and what we should do for them. It was at once apparent that not only we but the experts still had everything to learn. One specialist in endocrinology told us that all these men were suffering from pituitary disorders, and he exhibited photographs of their "cella tursicas" to prove it. The next lecturer told us the men were simply suffering from the "psychology of discontent" and he brought in to prove his case the same individuals whose "cella tursicas" we had just been shown. The third expert had been analysing dreams and was convinced that the men were suffering from suppressed complexes, probably in the main "the wish for death", and we should go on analysing their dreams. Still another told us that our cases were all indistinguishable from malingerers, they were simulating incapacity in order to escape disagreeable duty, and the proper treatment was to make duty more attractive to them than their present circumstances. And after this series of lectures we were left with our cases,—over 1200 of them during the course of the next few months.

FROM COCA-COLA TO CHEWING GUM

We Build Our
Own Canoe

Meantime in the Curative Work Shop we had printed up a set of test forms, which I had chosen as separately standardized on an age basis. The regularly adopted army tests at once proved unsuitable for our patients since so few could make scorable records on them, and anyway we could not get supplies until several weeks after the occasion for their use had passed. So we printed our own materials, and I taught the automobile mechanics and metal working assistants on my staff to help me give, and then to score, mental tests.

While we were setting up our school, shops, printery, looms, automobile training school (with a derelict car secured through the Red Cross), and supervising the young women "aides" who taught basketry and the like in the wards, I set about the study of a group of "cerebro-spinal meningitis residuals" who were gathered together in one ward. Physical examination showed these men to have recovered, organically, but they were still incapacitated. They baffled the neuro-psychiatric staff, and I was turned loose on them to see what a psychologist might learn about them.

I learned very soon three things about them. In the first place their present symptoms were all "vestiges" or "residuals", that is, they were complaints that had originally had justifiable organic cause. In the second place, they did not always exhibit these symptoms. One man who had a contractured arm under ordinary conditions was found on the back stoop of his ward, vigorously shining his shoes with both arms in full and free play, one Sunday morning when I unexpectedly came down the back alley, where officers seldom appeared. When I hove in sight the contractured arm flew up into its wonted cramp again, as if the sight of my uniform was what had done it.

Associate Professor
1916

A third observation was that this group of men did not give a normal distribution in their intelligence scores. They did not distribute themselves according to the bell-shaped curve found in the recruit army, and found also in such a hospital as Walter Reed, where organic injuries alone were received. Most of these men fell below average, but escaped feeble-mindedness in the technical sense, and a few scored above average. Where the 'average men' might have been expected to pile up in the centre of the graph, our graph was already rapidly tapering off. Already the germs of a theory of the neuroses began to grow in my mind.

As soon as I could I gave mental tests to my own staff, and got the ablest of them promoted to non-commissioned status, so that they could with some authority administer the various work shop enterprises, under my general eye and with the advice of the ward-surgeons. A particularly adaptable two or three were chosen to help me in a testing program which I at once proposed to the higher authorities and the neuro-psychiatric staff. Fortunately one of these men was Major A.J. Rosanoff, a well known psychiatrist, with whom I had already had cordial relations in civil life, and who was also interested in psychology, to which field he had made valuable contributions of his own. Without his friendly influence I am sure that my program would have made little headway. I was setting out to emphasise the research aspect of the problem, as well as the reconstruction end.

When a new group of men arrived at the hospital from the front, they had of course already passed through many observation hospitals, and had with them their case histories. They were again examined by the neuro-psychiatric experts at our hospital, diagnoses independently given, and they were then assigned to such physiotherapy, medico-therapy, electrotherapy, hydrotherapy, occupational therapy and the like as their conditions appeared to call for. They were then from time to time re-examined and their condition recorded.

By arrangement, the first thing after initial reception, assignment to quarters, and a cleaning up, all members of every group assembled for our group intelligence tests, and those doing poorly in these were subsequently called in for individual examination. We secured all the psychometric data we could on each case, and reported our findings, keeping duplicate records for our own study. We were also allowed access to all case histories and permitted to copy any or all of these, to be put to our own scientific uses. We also began to use on all cases a "psychoneurotic inventory" that was just being developed by Woodworth and his associates and which became the basis of a great array of such "personal data" sheets in later years.

Incidental observations also proved valuable. Thus when it was required, this being a military hospital and camp, to fire a salute of repeated guns upon the death of an ex-president, we noted how with each gun salvo more and more of our partially recovered cases would relapse back into their former symptom picture, so that by the time the salute was over, the apparent restorative work of weeks had been quite undone and we were back where we started with many of the cases. Individual observations suggested also that the symptoms were not always present, but came in response to certain situations or stimuli, which could often be identified by us, and even experimentally employed. And reference to the case histories showed that just as in the case of the cerebro-spinal meningitis cases, these symptoms had been part of a more severe behavior pattern in some previous collapse, under more justifiable provocation.

Mid-way of our work the Armistice occurred. Many of our cases recovered over night and appeared before the disability board without their symptoms and clamoring to be discharged. They usually had naive explanations to give for their recovery, they had eaten an apple, or the ward surgeon had prayed for them, or the doctor had passed a magnet over an arm, or an electric shock had just been administered, or they had had a striking dream, and so on. The same "miracles" appeared that filled the literature of the description of neuroses of civil origin, and the books on psychotherapy.

We continued to examine in the usual way the cases that continued to arrive after the Armistice, who had been on the road to us before this event occurred. We found them strangely free from many of the pictures presented before the Armistice, and the "neurotic inventory" disclosed that their condition was not only different but that even the reported "heredity" of cases now arriving was different. The Armistice had been one magnificent therapeutic event, and had the same influence that any change in insight or motivation or understanding had been found to have on neurotic patients in civilian clinics and practise.

When we now assembled our collection of intelligence scores we found very striking things to be true. Our patients as a whole were below average intelligence; this was not due to their present incapacity either, for their school records showed that they had always been just such people; moreover, the various diagnostic groups showed quite different average intelligence levels, although of course there was much overlapping.

Chief of Educational and Psychological Service

Shortly after the Armistice the curative work shops lost even such vogue as they had formerly built up and even the "bedside aides" lost their initial attractiveness for the men. The men still came out to the shops, but only to get lumber to build boxes in which to pack their things, in preparation for the journey home. We recommended promptly that our whole establishment be discharged, and began to give our attention to working up our records and data.

WHY I DEVELOPED A RUBY RASH

Whereupon a delegation of some dozen or more psychologically trained workers was sent to us. Although we had struggled through the winter in cold tar-paper barracks, with which we were now through, a contractor and architect appeared with instructions to build for us an elaborate structure to house our activities. Six months after we had begun to print our own test blanks to make any progress, and now that the war was over and the men in process of being discharged, we were to be treated to adequate equipment and to trained personnel,- for just none of which we had any need whatever. Even two additional Captains appeared to join my staff, as if the troubles of one Captain among an authoritative group of Lieutenant Colonels had not been enough for one military hospital.

No end of entertaining tales could be told of these days at Plattsburg. The episodes were not all amusing when they occurred. The experience as a whole was so distressing that after I had finally been discharged my whole body broke out into a ruby rash, my skin scaled off in great flakes and left a powdered wake behind me as I walked, as if to shake off every possible vestige of the affair. But many things, distressing and baffling enough at the time, are now funny enough to remember. Here again is material for my early paper on "The Obliviscence of the Disagreeable."

There was for instance the time I was locked out of the quaurters to which I had been assigned because ############ a new captain (one Goodrich) and his wife wanted to use the whole house. The Colonel who was Commanding Officer offered to "go to the mat" for my cause but I refused anyway to live in the house thereafter.

There was the man who was sent to us when we requisitioned a badly needed pharmacist, and who reported that yes, he was a farmicist,- he had worked on a farm all his life. He had been sent to us from headquarters with these qualifications.

There was the time I was called before the Commanding Officer and required to apologize because, in a letter asking for the nth time for better electric lights in our "curative" barracks, I had remarked that the eyesight of the men was at least as valuable as the fate of the tar-paper barracks, which were being carefully preserved from danger by stringent fire laws.

Much amusement was caused among us by the work of one of the new Captains assigned to our group. In keeping with regulations he had to take his turn as "Officer of the Day". He buttoned on his army pistol and marched through all the wards, filled with patients whose symptoms were easily enough re-instated by the sight of a pistol. Not content with this exploit, he even took his pistol from the holster and began to flourish it and examine it in their presence, so that we had finally to drag him almost bodily from the wards.

This whole business of being "Officer of the Day" continued to have its entertaining aspects. Although no military training had been exacted of me upon appointment, I was regularly called on, as were other officers, to take my turn at this duty. All day and all night I had to be on call, with pistol at my side. I had to inspect the camp and hospital grounds periodically, day and night,

Officer of the Day
1918

in true military fashion, although this was really a hospital. The sentries had to be challenged, required to recite their long list of duties. I was in charge of the guard house and was to "turn out the guard" when needed. Meanwhile our psychological and reconstruction work halted while the man in charge made his military round, and duly reported on the state of the camp and the activities of the enemy. There was even resentment expressed in some quarters because I did not regularly drill my staff and march them to duty in proper formation.

The non-commissioned officer who was my chief aid and ally throughout all this work had been severely disciplined in his day for reporting to civilians some of the undesirable features of the local situation. He and a fellow sergeant often warned me that it was a mistake for me to be seen walking up the street with them or having them to assist me in my room at night at our never completed work, because this was an infraction of military etiquette. I was often enough hailed before the Commanding Officer and expostulated with, but never actually on these grounds. Usually it had to do with the tone of some of my communications, or with things that had not been done through approved channels. My propensity for writing "impudent letters", which my early literature professor had pointed out to my prospective wife, was the thing that most easily brought me up on the carpet.

The whole situation was mitigated by the occasional visits that L.S.H. was able to make to the Post. Although given no quarters for man and wife, she was allowed to share my couch with me in the room at officers quarters and to come to officers' Mess with me. And she would regularly keep me informed on the state of things at the University and elsewhere in the nation. Lorle Stecher had come to Barnard to take my place during the military absence, and she and Georgina S. Gates who had become Lecturer and then Instructor as time went on carried on not only the Barnard work, but Georgina undertook also the evening courses to the business men on advertising, which were still under way. She continued in this department for many years, becoming assistant professor and doing distinguished work in her field until she resigned, to devote her whole attention to her own life and home affairs.

A THEORY OF THE NEUROSES

From my own point of view the chief accomplishment of our work at Plattsburg was the development of a description of what was psychologically going on in these men. I had found that on the whole they were men of less than average intelligence; that their symptoms were reactions to specific stimuli in their present situation; that these stimuli had been partial features of earlier contexts to which they had also reacted in just such manners, undermotivations that gave the stimuli their special meanings. It seemed to me that now they were simply responding again, to partial elements of these earlier contexts, in ways that had been appropriate enough to the whole situation then, but were not appropriate to the present situation in which the stimulating detail occurred at the later time.

On this basis I formulated a theory of the neuroses, which involved a specific intellectual weakness (lack of scope or sagacity); a past distressing episode; and the present effectiveness of partial features of the old episode in reinstateing the similar picture of distress or incapacity. I selected cases from the files to illustrate this concretely; assembled the data from our tests and inventories, and during the months after I was discharged from the army but could not yet resume full duty at the University because people had been appointed to carry on my work there for the full year, I organized all this material into a book. Authority to publish this volume was granted by the Surgeon General's Office, and it was published in 1920 by Appleton, under the title "The Psychology of Functional Neuroses."

I still had much to learn about functional neuroses, and as time went on and I became better acquainted with the literature, I found that even my own formulation had been tentatively ventured by others, who had not however stayed by it or had been unable to support it. The book was reviewed in a variety of ways. The medical reviewers inclined to think it could not have anything of value in it because I did not have an M.D. The mechanists thought my theory was entirely too introspective and spiritual; the purposivists thought the account was entirely too mechanistic; others felt that I could have said the same thing using different words; still others thought that however apt the theory might be for some cases, it had been a mistake to generalize it to cover all the field of the psychoneuroses.

It is true that as years went by I was able to formulate my interpretation in somewhat sounder ways, and in closer consonance with my own systematic viewpoint. Nevertheless in that volume the ground was laid for a developmental trend that occupied me through all the rest of my professional career and brought my own thinking, not only in abnormal psychology but in other fields as well, to what satisfied me as a sensible, naturalistic and workable point of view.

In the year that this volume on "Functional Neuroses" was published, L.S.H. became Assistant Professor of Education . The year following the book was awarded the Butler Medal by Columbia University, and the next year I was advanced to a full Professorship .. We had definitely 'pulled up stream' and were ready for 'full steam ahead.' Beginning with 1920 prolific contribution to the literature of psychology and education began again. It had been twelve years since that wistful evening when Rev. Martin Walker had pronounced us man and wife, and sixteen years since the memorable day at the University of Nebraska when we had declared our mutual intention sometime to pitch our tent together. We had come about half way since then, for, as it turned out, we had still about eighteen years of full professional life together before us.

PART IV

~~FULL STEAM AHEAD~~
FORTISSIMO

PART III   F O R T I S S I M O

Pause for Consideration

Before proceeding with the story of my life during its next period it may be instructive to consider briefly some of the more subjective features of our situation. It was unusual in those days for man and wife both to hold professorships in the same institution. Since then things have changed and this arrangement has sometimes been wittingly made by the authorities and recognized as having certain advantages. There are now several such pairs of psychologists working not only in the same institution but even in the same department.

Our own situation, although not so flagrant as this, was nevertheless anomalous; we held jobs on different faculties but still in the same university. We were often enough made aware of this. One colleague even had the effrontery to tell my wife that she was "just taking the bread out of some other family's mouth." Few of the indications were as crass as this one, but we were good enough psychologists to sense them, even when they were only implicit and indirect.

Perhaps we became so sensitized to such signs that we often seemed to find them even where they were not. Still, envy is a rather easily discerned reaction, although it often takes devious routes in its expression. We did not want to flaunt our good fortune before the eyes of others nor to invite any more ill feeling than might unavoidably arise. We therefore systematically soft-pedalled our relationship as much as we could. That we to some extent succeeded in doing this was indicated by the fact that more than once L.S.H. was referred to as my daughter.

Only under urgent necessity would we attend a university function together. We avoided teas and receptions to which faculty and faculty wives were jointly invited. When required to attend Commencement and similar exercises we kept apart and marched in different contingents. When, as was sometimes the case, this pretended coincidence of our names could not be carried through and we did appear together at a dinner, a funeral or a celebration, we were uncomfortably self-conscious and endeavored to remain on the side-lines.

One of our embarassments in this connection arose when, because of a peculiar administrative arrangement, I became responsible for the course in Educational Psychology in Barnard. According to the university charters all courses in education must be given by Teachers College, so that I had to be assigned to a seat on its faculty, as well as to my place on the faculty of Barnard College. Whereupon both of our names appeared in the catalogue and we were thus forced to wave a red flag in the very faces of our colleagues. Still later L.S.H. was assigned to the Graduate Faculty of Philosophy. in which I also was listed. We seemed to be going out of our way to do just the things we had always so morbidly avoided.

This situation did little to temper the obnoxious introversion and bashfulness that I had brought with me from Nebraska. If anything it only reinforced a reclusiveness which had in part grown upon me because of my earlier felt inferiorities and had perhaps in part been in my native constitution.

L.S.H. was less affected; she was more inclined to take things in her stride and make the best of them. However we never entered whole heartedly into the social activities of the university community; avoided teas and receptions and committees and rejoiced not to be elected as officers or representatives for this or that local affair.

Except for a few intimate friends among our colleagues who we believed liked us for our own sakes and whose friendship we should have wanted regardless, we came to know few of the faculty families. This outcome was favored by the difficulties of social contact at Columbia, due to the widely scattered places of residence of the staff and to the repellent barriers of apartment life which ruled out all ordinary "calling." All these things resulted in our building up circles of acquaintanceship from other than University connections and in our remaining relatively unknown in such social activities as did get under way among the faculty members on the campus.

For the same reasons we each avoided the social activities and student affairs within the walls of our respective institutions, the colleges. When wives were expected and usually attended (as at the annual Trustees Dinner) it was easier not to go than either to go together or, alone, to be asked repeatedly "And where is Mrs. Hollingworth ? Or should I call her Professor Hollingworth ?"

I doubt if the Dean of my own college, where I have been for over thirty years, for nearly forty, in fact, would have known L.S.H. had they met by some accident. I know well enough that I would not be able to recognize the wife of the Dean of Teachers College or Mrs. Nicholas Murray Butler, even if I met them at one of their own receptions. I say this with genuine regret, fully conscious that the ladies have suffered no appreciable loss through these circumstances. I am simply trying to see, by a review of the past, how things have come to be the way they are.

At an earlier point in this narrative it was intimated that certain boyhood experiences have probably kept me from kinds of activity and perhaps from forms of leadership that I might otherwise have enjoyed. It now seems probable that these later developments in our joint professional careers conspired with these earlier influences to give the peculiar social obscurity that I have acquired in my own institution. For it is indeed a peculiar outcome when one is better known and more at home in other institutions or in foreign parts than in the place where his life work has been carried on.

Certain Temperamental Traits

Other temperamental traits that have clearly emerged in my make-up might as well be ventillated here. Perhaps they are entangled with some of the influences that have just been recorded. I have been and still am strongly disinclined to group enterprises. Of all things that I abominate a conference is one of the worst. Socialized research programs, things to be done by councils, committees and cooperative effort do not leave me cold,- they stir in me a heated expostulation and a refractory negativism. I should not be at all surprised if my colleagues call me stubborn,- perhaps they use even stronger epithets.

All this appears to boil down to the fact that I am not socially minded; I am at least a chronic even if not a rugged individualist. The facts of individual differences bear down on me with full force. Although my history might have been expected to make me democratic, and although to my everyday behavior that term may be applicable enough, I am intellectually egocentric and impatient. Is that being snobbish ?

I think not. My habits of life are plain and even austere. My needs are simple. I get along with manual workers, tradesmen, mechanics, and the average man. But I know them for what they are and I have no great concern over the fate of the man with the hoe. I well know that too many of those ### posing as leaders and intellectuals should in all good conscience be wielding that implement instead of the fountain pen. And I do not mind this. "I accept the universe", but I do not want to spend many hours "in conference" with it .

My sympathies and loyalties are limited and narrow. I cannot get excited over the fate of Abyssinia; am allergic to all organizations for "international conciliation ; and have little or no interest in trying to change our institutions any more rapidly than they will change anyway. My primary concerns are not with the cosmos, nor even with the "brotherhood of man", but with the more immediate fate of my personal friends, my very, very local community, my closer associates, and the very few human beings for whom I have real affection.

And so I am not a joiner . As the years go by I belong to fewer and fewer organizations, although societies for this and that have multiplied like rabbits during my life time. I even went so far one day as to draw up a manifesto calculated to put out of business (the word is carefully chosen) the American Association for the Advancement of Science, on the ground of its having degenerated (expanded) into a mere paper organization. But personal loyalties again prevailed over cosmic interests and the manifesto never went to press.

When I ask ~~myself~~ how this social negativism has come about it does not seem adequate simply to ascribe it to a congenital selfishness. I am not really selfish, but am undoubtedly egocentric, and the circle of my genuine interests has a short personal radius. As I review my development up to this point it appears that practically every influence has conspired to slant me in this direction.

Uncertainties about my parentage, lack of family confidence, resentment at paternal domination, the unaided struggle with penury, utter self dependence for every inch of escape from the boyhood trap, the lack of concern over me shown by the social machinery with the real kindnesses always at the hands of purely individual friends, a lack of ease in entering into social relations except with individuals, and the realization from youth clear through the "gasping period" that society at large showed no interest in my destiny,- all these seem to have induced in me an apathy for the interests of society at large.

For strictly social purposes I have become a liability rather than a resource. Yet I feel that as an individual I can look any man in the face and challenge him to show a duty better done. I believe that as a friend I can be counted on. Here and there even small communal gains may have accrued from my having lived. But the motivation of that life has lain in my individual distresses and their alleviation, not in any inner picture of the "City of God" realized on earth.

This seems to have eventuated not from any inherited necessity, but chiefly from the lesson that where I was born and where I have lived the individual held his fate in his own hands. Perhaps this is all sheer rationalization of a constitutional inadequacy. I do not know. The matter is reported here only as part of the recollection of the ways I have felt and the thoughts that these feelings have sometimes provoked.

Another deplorable characteristic of my adult make-up I have realized more and more as life has advanced,- and that is the sluggishness of my emotional reactions. Long after an insult has been received and emotional reinforcement has lost any possible utility that it might have had, I find myself boiling with rage. Since the occasion and the opportunity for expression are past, this feeling can only smoulder as a chronic resentment. Similarly my grief and sense of deprivation lag too far behind the loss that was responsible for them. I have therefore little immediate emotional experience but a great deal of moodiness and my recovery is as slow as my break-down.

As to the origin of this trait I have wondered a good deal, but with little instructiveness. Perhaps it is just a phlegmatic constitution, dependent on a relatively inert endocrine system. If so, I do not appear to resemble my closer relatives in this respect; on the whole their emotions appear lively and prompt and they are on the scene in time to count. Mine drag along to appear only as a mocking echo, and hence they play no social role, for others do not know that they are there at all. I am therefore judged indifferent, unresponsive and unsympathetic.

There is just a possibility that the tardiness of my feelings can be traced to an honest acceptance of Biblical injunction in childhood. The Scriptures are full of slogans about the desirability of curbing and controlling impulsiveness.

> "He that is slow to wrath is of great understanding, but he that is hasty of spirit exalteth folly."

I well enough recall taking these pronouncements seriously in my youth. Many a delicate morsel has accumulated dirt in my pocket while I derived some satisfaction from resisting strong impulse to devour it, or at least felt that in thus resisting I was acquiring merit.

It is true enough that, systematically regarded, emotion can be considered only as a collapse reaction, a sign of some break down or inadequacy in the repertoire of adaptive adjustment. But the functional value of a fact is often enough left out of account in its mere systematic description. Whatever may be the genesis of my phlegmatic behavior, I am now persuaded of its undesirability in a social setting. I freely renounce the stoical philosophy, whether inherited or acquired, and envy the man whose immediate emotions are sharp and vigorous, and who promptly "tells the world". But it is futile for me at this late date to try to imitate him.

MORE "IMPUDENT LETTERS"

Perhaps connected in some ways with the foregoing characteristics are certain unfriendlinesses that have resulted from some of my many book reviews. Although I do not converse easily with my colleagues about their work, nor comfortably fraternize with other members of my profession at our association meetings, I have always enjoyed writing out my evaluations of their work. And so, often to my sorrow, I have readily been seduced by editors into writing reviews of the books of others. Since scribbling is so congenial to me and a critical approach has always been interesting, I have really enjoyed the writing of reviews. About forty such reviews are listed in my bibliography.

All has not, however, been smooth sailing in these waters. I have tried to be impartial and fair in my evaluations and have hoped that others would be equally fair in their appraisals of my own writings. Some times I have cemented good friendships when it happened that a book met with my enthusiastic approval; when this was the case I have never hesitated to voice tthe approval and always welcomed an opportunity to turn in this kind of a review.

But the occasions were not always propitious, and in these cases I have been impelled to write with equal candor. Titchener was so insulted by a review I wrote in 1911 of one of his books that he publicly demanded a public apology. His demand and my response thereto were published in the same journal that had printed the review. For many years he would have nothing to do with me. On one occasion I visited the Cornell laboratory and his colleagues telephoned him concerning my presence. He insisted that I come over to his house to see him. When he appeared at the door I extended my hand in amiable greeting, but he held his down at his side. Shortly he extended it with a jerk and exclaimed-"Well, I never thought I would be shaking hands with you again." Whereupon he invited me indoors, gave me a cigar, and we had a wholly pleasant hour of conversation. I never reminded him of the day he so discouraged me in the middle of the work for my Ph.D. dissertation, nor of the hours I had spent leading him about the Columbia campus and the stores of New York City. He was apparently wholly disoriented in the geographical environment, and asked me even to lead him from his room in the dormitory to the wash room, and then wait for his reappearance to lead him back again.

My early propensity for writing "impudent letters" may have appeared again in some of these review activities. I was prompted to write a vigorous protest against a review by Tait of the dissertation of E.K.Strong, which had been accomplished in consultation with me, and in this review I made some disparaging comment on "the psychology that Mr.Tait appears to have been taught". Immediately appeared an expostulatory letter from Hugo Münsterberg, pointing out that <u>he</u> had been responsible for the psychology the reviewer had been taught. Whereupon Münsterberg refused to serve with me on a committee of award for a prize that had been offered for papers by college students on "the psychology of automobiling", and insisted on being the sole judge. To placate him I let him have his way, but he never became my friend.

McDougall also showed signs of offence at some of the impudent things I said in a review of one of his books; and I know that Terman, whose friendship I always valued in the highest terms, was at least sorely grieved when I was forced to state my candid judgment concerning the published results of a study of the correlates of marital happiness which he, along with others, had published.

Other instances could be cited, but these should suffice to show what I have in mind. In my reviews, which I have enjoyed doing because I write with so much greater facility than I talk, I seem to have appeared too often as an obstructionist. But if all of my reviews are surveyed impartially I still feel that it will appear that the only mistake I have made was in being always candid. The many words of approval that those reviews contain have been given less attention than the cases of apparent impudence, and it is the latter that have led to the most positive changes in attitude on the part of others. But it is the "psychology of the other one", not of me, that is responsible for this outcome.

However, perhaps I am not the best judge of such matters. There is a possibility that the negativism I have recorded in the earlier paragraphs of this section has welcomed the chance to spring out in the private writing of a book review, so that my savagery has been too obvious and my appreciation not sufficiently emphatic. I have not wholly ignored the possibility of this danger, and desire to record here at least the fact that I have given it some consideration in my reflections

As I finish the writing of this section it is by chance necessary to spend the night in town instead of going back home as usual after the day's work at the college. As in the old days I have come up to the laboratory in Milbank, to write in it's solitude. For years, in the evening hours, L.S.H. and I would haunt this place because of the beneficent opportunity it gave to work at night. With all the laboratory tables available we could spread our data out before us and work until drowsiness finally drove us home. Then we would wander down the dark hallway, down the four dark flights of steps, out upon Broadway and across to Amsterdam, near which we always lived in the city.

Some years ago we ceased this lonesome habit, as we came to have room enough to work in our own apartment or in the country. But again I am here tonight, and it brings back vividly the peculiar tang of those old days,-L.S.H. and H.L.H., by their lonesome selves, working out their destiny on the bare laboratory tables. I cherish that memory and think that I shall occasionally come here ~~~~~~~~~ from time to time to revive it, just as I shall often visit the spot in a far western state which she chose ~~~~~~ for her last resting place.

But it was never really lonesome then, for her vivid spirit was there to quicken and illuminate our hours of work. Tonight it is really lonely. "Uncle Holly is a lone wolf", one of my nieces used to say. A lone wolf in psychology,- is that what this pause for consideration seems tp show me to have been ? But this would not be news to me. Even as a child I was lonely, in the midst of my fellows. I was always among them, but never quite one of them .Perhaps this is not an uncommon experience; Perhaps it is a feeling that many people have; but it is none the less real.

I well recall/adopted as ~~~~~~ ~~ favorite mottos, in my youth, the declaration of Francis Bacon that he intended to be only " the spectator of other men's fortunes". Even this act may be a familiar one, at least to such as in their youth become acquainted with such spirits as Francis Bacon. I believe there is something benign about such an attitude, if it can be maintained, and that to the extent that it can be thus maintained it gives one a fortitude in meeting life's reverses.

But I found it difficult to maintain this attitude, as my own fortune became entangled also with that of another. In the same way I was led to renounce an early declaration, recorded in ~~~ college days, that if I only had the assurance of $250 a year for life, I should be quite content to devote all my time to study and research !

At any rate, my niece spoke more truly than she realized, and she little knew how lonesome a lone wolf can come to be.

THE NEXT FIVE YEARS

So far as contributions to the literature of psychology are concerned the year 1920 was a fruitful one, and I did my own share toward adding to this harvest. Many of the studies based on data accumulated during the war, or for the time being held up by its occurrence, then saw the light of day. It was in this year that "The Psychology of Functional Neuroses" appeared,-the single volume that seems to have had the most significant material influence on my career. In the same year an enlarged and revised edition of "Applied Psychology" was published.

The "four horsemen" also combined in this year to produce an abbreviated students' edition of the original"Advertising", making a volume more suitable for class room use, entitled "Principles of Advertising." Since I had by this time gone out of this field of work and had nothing new to contribute, my own duties in connection with it were mainly editorial.

There appeared also in this year 1920 a "Manual of Psychiatry", to which I was one of five contributors. Rosanoff had been bringing out from time to time American editions of such a manual by DeFursac. He now requested several of us, with most of whom he had been somewhat closely associated in the Plattsburg episode, to contribute sections on our own specialties. The volume was no longer a mere edition of DeFursac but a wholly new manual by Rosanoff, with our own special sections. I was responsible for the didisions on mental measurement and its applications in psychiatry.

Although never professing to be a psychiatrist, I had for a long time been interested in abnormal psychology, the study of which I had begun with Bolton at Nebraska. Since that time I had read widely and tried to get a second hand acquaintance with the subject. I had for some years attended the clinics and some of the staff meetings at Manhattan State Hospital, when Adolph Meyer and August Hoch were active there. I had taken a course in psychiatry with Peterson, and also courses in neuro-anatomy with Strong and with Ames, and a course in clinical neurology, with clinical demonstrations, by Tilney and Strong I had done voluntary service in clinics for the feeble minded and was a certified examiner in mental defect in the State of New York. My Plattsburg experience, with psychoneurotics usefully supplemented these experiences with the psychoses and with intellectual deficiency. It is not to be wondered at then that I was glad to have a hand in a manual of psychiatry, and that in due time I should become the author of a textbook of Abnormal Psychology. But this, in 1920, was still a decade away.

The only book that I produced during the next five years after 1920 was a volume that combined my old interests in judgment with the work in vocational analysis. It was entitled "Judging Human Character", and was in part a survey of the modes and sources of error in such judgment, and in part the report of new experiments in this field carried on in the laboratory with my students. The emphasis was, I should say, more definitely on the topic of judgment, with little immediate bearing on practical personnel problems. Yet, it was an endeavor to improve and clarify personnel techniques in the light of the more abstract study of the ways in which judgments are made and the factors that influence them. It is easy to see that the "Experimental Studies in Judgment" and the "Vocational Psychology" of earlier years were here coming together.

As time went on, the "character" aspect of this volume was combined with the older "Vocational Psychology" in the form of a new book (1929) called "Vocational Psychology and Character Analysis". But the interest in judgment was at a whiter heat, and it soon flowered again, in 1926, in the "Psychology of Thought", about which I shall at a later point want to make a few pertinent remarks. I am here limiting myself so far as possible to the work of the five years after 1920.

Contributions to the technical periodicals during this period fall into three fairly definite groups, although there was no clear realization of this at the time. There was a miscellaneous collection of minor articles on psychological work in reconstruction, scientific selection of personnel, the study of drug effects, and the sense of taste, all harking back to earlier work of more pretentious scope, and in a sense representing the last hang over of the interests in applied psychology.

More imposing was a series of articles dealing with the thought processes and with systematic issues in psychology,-on "Meaning", on the "Psycho-physical Continuum" again, on "Symbolic Relations", on the "Definition of Judgment", and the earlier paper, presented first in abstract in 1915, on "Logic of Intermediate Steps" now appeared in full and elaborated form. All these represented the continued interest in the more abstract and theoretical problems, with a strong leaning toward the use of philosophical terms.

The new note is represented in a series of papers, totalling some 84 pages, on the immediate psychological effects of alcohol. But this is after all not a new note,-it represents the straightforward experimental approach of the psychologist in the laboratory. Even the world war and the shedding of skin under the influence of the ruby rash had not wholly eliminated the trifurcation of personality .

THE ALCOHOL EXPERIMENTS

The investigations of the immediate effects of alcohol on the mental and motor behavior of human beings was carried on in 1919 and 1920, some nine years after the work on caffeine. This problem arose in connection with the conflicts and arguments over prohibition, and a particular problem had to do with the alcoholic content that "near-beer" might contain without being considered intoxicating. The brewing industry was interested in this question and members had sought scientific evidence in various ways, to little avail. A psychiatrist who had been asked for evidence held a banquet of his friends and associates, invited in a few college boys and had them drink beer with known alcoholic content (unvaried) and then called a vote as to whether or not the boys had become intoxicated. This naive pseudo-scientific procedure disappointed even the brewers.

I was thereupon invited to make whatever investigations were needed to throw light on this question, and so we set up once more the technique of the original caffeine experiments, using alcoholic and control beverages instead of the caffeine and the sugar-of-milk controls. Six men were hired to serve as experimental subjects,- to drink or not to drink, and to work steadily throughout the day at our tests. From time to time we measured such functions as steadiness, coordination, motor speed, speech control, mental alertness, logical thinking, learning ability, memory, and pulse rate.

Each man also kept a subjective record of the state of his feelings from time to time and the experimental assistants made periodical records of their judgments and observations, aside from the measurements. In this investigation I was fortunate in having the co-laboration of Prof. Woodworth and Drs. G.S. Gates and F.E. Carothers as experimental observers.

The experiments were not as dull as they may sound in this description. Since we had already moved to the country for the spring and summer, we set up the experiments originally in our apartment on the second floor on 118th Street. The daily cargoes of beer bottles that were delivered made the neighbors suspicious of the goings on in our apartment. The noon drinking period, when the "doses" were administered and the men encouraged to spend the hour in conviviality, just as they might at an ordinary drinking session, aroused further doubts. When finally, under appropriate dosages, one of the men began to swing back and forth in pendular fashion the heavy dining room chandelier, we agreed with the neighbors that it was time to remove the investigation to more appropriate quarters. So we continued for the remainder of the two weeks which the experiments lasted in the laboratory in Schermerhorn Hall. Even here there were frivolous moments, as when one of the subjects, under appropriate dosage, began to stick gummed labels on the top of Prof. Woodworth's bald head.

Scientifically the investigation was a complete success, and I do not think I shall ever see a set of curves as striking and convincing as those resulting from our analysis of the data from these experiments on alcohol. The report of the findings was published in installments in the Journal of Abnormal and Social Psychology, in 1923 and 1924. Once more the industrial interests permitted the publication of the results regardless of their outcome, and it has seemed to me that this is the best way to guarantee validity for the results of investigations supported by commercial interests.

The duplication of the caffeine technique, in part, in ths alcohol investigation, made possible certain further comparisons that had not heretofore been made. We could show, under the same or closely similar circumstances, the ways in which the two different agents, caffeine and alcohol, influenced identical forms of behavior, and studies of this sort were made and reported in later articles in the journals. We were enabled to make useful observations concerning the individual differences in susceptibility to such drug influences, and to relate these in interesting ways to idiosyncrasies in other respects. In fact the drug experiment, it now began to appear, might serve as a neat laboratory paradigm for life itself, and disclose in measurable ways important variables that influence human type and conduct in general. We were also able to make a comparative study of several different ways of measuring or estimating the presence of intoxication and were able to bring clearly to light some of the difficulties involved in the definition of such a term. As late as 1931, a good ten years after the alcohol investigation and twenty years after the caffeine experiments, I was still going back to the barrel of data provided by these two inquiries for material for special reports and articles. And it may well be that the end is not yet. Although both of these investigations were sponsored by industrial interests, I have never considered them to lie in the field of applied psychology. They were from the beginning straightforward efforts to discover the nature of certain facts and relationships, and the chief interest of the findings has never been in any industrial or commercial application of them.

The most interesting things coming from these drug experiments were collateral results, of no concern whatever to the sponsors of the investigations. The data accumulated in such researches could be utilized to throw light on any number of topics not even dreamed of when the experiments were made. Thus I was able to try a check analysis in order to see if my data verified McDougall's declaration that introverts and extroverts are differentially susceptible to toxic agents. Other comparisons showed that individuals more unstable and variable in their normal work were the ones most easily influenced by a given dosage. Intelligent subjects and good learners in the type of work used were the most resistant to drug effects. Subjects showing the least disturbance in work scores showed the most striking changes in pulse rate. And so on.

These results tied up neatly enough also with those from the study of war neuroses. In the drug experiment, I became convinced, the human being exhibits in a laboratory setting the same make-up as that with which he confronts the world at large. The question as to what a particular drug does to one's behavior becomes trivial as compared with the more general principles and relationships which such experiments reveal. Thus I was able to devote a whole chapter in my volume on "Abnormal Psychology" to the systematic and strictly psychological significance of studies of the immediate effects of toxic agents. In all this occupation with pharmaco-psychology I have learned little or nothing about drugs, but a great deal, I believe, about human nature and mental organization. There are numerous side analyses of this sort in my files that have never seen the light of publication.

ON THE WITNESS STAND AGAIN

During the early part of the five year period here reported my Plattsburg experience was the occasion of a second appearance in the court room as a psychological expert. The first such appearance had been at the hearing at Chattanooga. On this second occasion a former Plattsburg psychiatric colleague had undertaken to advise the attorney for the defense in a murder case. He asked me to give the defendant a psychological examination and to report to the court my findings as to his level of intelligence. Visiting the defendant in his place of detention I spent a half day appraising his mental level by means of standardized tests.

I found him to have a mental age of about nine years, and satisfied myself that all possibilities of incooperation and of malingering had been covered and was willing to take oath on my findings. What I intended to do was simply to lay before the judge and jury these results, show them how the defendant, in degree of understanding and insight compared with the average adult and with children of different ages, and in this way let the facts contribute whatever they should toward justice.

But difficulties arose from the moment I took the chair. In the first place I had to qualify as an expert, and in the state in which this court sat there seemed to be inadequate precedent for recognizing a psychologist as an expert. The attorney for the defense tried all the tactics he could think of to satisfy the court that I was really an expert. He showed how many students were enrolled at Columbia University, where I taught, but this did not satisfy the court. He then showed how many psychological examinations I had given in my whole life; cited the number of my published books; my years of teaching. None of these or other devices seemed to fulfill the demand for a precedent. My having been commissioned an officer in the Sanitary Corps and appointed by the Surgeon General's Office to responsible ##### duties of a psychological sort seemed a little more convincing, still, I had no medical degree, and how could a man be an expert without this ?

Finally the judged ruled that there had to be a first instance of everything, for otherwise there never could be any precedents established. He decided that this occasion was going to become a precedent for the recognition of qualified psychologists, and my testimony was permitted to begin. But the troubles were not over. I was first required to describe the tests I had used, with no reference to my conclusions. Then I was asked to prove that my tests were valid. I set out on a naive seminar-like proof, citing the history of the tests, the method of their derivation and standardization, and quoted figures on their degree of reliability and the magnitude of their probable error. All through the morning hours I tried in this way to demonstrate the validity of my tests, to no judicial avail.

I was then dismissed for an intermission. Before I took the stand again after lunch I was in the court room when a veteran court expert in another field was likewise requested to "prove" the validity of the methods he had employed. He simply replied that from his own knowledge and based on his own experience he knew them to be adequate. This was enough, and he proceded with his testimony.

Whereupon, having taken the stand again and being once more invited to give evidence of the validity of my tests, I promptly asserted that I knew them to be valid from my own knowledge and experience. Well", said the judge, "Why couldn't you have given that evidence hours ago ? Proceed with the testimony." This legal conception of evidence as only the sworn assertion of a witness was not wholly new to me, yet I had never considered the possibility of demonstrating the validity of scientific techniques in that way. I am sure that Prof. Cattell would never have admitted that kind of proof in his seminar.

Even then my legal experience was just beginning, and it required two days before I was allowed to report even my own opinion of the meaning of the defendant's test scores. For it was not permitted clearly to state my conclusions and I was not allowed to state the man's 'mental age'. Instead, it was necessary that I listen to a long 'hypothetical question', terminating with ,- "'In the light of these evidences and of your examination of the defendant, was he at the time able to know the nature and quality of his act, and that it was wrong ? Answer YES or NO ."

I protested that##### no such categorical answer was possible, ө that what I could do was to indicate the degree of his understanding, that there could be no sharp YES-NO line drawn in such a case. After long argument and much comment by the impatient judge, I agreed that I could answer "YES and NO"; - the YES meaning that he could understand the nature of his act, the NO meaning that he could not fully understand ### its quality. Although the attorney, taking the lapel of his coat in his hand, did his best to convince the judge that the nature of that fabric and its quality were actually two different things, and that likewise the hypothetical question was really two different questions, to which I had to give different answers, the judge remained unconvinced.

One precedent had already been newly set up in that court, but to permit another such novelty seemed to be going too far. The hypothetical question was repeated and repeated, and I persisted in my inability to give a single answer, much to the judge's disgust. Neither would he allow me, at my request, to state just what it was that I might be able to contribute to the understanding of this case. I must say either YES or NO.

Upon being dismissed, to continue next day, I thought I had a bright idea, and conferred with the attorney who was just about to abandon all hope of getting any of my evidence before the jury. I explained to him that if he wished, and if he could convince the judge of my meaning, I was now ready to give a categorical NO to the hypothetical question. He was to ask both parts again, as the law apparently required, and he was to emphasize the conjunction "and" when he read it. "Did he know the nature <u>and</u> the quality of his act <u>and</u> that it was wrong ?"

My NO was to be a denial of this proposition taken in its <u>totality</u>, on the ground that although part of it was true, part was not, and if I were being asked "Are <u>all</u> these things true ?" I could conscientiously say NO. He was satisfied. Putting me back on the stand the next day he repeated the hypothetical question, emphasizing the "and", at which the judge looked up quizzically. I said "No", but was myself surprised to hear my own declaration given in such a weak voice that the judge in astonishment and disbelief asked me to repeat my answer. He then demanded that I explain why today I could give a single answer when for two days I had declared my inability to do so .

Although he was disgusted with my explanation, and had no more use for that given by the attorney, the jury had at least been allowed to hear my verdict. It seemed doubtful however whether they knew what the two day dispute had been about. At least it did the defendant no good, for he was convicted and condemned, in all or none fashion, just as if there had been no debate over the issue as to whether degrees of understanding are discrete or continuous. And it is possible that the judge may have regretted that he had ever violated precedent and allowed such a person as a quibbling psychologist to qualify as an expert. Certainly the issues are often decided in a court of law in ways very different from those popular in Hinman's seminar on advanced logic.

THE GAY DECADE

Before the end of this five year period (in 1923) L.S.H was again promoted, to become Associate Professor of Education, amd our income thus advanced again. Books of hers appeared, and royalties along with them. My own books in those days were filling a modest demand. L.S.H. was often called on for profitable adventures in public speaking, and she maintained several clinical connections that contributed in important ways to her work, and she had begun one of the cooperative experiments on the education of gifted children for which she subsequently became so well known. By the end of the five year period I have just described she had published some 28 papers in the technical journals, and four of her books or monographs had appeared by that time.

In 1925 we had promoted ourselves to a Hupmobile sedan, in place of the old Chevrolet touring car, and we were much impressed by the mighty roar it made. That roar seemed to us to be a token of power. But before we turned it in nine years later for a new and improved vehicle, we had become sceptical of our impression. We seemed to understand better, however, why the lion had established his reputation as the "King of beasts", and we had by that time observed parallels to this situation in human relationships.

It was in 1924 that Francie abandoned us for the greener field of Porto Rico. That was the year that the Weischer's, now so well known to all our friends, entered into our lives. Josefine the mother and Virginia, as a six year old child, came to

FROM COCA-COLA TO CHEWING GUM

Josefine and Virginia

assume the genuine management of our housekeeping just before we left 118th Street for what we considered a fairly grand place to live on Morningside Drive. And grand in many ways it was. It had eight rooms and all windows were on the outside, with not a single court for radios and cats to howl through.

The changes in our ménage became conspicuous. ########## Josefine, full of energy, exceptionally intelligent, with a cosmopolitan background, a passion for cleanliness, and fond of good things which she could make with skill to satisfy an epicure, at once took off the shoulders of L.S.H. the cares of marketing and planning. She and her work became the heart of our household, and she became famous for a variety of things that our friends knew they could enjoy if they came to visit "The Holly's".

And the little six-year-old who more or less toddled into our apartment in those days, answering to the name of Virginia, has now absorbed a college education, grown into a steady and self-reliant woman, cooperated with me in a piece of research, *married,* and goes productively about her own professional activities.

Early in the gay decade I was elected President of the American Psychological Association,- one of the scientific honors that I most highly prize. The next year we were due for a Sabbatical and we had at last our longed for trip to Europe, all by ourselves. While in Europe we received the welcome news that important increases all along the salary scale had been made at Columbia, so that both of us were assured of an appreciable increase in resources in the following year. Shortly after my election to the presidency of the American Psychological Association my college also saw fit to elevate me to the special status of "highly paid professor". We were on the crest of the wave; we had become known, and no longer need we shout to each other the early morning slogan about the "pants".

We left on our trip for Europe without thought of economy. We had waited and waited and saved for this opportunity. We took one of the biggest and swiftest boats and made ourselves comfortable thereon. We went to London and saw it to our heart's content, meeting also many of the British psychologists. We visited Melbourne, the ancestral home of my grandparents. We toured Ireland and acquired a stock of amusing anecdotes there that lasted us for many years. Then we crossed over into Scotland, and acquired more anecdotes.

We went to Hamburg, where L.S.H. visited all kinds of special schools and hob-nobbed with the educational experts. In Berlin we visited at the University and revelled in the special comforts of a glorious hotel we found there. We hired motor cars and drivers and went to the Hanseatic cities, went through the Black Forest, put up in the coddling atmosphere of Baden-Baden; came to Cologne, explored the Rhine; drifted through Belgium and homeward, on another huge and swift boat.

We did just what we wanted; we went everywhere, to many good spots (such as Nürnberg) that I have not mentioned; we took photographs of each other,-in jaunting cars, on the Giant's Causeway, in ruined castles, at the Heidelberg Fair, on boats, in deep forests, in national capitals, alongside palaces. And we came back to collect

FORTISSIMO

A Glimpse of Ancestral Derbyshire

royalty checks and salary advances that put us right back where we had been when we started out on our grand spree. The grand decade of inflation was under way and we were under full steam ahead. In the following year L.S.H. was promoted to a full proffes-sorship.

We came back to find many of our friends deep in the stock market, which was sky-rocketing while they accumulated vast paper profits. But this was something we had not learned much about, and we were wary (then) . We had put our small and carefully gleaned savings into real estate, in Washington where the folks had supervision of it; or we put them into what we called gilt edged national bonds (Peru, Brazil, Argentine, and Chicago school warrants); or we had bought that conservative investment of the widow and orphan ,-"guaranteed real estate mortgages"; and we had a sprinkling of Liberty Bonds and a few municapals , and here and there a savings account. For the time being we seemed secure, and were content with no paper profits .

The freedom that we had long wanted, to forget the little dabs of income and the deficits on the budget, was upon us. We were ready for two great consummations. One of these, we were shortly to be informed, was to be forever denied us. The other was ours to command, so that we launched with full energy again into our professional work.

FORTISSIMO

~~167A~~
167a

Somewhere in Ireland

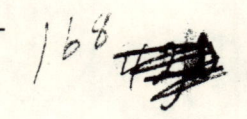

So strong was the intellectual impetus, upon being so completely freed from economic distress, that in the ten years after 1925 I published a new book nearly every year, in addition to a trickle of articles in the journals. "The Psychology of Thought" appeared in 1926; "Mental Growth and Decline" in 1927; "Psychology, Its Facts and Principles" in 1928; "Vocational Psychology and Character Analysis" in 1929; "Abnormal Psychology" in 1930; "Educational Psychology" in 1933; and "Psychology of the Audience" in 1935. There were thirteen of the articles, besides, in the psychological or other journals.

As the result of suggestions growing up in connection with the 1920 volume on "Functional Neuroses", I was formulating a point of view in psychology. Most of these books reflected this systematic view-point, as applied to one or another of the major fields in which I had worked.

The educational freedom that was permitted to the teaching staff of Barnard College was one of the things that made all these volumes possible. I was free to give whatever special courses I wished, once the fundamental introductory course and the experimental course had been taken care of. Before long additional instructors were provided who ably handled these fundamental courses, which rapidly grew beyond the capacity of one man to handle. This gave me still greater freedom to develop special fields according to my changing interests. The freedom from administrative domination at Barnard has been a great incentive to scholarly work in that institution. Practically every one of my courses grew into a book which some publisher was willing to take a chance on. To the enlightened and liberal administration of Barnard College during my years there, my scientific productivity owes much.

A SYSTEMATIC VIEW- POINT DEVELOPS

The study of the functional neuroses resulted in an interpretation that has come to be generally known as "redintegration." But the use of this term was unfortunate and has led to a common misunderstanding of the doctrine advanced in "Functional Neuroses". What impressed me was to be sure that these patients were unduly influenced by trivial details of earlier contexts. Such details led to responses such as had been formerly made to the more elaborate early contexts.

But such reactions are also characteristic of normal perception; that is the way we judge space; the way we understand what we read; the way we get enjoyment from poetry; and so on. The essential trouble with the neurotic I conceived to be not this fundamental mental process, but his obliviousness to the new circumstances in which the effective detail now appears. This limitation I called lack of "scope" or "weak sagacity". It is this failure to "com-prehend" the effective detail or symbol, along with its present setting, that makes the individual neurotic.

I had thus however hit upon two processes or features of behavior that seemed to me to be significant. One was "redintegration",- that is, the effectiveness of slight cues in producing impressive reactions. The other was "degree of scope",-which reflects the openness of the individual to the present environment that is, socially regarded, bearing down upon him.

Redintegrative behavior, that is the tendency to react to slight or attenuated cues (symbols, signs) I conceived to be the essential thing about mind. Those who lack this capacity cannot learn and we call them feeble in mind.

Undue limitation of "scope" is what I conceived to be the picture presented by the neurotic. The healthy mind is just a redintegrative system that ######### operates under an optimal degree of "scope." The problem with the neurotic is therefore to discover what cues in the present <u>function for</u> past distresses (without in any way "re-producing" them) in determining the undesirable conduct (symptom or complaint). To discover, next, for what past contexts these cues now function as surrogates or symbols. The therapeutic procedure then, is to re-train these cues to function for more propitious contexts. The various systems of psychotherapy it seemed to me represented only various ways of effecting this re-training. Such an account, I was able to show to my own satisfaction, renders intelligible the bizarre accounts rendered in figurative language by other theories of the neuroses.

To these conceptions I had to add only some account of the nature of "motives". All motives seemed to me to be essentially irritants or distresses. Life is a flight from goads, not a struggle toward goals. The goals, when they are at all represented, are but fancied techniques of escaping or reducing the initial distress.

Cue reduction, scope, and motive, thus gave me three fundamental concepts with which to operate. The various books to which I have referred were the records of my original fumbling efforts to show how these three principles provided the systematic basis for the analysis and investigation of all psychological topics.

So far as publication is concerned, the first step toward generalizing these three leading conceptions was in the "Psychology of Thought." The original intention was to call this volume "Sleeping, Dreaming and Thinking". I wanted first of all to clear the ground of certain encumbering notions about sleep. This phenomenon, which appeared to me to be one of the severest of human tragedies, I found the human race indifferent to. Vast fortunes were devoted to the investigation of hookworm and other minor ills. But sleep seemed even to be considered a boon. I wanted first of all to call attention to this strange situation. But I found that nearly every one took my suggestions as being jocular rather than made with serious intent.

I wanted next, starting with the earlier observations of drowsiness experiences, to show how dreaming offered all the characteristic features presented by more deliberative thinking. Especially I was interested in showing that thoughts are wholly <u>natural</u> things,- they are reduced cues or symbols, operating effectively as surrogates for other contexts, of which they have once been part . That is to say, I wanted to show the redintegrative character of rational activity, using the dream as a psychological instrument in this endeavor.

I next wanted to show how such mysterious topics as "meaning", "judgment", and "reasoning" could be understood, as the play of such symbols, actual occurring items in experience, such as words, images, gestures, relations, and the like, without the necessity of introducing "universals", "faculties" and "soul structure".

But the publisher did not like the title I had chosen, and agreed to bring the book out on his list if I should change the title to "Psychology of Thought". The other topics, which as a matter of fact open the volume, seemed to sit strangely under this title without explanation, so that I had to write an introductory chapter to show what in the long run I intended to do in the book.

In addition, in this volume, I felt the necessity of sweeping away a lot of cloudy notions that psychology had inherited from the days when it was a carefully supervised hand-maiden of philosophy. These dealt especially with such distinctions as those between subjective and objective, physical and mental, psychical and material, and with the much debated relationship between mind and body.

I tried to sweep these away in a high handed fashion, in terms of my "psycho-physical continuum". According to this notion all these distinctions ultimately fell back on that between the subjective and the objective. And between these I found no great gulf, but only a continuum of degrees of consistency of report. The difference between 'mind' and 'body' turned out thus to be but a statistical one, and no essential or intrinsic difference aside from this could be found. Subjective events are those on which the reports vary considerably; objective events are those on which there is little discrepancy of report. In between are all possible degrees of unanimity.

The traditional philosophical riddles, I urged, were therefore artefacts, dependent especially on the dichotomous character of our verbal language, which in turn probably went back to the influence of our bilateral symmetry on the development of gesture language. We could therefore forget them, and turn our attention to genuine psychological issues. The writing of this book gave me genuine pleasure and I am still very fond of it. No one else appears to be. Although the edition sold out and the book has been for some time out of print, I have yet to see any reference to it in psychological literature.

"Mental Growth and Decline" had been under way, and actually nearly ready for the publisher before all these points emerged in my thinking. This book had grown up as the result of a course we had started at Barnard on "developmental psychology", and I had not clearly enough assimilated the material in this field to my systematic position. The field of mental development, one then being neglected, shortly took a spurt so that new material accumulated so rapidly as quickly to put the volume out of date. I had intended to survey all the steps in the life span in a single bird's eye view. But each of the "ages of man" came suddenly to be so intensively cultivated that the prospect of summarising all the available results between the covers of a single book became more and more difficult.

In later years I carefully revised and again revised and enlarged the material first presented in "Mental Growth and Decline". I not only included the new materials as they came along, but more and more instructively I developed cue reduction, scope and motivation (distress) as the key principles in mental growth. New books in the field came out so rapidly and in such quick succession that I never took the necessary steps to urge upon the publisher these revisions. In my own thinking however, and in the course, which I still continue to give each year, the three fundamental principles are clearly enough exploited as underlying the phenomena of mental growth and decline. Some day I may summon up the courage to try this revision on the publisher again. For the present, it provides me with a wealth of material for my lectures, and the original book, once conceived as a text, is now merely a sketchy outline.

THREE FUNDAMENTAL PRINCIPLES

I may fairly be said to have announced the seriousness of my intention to formulate a systematic view point in psychology in a couple of articles that appeared in 1928. One of these was entitled "General Principles of Redintegration", in which there were mapped out certain principles associated with or characterising the kind of sequence I called redintegrative. The other was the publication of my 1927 presidential address before the American Psychological Association. I had devoted thoughtful care to the preparation of this address. It seemed to me ungracious to begin by saying "Fellow psychologists, listen to my own pet system." And yet I wanted to get the foundation of what was to come later in my work on record before them.

So I chose to begin with the elaboration of a somewhat special point of interest, showing some of the subjective factors that influence systems of thought. It was this introductory topic that gave the address its title,- a very misleading one, in point of fact. After the introductory topic was disposed of I launched freely into a brief synopsis of my view point. Although the address was well enough received, I fancied that no one took it very seriously. Coming home from the meetings, Prof. Cattell tried hard to compliment me on the address, but he could not do so wholeheartedly and he expressed some discontent with the fact that it had been so entirely 'verbal'. I began to expostulate that words and numbers (which he of course preferred) were alike nothing but symbols, but he impetuously stopped my flow of talk. Since I never argued with my teachers, but let their opinions flow freely in and out, I did not push my point,- although I continued to have my own ideas about it.

This was especially true because I conceived my "view point" to be merely a platform, from which to approach a whole program of research and interpretation. Later in the same year (1928) appeared the volume which I have always considered my masterpiece,- "Psychology, Its Facts and Principles". Here I undertook to survey the whole array of psychological topics, in each case reinterpreting the classical views and analysing all psychological activities in terms of my three fundamental principles,-

    a-That the effectiveness of partial cues in reinstating consequents appropriate to larger antecedent contexts is the essential thing about mental phenomena and processes. The "power of the symbol" lies herein, and this I conceived to be what had always been meant by "the spiritual".

    b-That degree of scope, as a characteristic in which organisms differ from one another, is an equally fundamental fact and a heavy determinant of what we call the "effectiveness" of mental processes. This I considered simply a natural variant for which no further explanation was yet available.

    c-That all motives are distresses,- that is, positive pangs, aches, hurts and discomforts, and that all action is in the endeavor to alleviate or to reduce these initial distresses. Instead of conduct being the "pursuit of pleasure", I conceived it to be a struggle <u>away from</u> goads.

In this way I seemed able to incorporate, to my own satisfaction, the contributions of the various warring schools of psychology, and to show, in straightforward naturalistic and descriptive terms what their analogies and allegories were all about. This volume did me personally a lot of good. It straightened out my thinking in psychology, heretofore muddled and messy, and it mapped out a path for all of my subsequent work to take. But it was never widely adopted as a text. This was perhaps in part because of its "heaviness" and "compactness"; in part also because no one not already conversant with the "system" could use the volume in the easy way in which class texts are supposed to be used. One of my colleagues described the book as having been written for myself alone.

I had now formulated my "view point" in a general way, in "Facts and Principles"; in "Functional Neuroses" I had put the germs of the view point to work in that special field; in my revised notes on "Mental Growth and Decline" the same point of view had been elaborated in the field of growth and development. Two years later (1930) "Abnormal Psychology" was published, and in this volume I tried to extend to the whole field of abnormal activities the same instructive principles that I had elaborated in the earlier volumes. I have always considered this a creditable volume; until it was superseded by later texts, it had a good enough welcome and seemed to be a dignified enterprise such as psychologists as such had not yet undertaken in the field of the abnormal. I have not yet seen any occasion to depart from the interpretations there laid down, and my personal belief is that next to "Facts and Principles", it is my best volume.

Meantime I had been responsible for a course in educational psychology, for students already introduced to the general field. The available texts lacked appeal, and on the whole the field of educational psychology seemed to me to be topsy-turvy and lacking in coherence. Introducing "Individual Differences" as a very naturalistic fourth principle, I now wrote out a systematic analysis of the tasks of the teacher and the problems of the learner, in terms of the four fundamental principles. I was able to state all these principles in simpler terms by this time, and in some respects "Educational Psychology" gives an easier account of my general point of view than do any of the other volumes. Moreover, it still seems to me to have introduced sense into that strange hodgepodge of material commonly called educational psychology. But again, perhaps because you have to believe a system before you can adopt the text, few have used it aside from my own institution.

The last volume of a general character to appear from my hand was "Psychology of the Audience", published in 1935, at the very end of "the gay decade". Actually I had this volume in my files for many years. It was really only an analysis of the performer-audience relations according to the same rules that had been applied years before to advertising, in my first general book. But I had steadily collected experimental and observational material until gradually a respectable manuscript came into being, although one that never seemed to me to have much fire in it. However the time came, when at an editor's request I turned the manuscript over and it appeared as a book, which a good many people seem to have found useful.

The occasion of the original drafting of this material was in some ways typical of much of my life. I had been requested to give a talk on the topic to a college group interested in debating. I did not relish this chore, but set about it with such good will as I could muster. Then having taken the first step, I determined to capitalize my calamity by really making something of the topic. I now find that a good deal of my productive work has come out of calamity; one way of combatting the calamity seems always to have been to turn it to some good end.

So, essentially, I wrote "Psychology of the Audience" because I was practically forced to make a speech on the subject; so also I had written "Advertising and Selling" because I had found it absolutely necessary to meet with my men's groups down town and spend hours weekly on this topic. The World War I actually put to good use also, since from it came "Functional Neuroses" which in the end was of considerable use to me, both practically and theoretically. It might even be said that writing these memoirs is an endeavor to turn my worst tragedy to some benign end.

Practically all of my other technical articles during this decade were written from the point of view of and in the interests of the system. In "How We Learn Our Reflexes" (1928) I tried to show how these principles might be responsible for learning before birth and that many of the specific capacities commonly attributed to heredity might easily enough be achieved through embryonic learning. A series articles on "The Nature of Learning", "The Law of Effect", Illusions as Neuroses", "Variations in Suggestibility" and "Omission of Intermediate Steps in Behavior", were all inter-related. Essentially, they attempted to apply the general principles of the "system" to the learning process, as I had done more generally in the "Educational Psychology".

Since 1935 there have been a few papers on more or less unrelated topics, such as gestalt theory, synesthesia, and perceptual fluctuation. But the main contribution since that date is to be found in the monograph and the several articles reporting my experimental investigations of "The Psycho-Dynamics of Chewing. This project and its results will be reviewed in a later section. There may also be included as an Appendix to this volume a complete bibliography of my publications which will facilitate the precise location of any of the papers that have been mentioned.

Perhaps this is an appropriate place in which to comment on the reception of this "system" by my professional colleagues. No one seems quite to have shared the author's enthusiasm over its principles. This is not wholly the system's fault, but in part the fault of my presentation of it. The widest discussion accorded it has been in connection with its application to the field of mental abnormality, and the difficulties here raised have been similar to those raised in other connections.

I should never have used the term "redintegration", although I thought that, since the word was now generally abandoned, I could resurrect it with a new meaning. This was an error. Resurrected, it has carried still its old historical connotation, and thus led to gross misundertanding of what I meant it to mean. Many of the objections hinge on this misunderstanding.

Quite aside from the choice of a term, I gave too much emphasis to the cue-reduction process, inadequately emphasing the importance of motives (distresses) and control (scope). Readers tended to respond to this over-emphasis and assumed my whole account to be based on the single principle , which, taken alone, is wholly inadequate to bear such a burden.

Finally, before launching the system, I should have devised a neat name for it, or at least a slogan. It should have been clearly recognizable as some kind of an "ism", so that others could refer to it easily and confidently. My endeavor to show that this account is "psychology", whereas other accounts are only "isms" may have succeeded in the class room, where I had the floor and graded the papers, but it is clear enough that my professional colleagues have not been wholly persuaded on this point. Since the main value of a system is to organize a man's own thinking and program of research, there is apparently nothing in this outcome to be regretted.

THE DECADE SOBERS UP

The general fate of this decade, in world history, is now so well known that I scarcely need relate it. It shows in the market graphs, in the trade indices, in the lists of bankruptcies, in the bank failures, in the suicide rate, and still asserts itself in the income decline of the endowed colleges. The strange antics resorted to for the relief of this fate are also still with us, in the national deficit, in the alphabet organizations and authorities, and in the way that the coddling of the shiftless (as well as of the unfortunate) is exacted of the industrious and the thrifty.

Out in the sand-hills of Nebraska it is well known how the subsidizing of the Indian has reduced him to a condition where he will not even hunt or fish, to say nothing of scalp. There is a saying there that I have heard from the mouths of dependable but well nigh exasperated cow-men that "This government is just makin' Injuns out of the white men." Since it lies outside my own field of expertness, I do not pass judgment on such a matter, but I think that I understand clearly enough what the cow-men have in mind.

At any rate, the decade that began so gaily in about 1925 gloriously cracked toward its end, in the early 30's. The gilt edge national bonds, with coupons still attached, were sold in order to declare an income tax loss; the guaranteed mortgages went up in smoke; we were advised by responsible officers in the city government of Chicago to sell our tax anticipation warrants for whatever they would bring on the open market.

Presumably responsible people, to whose rescue in their business emergencies we had gone with our Liberty Bonds, then went into bankruptcy. ~~and~~ We saw every dollar of securities that we still held decline to a value of 18 cents. All this, I am glad to say, did not deter us from going on with the full tide of our work. L.S.H. took it all with genuine serenity, confident that everything would come back. I was less certain about this, and a good part of my time began to be occupied in juggling our little investments, pretending to apply psychology to the stock market, and doing my best to <u>make</u> things come back by my own astuteness.

Sometimes I succeeded; often the experiences were bitter enough. The psychology often failed to apply, and the astuteness came severely into question. But, in the intervals between books, I devoted my whole energies in leisure hours, for several years, to this campaign for our "historical solvency". All I wanted was to be able to say that in the long run we had come out even.

L.S.H. thought I was much too preoccupied with these matters and I never could quite make her appear to understand that what I called my "self respect" was intimately involved, since it had been I that had assumed responsibility for our joint savings and their contribution toward our future security. I really felt quite deeply on this point, and not until we could finally say that we were "historically solvent" did a certain tenseness in my facial muscles give way to relaxation. At any rate, my scholarly work went on, and one book a year is enough for any man to write, — some people might say "too many".

For the time being, at least our jobs appeared to be secure, although "cuts" in salary were from to time threatened. In the institution where L.S.H. worked these "cuts" were more than once enforced and were never wholly restored. In my own institution, by what legerdemain of management I do not know, we were able to weather all the calamities and my own salary still stood at its peak. So that our present lives, barring future disasters worse than those we then knew, were secure enough, and we continued as vigorously as ever with our work.

We were however somewhat concerned over the remote future, which was what we had been saving for. We resolved to "cancel our denominator" in some respects, as the numerator continued to shrink, and thus if possible maintain the value constant. We decided once and for all to abandon our city apartment, which I had really always loathed anyway, rebuild our country place for year round occupancy, and move to the country, to become commuters.

Into this project I leaped with eagerness. All the old carpentering tricks were revived. I began to draw up floor plans and elevations, to unbutton the stairway again, and once more to remove partitions. All through the winter of 1932 and into the spring of 1933, when the banks were closing and ruin could almost be heard falling around us like dry leaves in the autumn, I would trot back and forth to Montrose to supervise the rebuilding of our house, and to transform it at last into the place that we could call "home."

WE BECOME PERMANENT COUNTRY FOLKS

We dug under the one corner of the place that did not rest flat on a rock ledge, and with pick and sledge and wheel barrow we mined a cellar under almost the entire house, which was meanwhile propped up on stilts as we rebuilt and reinforced the foundation. We tore down one wing and enlarged it into a two-storey addition; we remodelled practically every room ,moved nearly every door and many of the windows. We re-wired the place in a suitable fashion, and installed an oil burning furnace with a plethora of radiators and an abundance of hot water. We lined the interior in ways that were not conventional but that satisfied us, and insulated the floor of the attic. We added room after room,arranged buffers for privacy, and whenever we could think of nothing else to do we added another bath room !.At last one of my life long bug-bears was to be taken care of in appropriate fashion.

And then we hired trucks and carted all our belongings out to the Montrose colony, where we became permanent residents ,- winter and summer. Before long some of our friends became more and more country minded. The Gates's ,with whom we had formed one of the closest of friendly associations, before long built their charming Windways and no winter weather could frighten them from a week end there; summers they were there always. The Poffenbergers,another pair whom we had come to enjoy most heartily,soon installed heat in their place adjacent to us, and were more often than formerly to be found there,even on cold days. Helen Hull and Mabel Robinson built their picturesque cottage on a rocky shelf and made it their winter resort. L.S.H. had been attached to them ever since their common days as graduate students.

FORTISSIMO

183a

The House at Hollyneyek

Before long the genial Jersilds, whom we had all long wished could become members of the colony, decided to do so and they were promptly admitted to the "trustees; their own delightful project is still progressively expanding. The Reisners took to spending more time in their place, and the young Thorndikes took over one of the most imposing of the colony places when the Woodbridges were impelled to move back to the city..Ruth Strang began to appear at her cottage in the summer time at least. The Keppels and Evans's and Bagster-Collins's continued as before to be all the year residents. The colony became the best place in the world to live.

L.S.H. joined a bridge club in Peekskill where her old friends the Donald's continued to live. I could now wear out all my old clothes wrestling with rocks and timbers and running close second to the Kaiser with my axe. Fortunately the Weischers, both Josefine and Virginia, loved the country and the woods as much as any of us, and we settled down in complete comfort to enjoy, along with a coterie of friends who were just the ones we should have picked had we had it all our own way, the rest of our "forty years."

Very little "shop" was talked in our get-togethers. This sometimes surprised visitors who had expected high flown and pedantic conversation, full of science and philosophy and educational objectives. Instead we talked about the plumbing, or the wood piles, or somebody's vista . Over a highball at the Gates's or the Jersild's, or over a bit of "aged Scotch" at the Poff's we discussed and debated our projects ,-where we should move the garbage pit to, how best to drain the swamp, whether or not to turn the tennis court into a vegetable garden, and ever and anon how to keep the community dogs (of which ours was always one of the worst) from undesirable depredations and nuisances. I had **never** had a dog before in my life ! Neither had I ever had a genuine leather baseball mit, so I straightway bought two !

We had moved to the country, among other considerations, in part to save the exorbitant rent charged for city apartments; for we were being charged the whole salary of an assistant professor merely to occupy the ungainly and slovenly built and execrably painted apartment where we finally landed on Morningside Drive. We were never actually able to determine whether we had really effected such a saving, because we immediately felt impelled to expand and to enjoy our new found freedom to the utmost.

We indulged in a "second car'; then of course we had to enlarge the garage ; then our enterprises about the grounds, and the necessities of marketing and caring for things in our joint absence at duty made it seem desirable to have a man ; then we were impelled to have him stay on the premises, so that the garage expanded again. Then the water district was formed, and not to let any good things go by us, we added this inexhaustible, even if precariously stable , supply to that of our artesian wells and cistern.

No sooner had we gotten nicely settled into the place we now named "Hollywyck" than I got the real estate and building fever. I bought up old barns, old houses, vacant lands, and began to rebuild and modernize and became, in my spare moments, a speculative working landlord. Almost before I knew it I had acquired three tenant houses, in addition to the village like cluster of buildings which we called "Hollywyck." The man was useful also in these enterprises, and first Hennessey and then William came to be our mainstays.

By the end of the "gay decade" then we had in some respects drawn in our horns , and in other respects extended our boundaries . When 1935 came around we had settled down into the deepest comfort we had ever known, and were able to have our friends and relatives visit us under such circumstances that they could be contented and happy even if we left them entirely alone. It was in those years ,and shortly thereafter, that the guest book began to show its full complement of interesting names. And to the community at large we shortly became known as old settlers for actually we had been in Montrose at least part of the time since 1916.

No longer was it necessary to store our books in boxes under the bed or to leave them over at the office or in the laboratory". We piled them up all around us, and every corner of nearly every room housed a book case. There was even a library. We had desks wherever we wanted them, and no longer was it necessary to trudge over to Milbank at night and up the four dark flights of stairs to find a place to work.

It is true that since that time my productivity" has waned. But my physique and my health have improved, and my disposition is infinitely better. I have written but one "impudent" review since moving to "Hollywyck." Moreover, and this is the real crux of the matter, I had already formulated my system and arrived at a satisfactory weltanschauung . Hereafter it seemed to me that I knew the answers almost before the questions were posed. I was subjectively complacent,and content to elaborate my illuminating vision to my classes,without any longer trying to convert the literate world to my views.

This outcome fully justified the "system" so that there could be nothing to complain of. My frantic intellectual fumblings had all represented the endeavor to alleviate the distress of doubt and uncertainty. To be in an intellectual muddle was always for me the strongest of irritants,- that is, the most powerful of motives. I had now achieved, if you like, "a formula" which was in my experience so uniformly applicable and relevant that intellectual distress was almost wholly abolished. According to the system, therefore, since the irritant was alleviated, no action should ensue. And this is almost exactly what has happened.

I have come to have a strong feeling of kinship (can I say it without appearing arrogant or boastful) with poor fellows like Spencer, and Hegel, and Kant and Schopenhauer who could not rest until they had achieved a satisfactory "formula". And who when they had once discerned it, went about belaboring everything they saw with it. My kinship is in my behavior, not necessarily at any rate in the authenticity of my "formula". In the old days I recall that I diagnosed such men as mild paranoiacs. Perhaps they were, although the diagnosis, in the light of what I have just said, now sits uncomfortably on my own head.

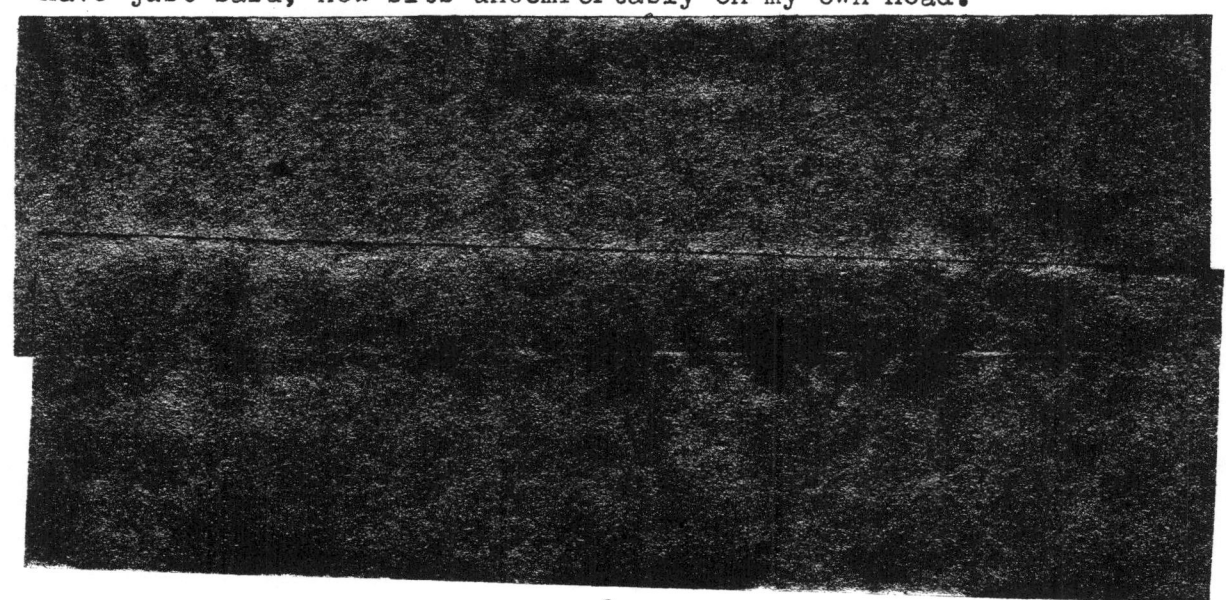

FROM COCA-COLA TO CHEWING GUM

187a

At Hollywyck

A STUDY OF PSYCHO-DYNAMICS

For the time being the matter was settled by another turn of fate. I was not left wholly to bask in contemplation of the system but was jarred from my dogmatic slumbers by the request to do another large scale investigation. The success of the caffeine and the alcohol experiments had led to several suggestions of similar studies of one or another topic. Most of them seemed to lack genuine scientific interest and since I had lost my interest in mere psychotechnology, they were turned down. But this new proposal did seem to open up questions that had some psychological and perhaps some social significance.

A manufacturer of food products had developed intellectual curiosity about the rapidly growing market for his chewing gum (it shall hereafter be described as "confectioner's chicle"). This man had long been accustomed to seek for scientific enlightenment on some of his problems, and he had more faith in inquiry than the usual manufacturer exhibits. In my "applied" days I had already made for his concern a considerable number of experiments and reports on this and that.

He now inquired whether we could ascertain the exact nature of the satisfactions that people derived from using the conventional masticatory and whether we could measure any possible effects that its use might have. In the beginning I was sceptical, and declared that whatever effects might be present were probably too subtle for our present methods to detect. But this man had more faith in science than I seemed to have. Two years later he made the proposal again. By this time it seemed to me that something might be accomplished along the line of his interests.

At the very end of the gay decade, during the Christmas holidays of 1934, we set up ~~again~~ the technique of the caffeine and alcohol experiments once more, but considerably elaborated. We added a variety of procedures, including subjective ratings of tension and strain, and we posted observers to make more objective records of restlessness and nervous behavior. Then we planned a schedule of systematic chewing, controlling these observations by tests when a flavored mint wafer was held in the mouth, by days when nothing whatever was "administered", and by other varieties of check..This was a drag net experiment, designed first of all to discover whether the act of chewing really produced measurable changes in any respect, and if so, in what respects.

Our Work scores, which had yielded the most definite results in the earlier investigations, turned out to show no clear influence of the motor activity of chewing. But our indications of strain and tension, both subjective and objective, were more interesting. There was strong evidence of relaxation under the influence of the motor automatism. This being the case, we had at least found the direction in which to look, and we therefore continued into the year 1935 further studies of this topic.

We engaged, in the usual fashion, a squad of experimental "chewers", and a suitable and proficient staff of experimental observers. For some of the things we undertook we had to call on the expert assistance of colleagues more proficient in those things than we were. In time Poffenberger, Rounds, Jackson, Foley, Simpson, took part in the investigation along with us.

We set up exact machinery for the measurement of muscular tension. We arranged regular psycho-galvanic measures of electrical potential in the body. We conducted metabolism measures of men working in a confining respiration helmet. We introduced devices presumably indicative of the general state of fatigue. We secured, unknown to our subjects, measures of the amount of energy they put into their movements as they worked at our standardized tasks. We measured the work product, in speed and accuracy. We repeated, for check purposes, our initial studies of subjectively felt relaxation. We duplicated the experiments in which observers rendered objective ratings of restlessness. We did repeated experiments in which pulse rate was measured. In addition to our more conventional laboratory tests, we studied changes in speed and accuracy of typing; and devised various new tests for our special purposes.

Our findings were consistent and definite. They were reported here and there in brief papers, and finally published as No. 239 of the Archives of Psychology, under the title "Psycho-Dynamics of Chewing", in 1939. The results are intrinsically interesting, and have some relevance as a systematic climax to my other psychological work. I quote here a few summary paragraphs from the last chapter of the volume.

"In general then we find that sustained chewing does provide relief from tension, and that the tension thus reduced is muscular. This reduction shows itself not only in direct measurements but also in the subjectively felt relaxation and in the decline in motor restlessness during sustained chewing.

As a result of this tension reduction, on an activity level appreciably higher than a basal resting state, the motor automatism is carried at little or no cost, as shown either by pulse rate or by calorie requirements.

There is evidence moreover that while chewing a surplus energy saving may result from this tension reduction. We have shown that at least part of such surplus may be unwittingly directed into the movements of the main occupation."

So much for the experimental findings of a straightforward psychological investigation. If anyone can find a useful application for the findings, well and good, and this result would be welcome in the case of any inquiry into pure science. The technologist has been eliminated, even though the investigation was supported by business and industry. The trifurcation of personality is at the very least reduced, at this point to a bi-furcation. If we can now only show that the system or the formula is valid here also, we shall have effected the complete integration of this long and sadly dissociated creature. Consider a few more paragraphs !

" Our interpretation of the mechanism of this total, very coherent picture is a very simple one. It involves no specific neurological hypotheses.......

The primary role of chewing is in the mastication of food. Eating is ordinarily a more or less "quiet" occupation. When we eat, we sit, or otherwise repose. Random restlessness is at a low point. We rest; we relax; and the general feeling tone is likely to be one of agreeableness and satisfaction.

An important item of the eating situation is the act of chewing. We suggest that, as a result of this contextual status, chewing .... brings with it, whenever it is sustained, a posture of relaxation.

Chewing, in other words, serves as a reduced cue, and to some extent redintegrates the relaxation of mealtime. The remaining parts of the picture follow from this redintegrated posture of relaxation. "

I derive a special gratification from the way in which the theoretical interpretation fits into the experimental facts. The diversity of interests already commented on is shown to reflect no warring set of attitudes and values, but a useful and consistent variety in a plausible unity of aim. The technological interest and experience brings one into contact with the problem and makes possible the organization of an investigation. The straightforward experimental interest and experience direct the investigation in such a way that verifiable and consistent results accrue. The systematic interest provides a theoretical explanation for the experimental results that is in harmony with other applications of the general theory.

There is therefore no real split personality involved in the simultaneous entertainment of interests so apparently diverse as those of technology, experimentalism, and systematic theorization. All these interests may usefully sypplement one another in the work of science.

There is however a point that has become clearer and clearer to me in recent years. It may to some extent explain and extenuate the presence of such diverse interests in an individual student, and it has to do with the relationships between the sciences. There is really no conflict between the various sciences and therefore no reason why varied view-points should not be cherished by a single individual. The various sciences differ primarily in their degree of remoteness from the data of observation, the facts of nature, which they all alike investigate.

The chemist gets right up into the tissues and fluids and applies his close-range techniques. The biologist takes up his position farther off, so that he misses the atomic and molecular details but discerns the morphology of a creature and the functional aspects of its special organs and systems. The psychologist, still farther away, is for the most part concerned with the individual as an integrated unit, and that is about all that he can soundly observe and discuss. The sociologist, in turn, is so distant from the original data that he can see men only as trees walking, and he can scarcely say anything relevant about individuals. While the philosopher is so remote that all he can observe is these other observers, and he is chiefly occupied with their procedures, assumptions, concepts, and conclusions.

But since men are mobile creatures they do not preserve these posts of observation as fixed stances. They approach and peer; they retreat and ponder. And thus even a chemist may occasionally get so far away from the primary facts as to talk like a philosopher. For a psychologist the shift is but an easy step.

FORTISSIMO

L. S. H.

ASSOCIATIONS AT BARNARD COLLEGE

It has already been shown that I owe much to my association with Barnard College, both through the cordial relations with the department of philosophy and through the freedom of teaching and the democratic administration characteristic of the College during my ~~~~~ years of service there. Although never on intimate social terms with members of the Faculty, I came to know many of them in professional ways, and through joint duty on college committees. I could have welcomed less service on committees, especially on the time consuming Committee on Instruction, on which I seemed more or less perennially to be. But this committee was the active administrative organ of the college, and service on it seemed always to be a duty not to be lightly regarded. However, I never felt myself to be of much use on committees, and ~~~~~~~~~~ my Quixotic and perhaps obstructionist ideas sat awkwardly among the more sedate opinions of the members of that committee.

I was seldom able to persuade such committees in favor of my firmer beliefs. One of these was the conviction that the best thing that the Honors system could do for our superior students was to shorten their period of educational infancy, by abbreviating their college course, much as mine had been abbreviated at Wesleyan and at the University of Nebraska. But it was on issues such as this that I usually took a real stand. When it came to planning anniversary celebrations, and the like, I was just a dud on any committee. On the Committee on Honors, I was never anything but an obstructionist. I still feel that the best way to "honor" a bright student is to promote his or her educational adulthood.

One feature of our work in the department of psychology at Barnard had its ambivalent aspects. Since the college did not increase in size appreciably through all my years there, although there was a great deal of shifting about of the general lines of student interest, it was not usually possible to promote our instructors to professorial status. This meant that in our staff people continually came and went. It was gratifying enough to see them go always to posts of better opportunity, since this we could at least construe in our own minds as a compliment to the value of their experience with us. And it did mean getting acquainted with a great number of the younger psychologists and enjoying their individual differences. But it also meant that there was constant changing of personnel, and that usually there was no set of broad shoulders to share the trivial but nevertheless exacting details of departmental administration.

It seems to me of some interest to list the considerable number of people who have been my shifting colleagues through the years I have remained the one continuity at Barnard. I give them here from memory and it is possible that some fail to be recalled for the moment. But most of those who have seen some service at Barnard and continued their work as psychologists elsewhere are in the following list. Where it is known to me, I shall indicate also their present location.

H. Koster
Lois Adams Forbes

Dr. Edith Mulhall Achilles	Trustee of Barnard College
Prof. Anne Anastasi	Queens College
Dr. Dorothy M. Barrett	Hunter College
Prof. Charlotte Bühler	University of Vienna
Prof. John P. Foley	George Washington University
Dr. Georgina S. Gates	New York City
Prof. H.C. Hamilton	Temple University
Prof. Joseph Holmes	Hunter College
Prof. Elizabeth Hurlock	Columbia University
Dr. T.A. Jackson	~~Columbia University~~ *Indiana University*
Prof. A.T. Jersild	Teachers College, Columbia University
Prof. F.P. Lund	Temple University
Prof. H. Nissem	Yale University
Dr. Helen Pallister	~~Barnard College~~ *Washington D.C.*
Dr. Rowena Ripin	New York City
Dr. Metta Rust	Teachers College, Columbia University
Prof. Georgine H. Seward	Connecticut College
Dr. Audrey M. Shuey	New York University
Prof. Ray H. Simpson	Alabama University
Dr. S.D.S. Spragg	Queens College
Dr. Lorle Stecher	Honolulu
Prof. E.K. Strong	Stanford University
Prof. R.L. Thorndike	Teachers College, Columbia University
Prof. R.E.P Youtz	~~Oberlin College~~ *Barnard College*
Prof. Meredith P. Crawford	Vanderbilt University
Prof. R.H. Henneman	College of William and Mary
Dr. S.S. Sargent	~~Central YMCA College,~~ *Chicago* ~~Chicago~~ *Barnard College*
Dr. T.G. Andrews	University ~~of N...~~
Mr. Gelolo McHugh	~~Barnard College~~ *Duke University*
Dr. Wm. A. Shaw	University of Pennsylvania

Here are ~~over~~ thirty active younger psychologists who have at one time or another been associated with me in the work of the department of psychology at Barnard, and who are now effectively carrying on their work in other centers. It has been one of my greatest satisfactions to see these people getting their work under way, and sometimes to have been of use in opening to them an opportunity, in the same way that my own teachers and later colleagues in their time opened "doors in the East" to me in my early years. And it was often enough a sore trial to be compelled to see them leave, because we could not do better things for them and could not adequately recognize their often very distinctive work by advancing them in our own department.

Acquaintance with my own students at Barnard has also been thoroughly agreeable and stimulating. Of course most of our students did not bring professional interests to the department. What they learned from us was to be put to as good use as might be in their daily lives in other than strictly psychological fields. And we have always recognised ~~in our department~~ that our main task was not to prepare more people to be psychologists, but to make our courses contribute as much as possible to the understanding of students who were not themselves going to be specialists in this field. There have been enough evidences that we were reasonably successful in this aim so that I am as contented on this point as any college teacher can well be.

Nevertheless a great many of our students did acquire, or perhaps brought with them, intrinsic interests in psychology, and later went on to more advanced study, and often enough, to active work in the field of psychology. Some of them in their turn became instructors in our own department. At least twenty of the women students in my courses at Barnard continued their work to receive the Ph.D. in psychology, and most of these became professionally active in this field.

Over fifty of our Barnard students continued for at least another year of study, to receive the M.A. degree in psychology, and a good many of these have continued to work in this field, in clinical, personnel, or other similar types of work. Some of them later went on, to be numbered among the twenty or more who achieved the higher degree.

FROM COCA-COLA TO CHEWING GUM

Barnard copy

MEASURING REACTIONS IN THE PSYCHOLOGY LABORATORY

A List of Publicity for Barnard

We have been especially favored at Barnard by the close affiliations and cordial relations always maintained with the work of Columbia College, The Graduate School, and Teachers College. Throughout my work at Barnard, for example, I have had men as well as women students in my courses. Even the undergraduate course in educational psychology for some years provided both for the women of Barnard and the men of Columbia. From almost the beginning my graduate courses given at Barnard have been open to all qualified students in the University, and in recent years about half of the students in my advanced seminars and other graduate courses have been men. Many of the disadvantages of the traditional woman's college have not been present with us.

So far as that is concerned, my pleasantest relations, as a teacher, have been with my own Barnard students. The girls in that institution are a choice selection of able and on the whole thoughtful young women. I find my senior majors in Barnard well able to hold their own with graduate students from whatever source. In fact at one time the men students in one of my courses made a concerted protest, demanding that their papers be graded on a different scale because they could not compete on equal terms with the girls in the class.

We have had at Barnard College a great many transfer students who have had perhaps two years of work at other institutions and then come to us for their last two years and their major, which was very often psychology. We have thus become more or less unwittingly a senior college, welcoming from other places those who especially value the advantages of our particularly strong departments, and the affiliations with the University.

What I am really trying to say is simply that I like my work at Barnard College, and would not exchange it for any other place that I know. There have been from time to time invitations, and sometimes temptations, to leave it for places that perhaps offered more immediate prospects, and certain formal distinctions. But I have never regretted that we did not go. The floor under my desk chair in Room 420 Milbank is becoming sadly worn, as the result of years of foot shuffling and chair grinding. Recently I moved the desk into another corner of the room, and began to wear out a new spot on the floor. It is the very same desk that I was given when I first came to Barnard in 1909. But I had to ask finally for a new chair, when the original one went to pieces. Even the old piece of apparatus, so condemned by the Dean of American psychology when he inspected the work I was doing for my doctor's dissertation, still stands on top of one of the cabinets. Occasionally I feel old enough to take it down, set it together on a laboratory table, and tell the current students, none of whom were born when the thing was first put together, all about the "law of central tendency".

t my greatest dismay, to which I cannot get quite accustomed, comes when I begin to tell them about our Plattsburg results. I begin by referring casually to the World War, as much as to say "You remember how things were". Then it dawns on me, as I see their blank looks, that even these results are over twenty two years old. When these data were gathered, none of these students was yet born; and many of them, I am sure, think that I am casually referring to the World War that is going on in unmistakable terms in their own day. But I had forgotten the present War, and was living back in the old one, just as Peter Holt used to do in our town when his pension check arrived.

THE SPIRIT OF COLUMBIA

Having thus expressed satisfaction with my local situation I should like also to record the deep personal contentment I have found in the more elaborate picture of the University as a whole. In college days in Nebraska the name "Columbia University" had a peculiarly noble sound. It was voluminous, rotund, sonorous and full of promise. It seemed to be the name of a city that was set on a hill and could not be hid. There was to it an expansiveness that promised to hold many good things; it seemed to speak youth, growth, power rather than sanctity and tradition. It sang in the new voice of science rather than in the plaintive accents of reminiscence and antiquity.

Without trying to tell it all I can still speak the words "Columbia University" and get that compelling feeling tone that the name had for me 40 years ago. It did not have the bark and snap of Yale; the vague uncertainty of Cornell; the honey and full costume of Harvard; or the juvenile gaiety of Princeton. There was no other name like it. It seemed to be the proper name for the home of pragmatism, empirical realism, behaviorism, experimental education,- for the spirit of scientific inquiry.

Such early associations are of little moment and have the most varied origins. Yet they are founded in some kind of reality and are not wholly adventitious. At any rate the feeling tone of the name "Columbia" has not let me down. I found in the institution just such freedom, such opportunity, such open minded toleration and democracy as the sonorous name had originally led me to expect. I hear people from other institutions complain of the spirit, the administrations, the traditions, jealousies, rivalries and little obstructionisms in their own universities. All this seems unreal, so foreign is it to the picture of all the parts of Columbia that I have known.

I shall offer here no essay on university administration; plenty of rejected administrators have done that. But there is a certain psychological trait that characterizes the organization and activities at Columbia which I feel competent to record. It is one of the things inherent in the spirit of the place as I have known it; whether as cause or effect I am not sure. I fancy that much of it has arisen from the sagacity of the chief executive who during my years at Columbia has been responsible for the overall policies of the institution and for the choice of men to implement this policy. It must also have been favored by the caliber of the men and women chosen to sit on its faculties and perhaps also by the character of the students attracted to the institution.

The trait to which I refer is freedom from neuroticism. Institutions as well as individuals may exhibit neuroses. The essence of a neurosis as I here define it is that some act, feeling, gesture or attitude, once appropriate enough to a crisis in which it originated, continues to be evoked in the future by events that only remotely resemble the original contexts. Thus unsagaciously aroused and inappropriate to the present context in which they occur, they represent atavisms, vestigial acts and functions,-in other words, neuroses. Few institutions escape this encrustation by monuments of the past and among those in which they most distressingly occur are our schools.

Among the most familiar and obvious of neurotic symptoms in education are such things as vestigial student organizations, wasteful faculty meetings, extravagant commencement exercises, Latin diplomas, classical language requirements, celibacy requirements, selection of teachers on the basis of anatomy, inherited and outmoded curricula, long summer vacations, relative idleness of plant and equipment, and so on.

There are institutions that stagger under the weight of such neuroses. At Columbia they appear to have been pretty well put in their place. In spite of the size and complexity of the university it maintains a remarkable integrity. This appears to be due in part at least to the rigorous way in which Columbia policy has continued to face the present, reducing many of its salutations to the sacred past almost to brief symbolic gestures. This is the way of mental health in the individual. Perhaps it is also the way to eternal life in an institution.

Part IV DIMINUENDO

OUR SUBJECTIVE CLIMAX

It is easy enough for an event that does not stir a ripple in world affairs to be an exciting climax in the lives of individual men and women. As this narrative has unfolded it has shown clearly enough how intertwined the lives of L.S.H. and H.L.H. became in the thirty five years that followed their first acquaintance in the University of Nebraska in 1905. There were the tender ties of romance and all the strong bonds of attachment that develop from congenial married life. There were mutual admiration and devotion and a strong feeling of identity arising from closely similar backgrounds and childhood experiences. There were common faith in a chosen set of personal and social values and a common dedication to the things of the mind. And there was now the history of thirty years of living together, pooling our resources, meeting together the usual run of life's crises, and the development of absolute confidence and trust in each other. The contingencies of our joint professional careers had led also to constant gracious and facile adjustments of the activities and goals of one to those of the other, with the interests of our one merged being always uppermost. Although there were no children to provide such unifying threads as these may sometimes bring, I believe that our two lives were as closely integrated as the frailties of human nature make possible.

We both cherished a high sentiment for the region of our origin and for the institution in which we had first begun the tentative soundings that initiated our life together. We were fond of the people of Nebraska, valued such continued contacts with our early teachers as fate had decreed, and when there was occasion, we would visit the old scenes together and revive together our memories of the struggles we had both gone through to achieve our final union.

FROM COCA-COLA TO CHEWING GUM

In the middle of the gay decade we had been called to the University of Denver for a period in the summer. I gave there a series of lectures, and we were jointly invited to return for the following summer for common participation in the work of the summer session. The Chancellor of this enterprising institution was Fred M. Hunter, who had been elected president of our senior class at Nebraska in the absurd year in which I had been a candidate on the "barb" ticket while wearing my Alpha Tau Omega pledge pin.

Since we taught regularly in the Columbia summer school we could not accept the return engagement, but the first expedition to the University of Denver we made the occasion for a most satisfying series of visits about the vicinity of Lincoln and that part of the state in which I had lived, and L.S.H. had been a high school teacher. We had turned in the roaring Hupmobile and now sailed across the country in a really powerful Packard. The journey took us, for one thing, along the same trail that I had blazed years before on my old Tribune bicycle on the trek to Wyoming. We then acquired a strong appetite to explore some day the more remote corner of the state, where L.S.H. had spent her childhood.

She had been born in a dug-out some miles out of Chadron, and had been the first white child born in Dawes County after its organization into a political unit. Her ancestors had been "covered wagon" pioneers, who had reached that remote section in the early days and taken up land or gone into the cattle business. As she once wrote, in a brief autobiography she was asked to prepare:

" My early memories are of Texas long-horns, Sioux Indians, blizzards, sod-houses, our log-house, and the one-room log school house, where I attended from six to ten years of age."

She had in her childhood known poverty, even as I had. She also had lost her mother in her early years. Not all her memories of this region or of those times were cheerful. Since her extreme youth she had never been able to revisit the childhood scenes and we had often spoken tentatively of some day going there so that I could become as familiar with her background as she had become with mine through her days of teaching in "our town." But no suitable occasion for this expedition had yet arisen. Fortunately the pleasure of this adventure had been delayed so that it could become an intrinsic part of our joint subjective climax, when that arrived in 1938.

In the spring of 1938 we simultaneously received through the mail impressive looking envelopes from the Office of the Chancellor of the University of Nebraska. Each of us was therein informed that the University, our Alma Mater, desired to confer upon us, individually but on the same occasion, at the coming Commencement, the honorary degree of LLD. To receive these degrees it would be necessary for us to attend the Commencement ceremonies.

I shall never be granted any deeper satisfaction than came from this act of our old University. The early struggles to survive and to study, on that very campus, would now be washed from memory. Almost on the very spot where we had pledged our "forty years" together, a grand new stadium and auditorium had been built since our days. On the platform of this auditorium, before many of our former teachers, and many of our local friends, and the people of Nebraska, L.S.H. and H.L.H. would stand side by side. The Chancellor would speak words of commendation about our work and would hang about our necks identical gorgeously colored hoods, in quaint but significant symbolism of the approval of our joint endeavors.

Although we had often enough hesitated to appear together before our colleagues at Columbia we had no qualms at all about standing side by side before the faculty at Nebraska. We accepted the invitation to attend Commencement, and were then informed that at Alumni meetings after the exercises we should be ready to speak. Louise Pound, one of the best beloved/former teachers of L.S.H., to whose alert proddings the sluggish communal mind most surely owed its present memories of us, was to be sponsor to L.S.H. and attend her to the ceremonial march. J.P.Guilford, now heading the Department of Psychology where Bolton had reigned in my day, was to do me this honor.

BACK TO NEBRASKA

We decided to make this the grandest of all occasions, and to visit all the scenes of our childhood, with all the comforts of modern travel. Having reserved rooms at the Cornhusker Hotel in Lincoln, when the first of June approached we asked for leave of absence from our institutions, and embarked in the Packard for the Middle West. We were equipped with the motion picture camera that L.S.H. had been using in her work at Speyer School, and we intended to bring back with us permanent records of as many of the old familiar spots as we could catch.

Across the country we took snatches of film to record our progress. Arriving in Nebraska we ran down the short straight stretch of paved highway from Omaha to Lincoln just as the Burlington Zephyr streamed along its road-bed beside us, as to convoy us back to the old haunts. Arriving at Lincoln we first renewed the acquaintance of many old friends there, then stored our main baggage and set out to see the old spots in south-eastern Nebraska, my own territory, before the date of Commencement.

We went down to DeWitt and on the way we stopped before the door of the little school house of District No. 149. The motion picture camera was unslung and I can now exhibit the lines and environs of this revered old building to such of my friends as deserve to see them. We went on into town and found my aunts, Ella and Mattie; we took them out into the country past the yellowish-brown house where my grandmother had lived, and on to the school house of Vroom District, No.73 .

But the old building, patched with geography backs, was gone, and in its place stood a new structure of alien and forbidding mien. Just the same we took a film of it, and of my aunts examining the grain for rust in the field across the road. There still stood the house in which I had taken my daily doses of Indian John's medicine from the $1 jug my father had so solicitously purchased. As we aimed the camera a modern farmer passed down the road between us and the field, driving one of the huge iron juggernauts with which fields in that section are now ploughed and cultivated. Nowhere in the picture do any domesticated animals appear.

On the way back to town we visited the old cemetery on the sandy hill and viewed my mother's grave. Then back to Lincoln, and to Wyuka Cemetery, where we purchased for ourselves a tiny plot of ground on the eastern slope of a grassy mound. L.S.H., in a mood that was strangely foreign to her up to that time, had become seriously concerned over the provision for our final resting place, and she expressed a desire to make such an arrangement now. The prescient nature of this act was then, by me at least, wholly unsuspected, and I little dreamed that in another eighteen months I would be bringing her there to rest forever in the spot she had chosen.

Back at the University in time for Commencement, we found that the orator of the day was Dean Ackerman of our Columbia School of Journalism, and that another alumnus to be given an honorary degree was Professor Watermann of Columbia. Much to the surprise of the Nebraska faculty, who did not wholly understand the conditions of life at the highly urbanized university of Columbia, we knew neither of these colleagues, and neither of them knew either of us.

We sat together on the platform and we stood in turn before the people of Nebraska, the only state in the Union that can have no bonded indebtedness. There we received in humble gratitude the seals of their ~~####~~ approval,- two gorgeously colored hoods, conveying to the academic world the message "Doctor of Laws".

After the ceremonies these two silken symbols, given to us by the University of Nebraska, and paid for by the people of our native state on their indomitable cash and carry basis, were carefully folded away to be preserved for the very next formal occasion on which we could wear them before the world. Before that occasion had time to arrive L.S.H. was no more. There was never, in the short time left for us together, occasion for L.S.H. to wear her honorary hood. And I shall never wear mine..

We had received no precise instructions from the Commencement committee concerning their plans for us so that in the morning I had visited the administrative offices to get such information as was available. In conformity with the earlier suggestions each of us had prepared certain "words" to say when we were called on to address the gathering of Alumni. I was now told that there would be but one address from the honorary degree recipients at the Alumni dinner and that L.S.H. would be asked to give this. Except for this investigatory trip she would have found herself unexpectedly called on for an 'address' when all she had thought of was a few words.

We had prepared 'remarks' in somewhat similar vein, based in each case on certain facts and statistical data. She took mine over and used such of them as she needed to supplement her own, to make a four page address on "The Participation of Nebraska in the Intellectual and Artistic Leadership of the Nation." When her conversation with the Governor, who was her dinner companion, was interrupted by the request for her speech, she delivered this address in the ringing tones with which I had so long now been familiar, to the tumultuous applause of the audience of enthusiastic Alumni and state and University officials.

I can say without reservation that this was the most triumphant moment of my life, as I sat watching her, in the gorgeous hood that had not yet been removed, giving to the people of her native state her stirring message about their part in the production and conservation of ability, with the same wistful appeal and the same lilt to her gesture and carriage that the scarlet Tam-o-Shanter girl had brought with her into the musty stack room of the old library just a third of a century before.

So wholly won were the people of the university by her theme that the address was widely printed throughout the state, and in the university papers, and then separately published by the University authorities in a neatly bound pamphlet for distribution and circulation wherever it would be read.

After this Commencement day was over we packed ourselves into the car and drove up through the farm lands of central Nebraska, along and across the Niobrara, and into the sand hills. On the way we found, on an accidental detour, a surviving dug-out which must have been much like the one in which L.S.H. had been born, at Dakota Junction, outside of Chadron, fifty-two years before. We stopped and secured several photographs of this old land-mark.

Reaching Valentine, all her people assembled for a two day get together, and a picnic out toward Lone Pine Hill, where had once stood the rugged solitary tree that she had celebrated in a poem printed in the local newspaper when she was 14 years of age. Then we went on, still through the sand hills, this year exceptionally green, but on a substantial highway, toward Chadron.

We visited and photographed all the old sites that she could recall in Chadron,-the church where she had been baptized, the oldest house in the now thriving city, the cemetery where lay her mother and her sister Ruth whom we had taken there on the long journey years before.

I recalled the story related to me by L.S.H. that she had learned to read by studying out the large printed inscriptions on her under-wear in those days,- such legends as "Chadron Roller Mills." We passed these mills, and I stopped the car and went in to interview the miller, and to secure as one of my own souvenirs a fresh and unused flour sack bearing these familiar inscriptions. He demanded to know what I was up to, and I had to tell him briefly why I wanted one of his bags. It turned out that he was the same old miller, had known well the Danley family, the grandparents of L.S.H. and knew a great deal about her. Not only did he give me the souvenir bags, which I still have here in my desk, but he came out to the car and told many interesting things about what had happened since the early days.

Then we went on through the sandy wastes, looking for the spot once known as Dakota Junction, and for the site of an old dug-out, later supplanted by a more enterprising and ambitious log-house. We found the place, and in our wandering about it probably stood on the very site of the log-house. But everything was changed except the White River, which still trickled along between its sandy banks. The old home-stead had been swallowed up in an elaborate grading project, with P.W.A. men at work on it, which ran through the yard where the three Stetter sisters had played, and through the field where, L.S.H. ~~had~~ spent days moving the hand lever on the corn planter of her despairing grandfather. When there had been rain, in those days, and a crop had come, the grasshoppers usually gathered it in before it could be humanly harvested. Even now, as we walked through the patches of prairie grass that here and there appeared among the sand blown stretches, a new and tender generation of grasshoppers arose in swarms from where we stepped. Before fall, we were told, in the dearth of other fodder they would begin again to devour the very fence posts that still stood crookedly here and there around those agriculturally abandoned sections.

      We turned back from the sand hills and left the valley of the Niobrara; back across the rich fields of Iowa, and Ohio and Illinois, once familiar to our ancestors; through the smokey towns of Pennsylvania, through a corner of New York State to the Bear Mountain Bridge across the Hudson. And there we were again,- just a few miles from Hollywyck. While the sun was still high that day we rolled into the Montrose Colony, and back to the spot we had come to know as home, late in June of the year 1938, bearing the gorgeous honorary hoods with us.

T H E   E N D

We both felt then that a new turn had come in our lives, and that thereafter we might well be following through another era in our joint development. This was sadly to be true. The events of the next year or so are so ever present with me that they cannot possibly be construed as memories. They are pulsing perseverations for the partial alleviation of which this narrative was undertaken. All this belongs to the final period of my life; except for its painful beginning I do not know what it is to be like, and this narrative can therefore say nothing about it.

The beginning of the end came on a wild and stormy day early in November of 1939. During three weeks of misery L.S.H. had withdrawn from all social contacts and refused medical attention. When she finally relented and submitted to examination she was ordered immediately to a hospital for surgical exploration.

An ambulance was secured to bear her to the Medical Center, forty miles away. In a fierce onslaught of wind and rain the ambulance made its way with difficulty down the Post Road toward New York City, with its siren shrieking and a helper clearing the windshield by hand so that the driver could see his way. In an hour or two the verdict was ready, but the story of that tragic sequel has been briefly told in another place and need not be repeated here.

On a granite monument on the eastern slope of a gentle grassy undulation in Wyuka Cemetery, in Lincoln, Nebraska, there is deeply engraved a very simple inscription. It was the graving of this inscription that put an end to the ~~~~~~ last period of my life, so far as this story is concerned. And this inscription, which is not unlike the diagram to be given below, may also be the fitting terminus of this volume. It reads :

```
................................................
.                                              .
.  H O L L I N G W O R T H                     .
.                                              .
.      Leta Stetter                            .
.       May 25, 1886                           .
.     November 27, 1939                        .
.                                              .
................................................
```

Postscript follows .

POSTSCRIPT

The bulky manuscript of which this volume represents a part began with a preface and ended with a postscript. The preface gave some account of the circumstances that led to the enterprise and of some of the personal gains accruing through preoccupation with it. No such excuse is here included; what has been written is written. An autobiographical account is wholesome therapy for anyone shaken by unexpected disaster who has an inclination to write. It helps one understand a bit better what has happened; throws some light on personal traits and characteristics; suggests useful plans for future action; assists in the achieving of balance and perspective. It may even keep one alive. No excuse need be offered for the egocentricity of autobiography; that follows by definition.

The original postscript contained certain reflections on the manifold differences between life in the era here surveyed and the conditions of work and achievement in more recent years. Some of these observations may be in place here. As I now review this unexciting account of the experiences of half the life time of a simple man, certain facts stand out. They are facts familiar enough to students of social change but they have a special poignancy when felt in the personal flow of one's own existence. They have additional impressiveness when viewed in the light of the experiences of my youth, in the quarter century preceding the years covered by this chronicle. I shall but recite them briefly by way of bringing this volume to a somewhat gentle close.

The years in question appear to have been the closing epoch of our era of individualism. The paternalism of the New Deal, the state and federal concern over the fate of the indolent and incompetent adult, the penalizing of initiative, thrift and enterprise, the endeavor to scatter accumulated wealth, to equalize incomes, and in general to apportion available goods on the basis of our common needs rather than of our differential efforts and abilities,- all of these socialistic endeavors may be said to have terminated, more or less abruptly, the era which I have been describing.

Under the influence of such communistic developments the type of individual struggle here reviewed may seem primitive and naïve, or even improbable and fictional. From much of the frustration and penury here narrated the young of the new era may be protected and they may have unlimited opportunity to follow their interests and achieve their goals. Personally I view these trends with mixed feelings. I find the attendant regimentation and dependence repugnant, even though it may be the price of a guaranteed and relatively effortless subsistence level for all, a subsistence which accrued in earlier days only to families with competent and fortunate adults .

It remains yet to be seen to what extent this erasure of the distress motive will flatten out and conventionalize the activities of those responsible for our intellectual advancement and our scientific and artistic progress. If my own systematic account of human nature is sound, the dynamics of individual achievement will be severely diluted and an era of bovine comfort may follow the era of inequality now closing.

In that era it was the diversities of human nature that were primarily recognized and heavily rewarded, although there was manifest unfairness and marked injustice in the technique of identifying these inequalities and administering the rewards. In the era now upon us it is to be the similarities of men, rather than their differences, that shape our institutions and direct our endeavors, if, that is, endeavor is still to continue. It is to be a civilization based on the stomachs of men rather than on their brains, for men are more alike in the nature and strength of their appetites than they are in their individual capacities to satisfy these urges.

Unfairness may be just as manifest and injustice just as conspicuous as in the era now drawing to a close. Perhaps this communistic emphasis will have to run its due course before a social order can evolve that takes adequate account both of the similarities and of the diversities of human nature. Or it may be that such forebodings are merely the whim of an elderly and recently frustrated man, enamored of his past and reluctant to find anything promising in the prospects of the immediate future.

                                                                             July 10, 1940

The departure of L- seemed to let loose an avalanche of deaths among our friends and associates. For years no one close to us had died, but in these five years twenty eight or more have gone. Among them are these,-

 Menas S.Gregory,Director of the Psychiatric Ward at Bellevue Hospital,with whom L- had worked in her earlier years as a clinical psychologist.
 Mrs.Chase,mother in law of L-'s sister,with whom there had been tangled relations and negotiations in connection with miscarriages in the settlement of her husband's estate.
 Genevieve Buncher,sister of Mrs.Pickup who was almost a foster mother to L- during her college years. She was one of the old friends who had been present at L-'s funeral.
 Elizabeth Irwin,founder of The Little Red School House in New York City, for years L-'s friend and a fellow member of Heterodoxy. Claire Mumford, also a member of that dining and discussion club. Sarah Sturdevant,a Teachers College colleague and a sorority sister of L-'s who had been a loyal associate and often a guest at Hollywyck.
 F.A.Stuff one of L-'s favorite professors at the University of Nebraska,where she had been his Assistant in the Department of English for three years of her college course. He had also been my teacher there,and I had known him earlier at Nebraska Wesleyan when I was a reader there in the Department of English in my Academy days.
 Rudolph Pintner,distinguished colleague and friend at Teachers College, and F.H.Wickware of D.Appleton and Co., who had been the chief contact of both of us in connection with the various books of ours published by that firm.
 The young Fisher boy,one of the sons of L-'s cousin Anna. He was a conspicuous student at the University and we had come to be fond of him in our last visit to Valentine. Supt.Campbell of the New York School System under whose general approval P.S.500 (Speyer School) was established. Supt.Graham,of Pittsburg, also a loyal supporter of L-'s work with gifted children.
 McGeogh,Whipple,Beas, Rosanoff,Washburn, Jastrow,all scholars with whom one or other of us had cooperated in particular and friendly ways during our professional careers .
 My Aunt Mattie,the only one left of the immediate family of my mother; my brother Irwin; and L-'s father,John G.Stetter.
 Mrs.Poffenberger,one of our earliest friends in New York, our nearest neighbor at Montrose and for many years,with her husband and family,among our most congenial friends. Mrs.Warden,wife of an associate in the psychology department;the husband was also from Nebraska and his wife was associated with Teachers College.
 Capt.Douglas Donald,formerly of Valentine,the husband of L-'s oldest Nebraska friend in New York; also two members of the Peekskill bridge club of whom L- had been fond ,Mrs.Shirtzinger and Miss Powers; Jack Johnson, husband of a woman who was one of L-'s good friends and a former student of mine.
 F.P.Keppel,our neighbor at Montroseand a good friend of both of us;and finally J.McKeen Cattell,the man who had invited me to leave my job at Fremont High School and come to New York to be his assistant at Columbia.

There are others who also belong in such a list, but this is no attempt to present a complete necrology. The list as it stands is sufficiently striking to explain my feeling that the loss of L- touched off an avalanche of losses such as I had never known before in any corresponding time. There in the Montrose colony, where only one death had occurred in a quarter century, suddenly stood three empty houses side by side,- our own and those next to it on each side,- three houses in a row from each of which either husband or wife had gone in this brief period.

In many other ways also these five years since L-'s departure have been an epoch. For the first time in history our national executive has been elected for a third term and is even now candidate for a fourth. These years have seen us launched into World War II, with its incredible phenomena of regimentation, centralized and beureaucratic authority, rationing of goods and services, manifold limitations, restrictions and prohibitions, conscription not only of men over 17 years of age but also of property, implements, factories, mines, and means of transportation, with taxes so high that in some cases they exceed the individual's income, and they have furthermore to be estimated or guessed at in advance and paid before-hand. Freedom of movement, of action, of speech are threatened and the New Deal's conspiracy with the morons has been allowed the easiest and widest expansion under the guise of military emergency. Any objection to these developments is tabooed as interference with the war effort. Ludicrous manouevers, farcical rulings and exhibitions, and quaint rehearsals under the name of black-out and air-raid precautions have needlessly complicated the already burdensome life of rural districts. Preposterous over-organization of local communities on a hundred pretexts have kept the population in a fever and sometimes put us in a panic of foreboding or a mood of resentment.

Many of the prohibitions and restrictions appear to have no justified economic foundation but to be perpetrated in order to whip the people into a mood of irritation and hate, which may then be directed or projected into the aims of war.

Not only have eleven million men been put into the work of war. Women also in great numbers have received uniforms and commissions as members of the armed forces. Other women have eagerly and profitably undertaken types of work not hitherto pursued by them and have become welders, riveters, airplane pilots, lathe operators, truck drivers, engineers, and almost anything they might wish to be. The status of women has probably changed more significantly in this five year period than during all the rest of my life time. Or is it only that the previous changes have now had good opportunity to make themselves manifest ? L.S.W. would have been intrigued by these changes, but I sometimes think that she would also have found these five years full of anxiety and distress, and almost rejoice that she was allowed to escape them.

Finally, as if to round out this five year period and make of it a unitary epoch, I spent most of this summer in the hospital and emerged with various more or less permanent disabilities; and, to cap the climax, almost immediately sold "Hollywyck". I shall briefly record my activities and experiences, therefore, to bring this chronicle up to date, and especially to provide occupation for some of my leisure and more or less crippled moments.

The period falls naturally into two sections,-two years in which I continued to occupy the house at Hollywyck, and the remaining time after moving down to Linden Cottage with "Sephus",- a name gradually adopted for Josefine Weischer. During the first winter I continued to teach at the University and was busy getting in shape the things and projects that L- had left behind. Her former assistant, James Dunlap, was installed in the city apartment that had just been leased for a year. L's things from her office and some of the Speyer School materials were transferred to this apartment and Dunlap was engaged to help sort and identify them. Other things, especially those that I might later try to develop, were taken to Hollywyck. Dunlap often came to the country for a few days especially to identify and label the records, photographs and films from the Speyer project. He and Dr. Pritchard continued to work at Speyer School part of the time, assisting the new director of research to continue the projects then under way.

In addition to this work which went on all year, I had at home the sad task of disposing of L's personal effects. Over a score of cartons of such things were sent to her sister and niece, the two Margarets. Her letters, records, souvenirs, manuscripts, lecture notes and all kinds of materials and data for projected papers and books constituted a formidable pile of stuff, all of which had to be examined, identified, classified, and either filed, stored, or destroyed. The general gloom of life prevented any constructive use of these things at this time, and besides it was necessary to discover what was there before planning what use to make of it. Everywhere I looked for some message or memorandum from her, showing how well she understood what was happening to her in the last years of her life. Nothing of this character was ever revealed.

By early spring I had decided to salvage a collection of poems that had been assembled from various places; several I had already brought together in one of the drawers of my desk, unknown to L-. The collection of verse was printed by the Columbia University Press in a pleasing small volume called "Prairie Years." The copies were distributed to people who I knew would value them; only a few hundred were printed and they were not allowed to be sold.

There were also numerous public addresses for which manuscripts were found. These seemed to me sufficiently characteristic and distinctive to merit preservation. They were brought together in chronological order and published by the Science Press Printing Co., under the title "Public Addresses of Leta S. Hollingworth." Since nearly enough of these were sold to meet the costs of publication and others were available for distribution to relatives, colleagues, libraries and friends, I have felt that this project was worth the doing.

Both of these volumes were off the press by the late fall of 1940 when, a year after her death, the Memorial Conference on the Gifted in Honor of Leta S. Hollingworth was organized by Teachers College. The volumes were exhibited for the first time at this conference, along with a special number of the Teachers College Record called "Education and the Individual" which consisted of surveys of the various fields in which L.S.H. had worked, and her bibliography. In the biography to be later described a chapter is devoted to the account of this Memorial Conference. Meanwhile still other things were under way.

I found the winter depressing and lonely although Josefine Weischer took devoted care of me and I had frequent contacts with Tom McKay, the Gateses, Jersilds, Poffenbergers, as well as frequent sessions with Dunlap and other people from Teachers College and the New York City school system. I turned to writing,- the **Memoirs** that have now materialized as "Leta Stetter Hollingworth-A Biography", printed by the University of Nebraska Press, and the manuscripts called "Born in Nebraska" and "Years at Columbia". All of this helped, but I was still disconsolate and felt the need of company to keep from complete despair.

My nephew Ladd was invited to come from the Pacific Coast to spend the summer and next winter with me and profit in such ways as he desired from residence in or near New York City. He was just getting started in a job that seemed to be worth cultivating, so he could not come. My sister Gertrude, teaching music in San Diego, was invited to come to Montrose early in the spring and bring her son and daughter. Norman was in college and could attend Columbia Summer session. Barbara was just finishing High School. She was a gifted pianist and could spend the summer profitably at Julliard School of Music. Gertrude could just visit and see New York again, and together they would keep me company. In the fall the mother could go home to her music students, and son and daughter remain behind for further study in New York if the summer adventures turned out well.

All of this was done according to plan, My sister remained until fall. My nephew in the winter term took further work at Columbia and then returned to complete the year and recieve his degree from San Diego College. Barbara was awarded a very complimentary fellowship at Julliard in the Graduate School. We rented a grand piano for Hollywyck and Norman set up his big marimba. Sometimes Tom McKay would venture to bring his violin. All that second winter we had music beating, beating, beating through the house. It drove all other considerations out of my head, which was just what I had been hoping for. All this was excellent therapy and a most effective antidote to my misery.

I should add, in this report of the first two years, that in the first spring after L-'s death I had gone back to Nebraska,- to be near her, to visit our old haunts, and to give the Memorial Day address at my home town of DeWitt. This visit is described in the postscript of "Born in Nebraska". It was then that my sister and her children started from California. They met me at Lincoln and together we drove back East in the car I had driven to Nebraska.

Barbara is now in her fifth year on the Julliard Fellowship and aspires to a musical career in New York. She has a rare gift and is devoted to its use; with anything like a fair opportunity she ought to go far. Since the first year at Hollywyck she has lived in the city so as to be nearer her work and to the musical affairs of the city. Her brother, since graduating from college, has worked for a boat building firm on war contracts, has married, and is expecting offspring next month. Tom McKay is also married and a soldier in China. Dunlap has married, taken his professional degree from Teachers College and is engaged in a job of his own in an up-state city of importance. Speyer School is only a fading memory. I gave up the city apartment when the lease expired and since then have not spent a night in the city, except for a very recent period of hospitalization, of which more later.

The academic year 1941-42 was a fateful one. It was in this year, presumably in the spring, that we were to have had another Sabbatical year together. This was because of age, to be my last vacation of this character. We had tentatively planned a trip to the Scandinavian countries and L- was especially enthusiastic over this proposal. It seems to me since that at least some of this enthusiasm must have been spurious,-calculated to conceal her secret knowledge that she would probably not be there when the time came . But perhaps I am wrong there. At any rate, when the time arrived, she had already been gone for two years, the Japs had attacked Pearl Harbor, and we were at war with Japan, Germany and Italy . When the vacation came I used it to get things in better shape at ######## Montrose and to review and slightly revise the bulky manuscript of memoirs which precedes this postcript. In this revision it became three volumes, one concerned with L-'s life; a second describing my own life up to the time I left Nebraska; and a third reporting our joint career in the East.

By this time Josefine Weischer and I, taking care of each other in the rambling house at Hollywyck, had become better acquainted. I came to admire her courageous spirit, her cultural background, her intelligence, skill and loyalty. We became friends rather than employer and employee and agreed to remain together, getting what satisfactions we could out of the few years yet before us. But the house and grounds at Hollywyck were too large and too burdensome for just the two of us. Five rooms instead of fourteen were what we needed, and half an acre instead of five or six. So we closed the place at Hollywyck and moved into the little cottage at the beginning of Colony Road.

be used for the publication of other works by L.S.H. There has been enough demand for this book so that I am glad I undertook to finish it in L-'s name. It was one of her pet projects and it is a pity that she did not live to complete it properly.

It was during this time also that I separated the section of "Born in Nebraska" dealing with L-'s life from the rest of the manuscript, and prepared a single volume devoted solely to her biography, surveying her life and character and reviewing her work. Commercial publishers did not find such a volume acceptable for their lists and the Columbia University Press thought it too much of a memorial volume for them to publish. The University of Nebraska Press was glad to publish the book and 400 copies were printed. Most of these copies are now sold or otherwise distributed. I was particularly glad to have this book published by the University of Nebraska; I paid the publication cost and gave the book to the University with such proceeds as might come from its sale. I had it in mind eventually to establish there a fellowship in honor of L- and the volume would serve a good end in this connection if my plans worked out.

During this period also Virginia Weischer married, and both her mother and I were left alone. This still further strengthened our alliance, which developed in ways from which we have both derived much joy and contentment. The work frenzy that had characterized my earlier career was allowed to subside and I proceeded to lighten my load of responsibilities and to take life more lightly, squeezing from it such pleasures, whether sensuous, intellectual or emotional as might be extracted.

My teaching and research were reduced to a minimum and became for the time being, I fear, as perfunctory as the endeavors of many of my associates had appeared always to be. I began to have as much time for myself as they had always had for golf and chess and billiards and pool and bowling. Much desultory reading was indulged in and enjoyed. I became a radio addict and under the guidance of Sephus who was full of musical lore and had been an opera singer in Europe, I began to acquire a passive listener's interest in good music and to recognize the touch of some of the masters.

For the time being scribbling nearly ceased, after the manuscript of the biography of L— was completed. I spent as little time in town as necessary and became, if possible, fonder than ever of country activities, in which I could now indulge freely but with no compulsion. Except for frequent visits of Virginia and Ben, and occasional contacts with the Gateses and Jersilds, social life was nearly restricted to fraternizing with Sephus in our little cottage and garden. Only once or twice in these five years have I appeared at the Century Club, and then only to lunch briefly with Tom McKay or with T.L.Bolton. The death of Keppel and Mrs.Poffenberger so soon after that of L— helped to reduce the social activities of the colony to nearly zero, and the impact of war, with the young men away in service or in prison camps wholly completed this reduction.

As the months passed a new zeal to write and to experiment grew active. I turned to a long postponed project that L- and I had often discussed. She had urged me to do a book on ethics, showing how my systematic psychology would work out in this field. I had never felt quite ready for this undertaking but was sure that sometime the spirit would move me to it and I would reel it off in a frenzy. This method of work had become more or less familiar to me. This was what was now happening and in the summer of 1943 the pencils and Corona up in my study began to race again. A manuscript of some 300 pages resulted, which I called "The Psychology of Conduct". But I found that a long experimental exploration was needed to put my ideas to the test of reality, so that since then, as occasion offered, I have continued to plan and carry on these experimental studies on the measurement and analysis of ethical discrimination, and have interested some of my students in these studies by way of collaboration. It is this project that is now my main diversion and I find myself quite absorbed in it whenever the bodily ills that now annoy me make it comfortable to turn to it again.

These bodily ills may be briefly reported. In the spring of the present year (1944) I was found to have a malignant development (epithelioma) on the lower lip which required surgical treatment to the extent of excising about an inch of tissue from the lip. This was done late in June at the New York Hospital. During this experience my bladder suddenly refused to function and something had to be done about this too. Enlarged prostate was the cause, and I had at earlier times already suffered some inconvenience and discomfort from this. So that while my lip was healing I went again to the operating room for a trans-urethral prostatectomy. The first operation did not succeed and my pains and difficulties continued. A second operation was therefore undertaken, which appeared to remove the obstacles that had been causing the trouble.

By this time, with three operations, one under general and two under spinal anesthesia (which I abominate), all in the course of a week or two, I felt badly shaken. The whole experience was a trying ordeal, but after the third week in the hospital I was judged able to go home and appeared to have made a quick and favorable recovery.

Convalescence was steady so far as local matters were concerned, but as I again became active severe leg pains appeared which continued at night to keep me restless and awake. Suspecting these to be similar to aches I had once had years before, due to weak arches, I dug out the old arch supports and resorted again to the exercises that had so comfortably and permanently put me on my feet again on that earlier occasion, some fifteen years before. The pains disappeared in a few days, but apparently I was too violent in the exercises for a crippled knee suddenly appeared, putting a stop to the exercises and interfering seriously with all locomotion. This is still with me, after a month or two, and it is not yet clear what is to be done about it, beyond the constant wearing of a bandage that is supposed to enable the knee to recover of its own accord and in its own slow way.

The very week that I came home from the hospital the young Crampton's, long friends of people in the colony, offered to buy Hollywyck. We finally agreed on a price that represented a severe sacrifice but the prospect of selling to congenial people and of getting rid of this once cherished place that had now become only a burden and an expense was too inviting to resist. So Hollywyck is no more, although I still retain two pieces of land adjacent to the part that was sold, along with the buildings. I rented the garage and the rooms over it from the new owners and thus still have my study and shop in the old place, at least so far as storage is concerned. But I seldom go there, and when the war is over I may build a small place of my own, either on some of the land that was not sold, or down by Linden cottage where there is a half acre.

The hospital experience had shown me that it was not enough to trust to a last will and testament as a way of providing for emergencies. Those one wishes to provide for must be made secure even during the emergencies, which may be long drawn out. There was also the matter of the fellowship in memory of L— that I wished if possible to see arranged during my life time. I wanted to see Josefine Weischer provided for and the fellowship established while funds were definitely available, not left to the contingencies of what my final estate might or might not represent.

The Trustees of Columbia University were found willing to accept a fund, to pay the income therefrom to Josefine during her life time, or to me if I survived her, then finally devote it to the Leta Stetter Hollingworth Fellowship on conditions which I had outlined. This seemed to me an ideal arrangement for my two principal remaining aims would be provided for and no longer be left dependent on my own fate or fortune. An agreement was therefore drawn up and signed by both parties and I turned over to the University for this foundation the sum of $51,000, representing about a third of my remaining resources.

It gives me special pleasure to know that every year a promising woman from Nebraska will be enabled to accomplish a year of graduate work at Columbia with her whole way paid by this fellowship. What a boon that possibility would have been to L.S.H. in the days when she was too impoverished to pay tuition in the graduate school and had to postpone her professional interests for many years. It is also a matter of selfish pride that without a penny to start on I have been able, without undue sacrifice of my own welfare, to provide the means whereby such an opportunity shall be annually available to a young woman from the University of Nebraska who is judged by the faculty of that institution to be "most likely to emulate the character and career of Leta Stetter Hollingworth." I can think of no more appropriate way in which to leave a monument to all the things she meant to me during her life time.

The war is still on and we can only push ahead with our routine duties and wait impatiently for peace. Driving far from home is impossible because of restrictions on rubber and gas. Other means of transportation are crowded and accomodations precarious. With but two ration books to operate on, our wits are constantly busy managing to get our modest share of the available sugar, butter, meat, shoes and fuel in spite of shopping only two days a week in Peekskill.

At one time, while Keppel was still alive, there was a tentative plan for me to travel, during the Sabbatical year, in Australia and South Africa, assisted by the Carnegie corporation, and reporting on certain educational and scientific activities there. The necessary abandonment of the trip to Scandinavia made this prospect initially attractive, but war soon spread toward these very regions and civilian travel abroad was soon limited and regulated.

It is doubtful now whether I shall ever see either Scandinavia or Australia, or whether I should care to see them even if conditions changed. Here at home even the annual meetings of scientific societies have been reduced to skeleton affairs and during these five years I have attended but one such session. We are perforce learning to keep close to home and to find our satisfactions there, even as we were wont to do in the early years in Nebraska. It is not a bad way to live.

Subjectively these five years have been a strange period. At my age men are supposed to become retrospective, preoccupied with the past, enamored of their youth. My own trends in this direction appear to have been satisfied by the orgy of reminiscence that led to these volumes of memoirs. My attitudes since the completion of the foregoing manuscripts have again become prospective,- but peculiarly so, and some might say morbid. For I have been steadfastly looking forward to my own death, anticipating it, picturing it, and as it were, dieing in advance.

Irrespective of what the tissues of the body may have been doing, intellectually I have been gradually, deliberately and in an orderly and reconciled manner leaving the world. Incomplete projects have been rounded up; responsibilities discharged; records and resources simplified and put in order; papers filed and addresses compiled; memoranda and instructions prepared and placed in the proper hands; assets liquidated and put in easily manageable and identifiable form; gifts made and endowments established; new wills made from time to time as conditions changed.

Probable and possible modes of departure have been canvassed and some of their prerequisites made readily available in case they should appear expedient. In the hospital when things were most discouraging and a recurrence of malignant conditions appeared imminent, the relative merits of all the windows were tentatively explored.

Emotionally I died five years ago; intellectually I have been expediting my demise during the past three years; this summer even the bodily tissues appeared to become unduly aware of their mortality. And yet there is an amazing resilience in the organism. Now that the period is past, its activities drawn to a close, and even the house at Hollywyck being occupied and ruthlessly remodelled by strangers, I seem to be starting another life on "borrowed time". It is a strange experience, whether brief or long. For it is a life in which I am not an actor and there is in the apathy with which one in his own proper life observes the course of other men's affairs. It will be aimless and without dynamic urge, its events evaluated only by their own immediate feeling tone, with no reference to the final destiny of a self, and with no life plan.

In my own life I often fancied living under another name, and even devised several, from which to choose. I could easily and with some propriety adopt one of these now, migrate to a new region and live out this spurious second life there. There might indeed in time be a third volume of memoirs,— life in Nebraska, life at Columbia, and life in Shangri-La .
life in Weiss-nicht-wo .

No pp. 217-236

APPENDIX

BIBLIOGRAPHY OF H.L. HOLLINGWORTH

Books and Monographs

THE INACCURACY OF MOVEMENT - Archives of Psychology, No.13, Columbia University, pp.87, The Science Press, 1909

THE INFLUENCE OF CAFFEINE ON EFFICIENCY, Archives of Psychology, No. 22, Columbia University, pp.166, The Science Press, 1912

ADVERTISING AND SELLING, D. Appleton and Co., New York, 1913, pp.314

EXPERIMENTAL STUDIES IN JUDGMENT, Archives of Psychology, No.29, Columbia University, pp.119, The Science Press, 1913

OUTLINES FOR EXPERIMENTAL PSYCHOLOGY, A.G. Seiler, New York, 1913, pp.112

OUTLINE FOR ABNORMAL AND APPLIED PSYCHOLOGY, A.G. Seiler, New York, 1914, pp. 20

ADVERTISING, PRINCIPLES AND PRACTISE (With Tipper, Hotchkiss and Parsons) Ronald Press, New York, 1915, pp.575 (Trans. into German by H. Hahn, Springer, Berlin, 1928)

VOCATIONAL PSYCHOLOGY (With a Chapter by Leta S. Hollingworth), D. Appleton and Co., New York, 1916, pp.308

THE SENSE OF TASTE (With A.T. Poffenberger), Moffat Yard and Co., New York, 1917, pp.200

APPLIED PSYCHOLOGY (With A.T. Poffenberger), D. Appleton and Co., New York, 1917, pp.431. Enlarged, 1920; Revised and Enlarged, 1923. (Trans. into Swedish, Stockholm, 1923)

PRINCIPLES OF ADVERTISING (With Tipper, Hotchkiss and Parsons), Ronald Press, New York, 1920, pp.473. Revised and enlarged, 1923

PSYCHOLOGY OF FUNCTIONAL NEUROSES, D. Appleton and Co., New York, 1920, pp.259

MANUAL OF PSYCHIATRY (Rosanoff, 1920 Edition), One of five contributors, John Wiley and Sons, Baltimore, 1920

JUDGING HUMAN CHARACTER, D. Appleton and Co., New York, 1922, pp.268

PSYCHOLOGY OF ADVERTISING AND SELLING, Home Study Dept., Columbia University, 1923, pp. 43

THE PSYCHOLOGY OF THOUGHT, D. Appleton and Co, New York, 1926, pp.341

MENTAL GROWTH AND DECLINE, D. Appleton and Co., New York, 1927, pp.396

PSYCHOLOGY, ITS FACTS AND PRINCIPLES, D. Appleton and Co., New York, 1928, pp.539

VOCATIONAL PSYCHOLOGY AND CHARACTER ANALYSIS, D. Appleton and Co., New York, 1928, pp.409

ABNORMAL PSYCHOLOGY, The Ronald Press, New York 1930, pp.590

EDUCATIONAL PSYCHOLOGY, D. Appleton and Co., New York, 1933, pp. 540

PSYCHOLOGY OF THE AUDIENCE, American Book Company, New York, 1935, pp.232

PSYCHO-DYNAMICS OF CHEWING, Archives of Psychology, No.239, Columbia University, 1939, pp. 90

LETA STETTER HOLLINGWORTH - A Biography. University of Nebraska Press, Lincoln, Nebr. 1943. pp.250

Psychology and Ethics, Ronald Press Co. N.Y. 1948, pp. 247

ARTICLES AND PAPERS

1900- To The Class of 1900- DeWitt Times, DeWitt, Nebr.

1902- The Unconscious Element in Education, Word and Works, St. Louis

1903- The Optics of Life, No. 1 and 2. Word and Works, St. Louis

Innominata- Word and Works, St. Louis

1909- The Perceptual Basis for Judgments of Extent of Movement, Journal of Philosophy, Psychology and Scientific Methods

The Central Tendency of Judgment, Journal of Philosophy, Psychology and Scientific Methods.

Recent Applications of Experimental Psychology, Arizona Journal of Education

1910- Obliviscence of the Disagreeable, Journ. Phil., Psych. and Sci. Meth.

1911- The Psychology of Drowsiness, American Journal of Psychology

Judgments of the Comic, Psychological Review

Judgments of Persuasiveness, Psychological Review

Vicarious Functioning of Irrelevant Imagery, Journal of Philosophy, Psychology and Scientific Methods

Principles of Appeal and Response. Serially in Judicious Advertising Monthly

1912- Influence of Caffeine on Typewriting, Psychological Review

Influence of Caffeine on Sleep, Amer. Journ. of Psychol.

Caffeine and Efficiency, Therapeutic Gazette

Psychology and Public Health, Arizona Journal of Education

Psychology of Efficiency in Work, Efficiency Magazine

Efficiency in Thinking, Efficiency Magazine

The Psychology of Advertising, Psychological Bulletin

Influence of Form and Category on the Outcome of Judgment, (With Margaret Hart), Journ. of Phil., Psych., and Sci. Meth.

Caffeine as a Stimulant, Tea and Coffee Trade Journal

Caffeine and Efficiency, The Spice Mill

Articles and Papers, Cont.

1913- Psychology and Medicine, The Medical Record, N.Y.

Judgments of Similarity and Difference, Psych. Rev.

Correlation of Abilities as Affected by Practise, Journal of Educational Psychology

A New Experiment in the Psychology of Perception, Journ. of Phil., Psych. and Sci. Meth.

Characteristic Differences between Recall and Recognition, Amer. Journ. of Psych.

1914- Individual Differences Before, During and After Practise, Psych. Rev.

The Art of Remembering, Fortnightly Bulletin, Columbia Univ.

Prof. Cattell's Studies by the Method of Relative Position, in "Psychological Studies of J. McKeen Cattell", Archives of Psychology, No. 30, Columbia University

Comparison of Stylus and Key in Tapping. Journ. of Phil., Psych. and Sci. Meth.

Appeal and Response in Advertising, Proceedings of the Federation of Trade Press Associations

Variations in Efficiency during the Working Day, Psych. Rev.

1915- The Logic of Intermediate Steps (Abstract), Journ. of Phil., Psych. and Sci. Meth.

Advertising and Progress, Judicious Advertising Monthly

Articulation and Association, Journ. of Educ. Psych.

Specialized Vocational Tests and Methods, School and Society

Self-analysis, Judgments of Associates and Results of Mental Tests, School and Society

Psychological Analysis of 99 Successful Advertisements, Advertising and Selling Magazine

1916- The Psychophysical Continuum, Journ. of Phil., Psych. and Sci. Meth.

The Selection of Salesmen, Salesmanship Magazine

1919- Psychological Service in Reconstruction, Columbia University Quarterly

1920- Scientific Selection of Personnel, Business Personnel Magazine

Comparison of Alcohol and Caffeine, Therapeutic Gazette

Articles and Papers, Cont.

1923- The Scientific Study of Drugs, Columbia University Alumni News, April 11.

The Psychology of Idiosyncrasy, Australasian Journal of Psychology and Philosophy, September.

The Social Rite of Eating, Forecast Magazine, July

Meaning and the Psychophysical Continuum, Journal of Philosophy, Aug.2, XX, 16

Symbolic Relations in Thinking, Journ. of Phil. Sept.13, XX, 19

Psychological Influence of Alcohol, Part I. Journal of Abnormal and Social Psychology, October, XVIII

1924- Psychological Influence of Alcohol, Part II., Journ. of Abn. and Soc. Psych. January

Particular Features of Meaning, Psych. Rev. Sept. XXXI, 5

1925- The Logic of Intermediate Steps, Journ. of Phil. March

Correlations of Achievement within an Individual, Journal of Experimental Psychology, June.

When Is a Man Intoxicated ? Journal of Applied Psychology, June.

The Definition of Judgment, Psych. Rev. September.

1926- The Psychology of the Audience, Christian Advocates, July 22

1928- General Principles of Redintegration, Journal of General Psychology. January, pp.79-91

Sensuous Determinants of Psychological Attitude, Presidential Address, American Psychological Association, Psych. Rev. March, XXXV, 2, pp.93-117

How We Learn Our Reflexes, Psych. Rev. September, XXXV, 5, pp.439-442

1929- When I Was Very Young, Mentor Magazine, October. p.8 ff.

1930- Ethical Implications of Individual Differences, in "The Development of Ethics in Modern Business", Bureau of Personnel Administration, N.W.

On the Omission of Intermediate Acts in Behavior, Amer. Journ. of Psych. July, XLII, pp. 457-459

Articles and Papers, Cont.

1931- Experiments on Susceptibility to Drugs, Amer. Journ. of Psych. Jan. XLIII, pp.139-144

Affect and Affect in Learning, Psych. Rev. March, XXXVIII, 2, pp.153-159

Diurnal Variations in Suggestibility, Journ. of Appl. Psych. XV, 5, October, pp.431-435

1932- The Illusion as a Neurosis, Journ. of Abn. and Soc. Psych., XXVI, Oct.-Dec., pp.270-282

What Is Learning ?, The Scientific Monthly, July, XXXV, pp.63-65

1935- The Conditions of Verbal Configuration, Journ. of Exper. Psych. XVIII, 3, June, pp.299-306

1938- Memories of the Early Development of the Psychology of Advertising, Psych. Bull. May, XXXV, 8, pp.307-313

Verbal Gestalt Experiments with Children, Journ of Exper. Psych. July, XXIII, 1, pp.90-95

1939- Perceptual Fluctuation as a Fatigue Index, Journ. of Exper. Psych. May, XXIV, 5, pp.511-519

Persistent Alphabetical Synesthesis, Amer. Journ. of Psych., July, pp. 361-366

Psycho-dynamics of Chewing, Transactions of the New York Academy of Sciences, May. SeriesII, Vol.I, No.7, pp.113-115

Chewing as a Technique of Relaxation, Science, Oct. 27, Vol. 90, No.2339, pp.385-387

1946- Experimental Psychology and Ethics. - Trans. N.Y. Acad. of Sciences. II, 8. No.6. April 1946, 202-214

REVIEWS

Cook- Die Tactile Erschätzung, Journal of Philosophy, Psychology, and Scientific Methods, 1910
Titchener-Text Book of Psychology, Journ. of Phil. etc. 1911
Reply to Titchener's Protest, Journ. of Phil. etc. 1911
Scott-Influencing Men in Business, Psych. Bull., 1911
Scott-Influencing Men in Business, Journ. of Phil. etc. 1912
Myers-Experimental Psychology, Journ. of Phil. etc. 1912
Angell-Chapters from Modern Psychology, Journ. of Phil. etc. 1912
Psychological Aspects of Drug Action, Psych. Bull. 1912
Toulouse- Poincare, Psych. Bull. 1912
Binet-Simon-Scale for Measuring Intelligence of Young Children, Town's Trans., Journ. of Phil. etc. 1913
Münsterberg- Psychology and Industrial Efficiency, Amer. Journ. of Economics, 1913
Calkins-First Book in Psychology, 1913
Münsterberg- Psychology and Industrial Efficiency, Science, 1913
Yerkes and LaRue-Outline for Study of the Self, Journ. of Phil. etc. 1914
Gilbreth-Psychology of Management, Science, 1914
L'Anee Psychologique, Journ. of Phil. etc. 1915
Yerkes and LaRue-Outline for Study of the Self (Revised), Journ. of Phil. etc. 1915
Report of Committee on Academic Status of Psychology, Journ. of Phil. etc. 1915
Ziehen-Die Grundlagen der Psychologie, Journ. of Phil. etc., 1916
Dodge and Benedict-Psychological Effects of Alcohol, Journ. of Phil. etc., 1916
Calkins- Introduction to Psychology, Journ. of Phil. etc., 1916
Watt-Echo Personalities, Journ of Phil. etc., 1920
Pillsbury-Psychology of Nationality, Science, 1920
Hall- Senescence, Journ. of Phil. etc., 1922
Hurst- Functional Disorders of Special Senses, Journ. of Compar. Psych. 1921
O'Shea-Tobacco and Mental Efficiency, Science, 1923
McDougall-Introduction to Psychology, Journ. of Phil. etc.,
Platt-The Riddle of Society, Columbia Law Review, 1926
Fenton-Shell Shock and Its Aftermath, Journ. of Phil. etc., 1927
Maccurdy-Common Principles in Psychology and Physiology, Journ of Phil. etc., 1929
Psychologies of 1930- Journ. of Educ. Psychol. 1930, Oct. 552-554
Müller-Freienfels,-The Evolution of Modern Psychology, Psych. Bull. Dec. 1935.
Keller-The Definition of Psychology, Psych. Bull. Jan. 1938
Allport-Personality, A Psychological Interpretation, Psych. Bull. 1938
Terman et al- Psychological Factors in Marital Happiness, Psych. Bull. March, 1939
Koehler- The Place of Value in a World of Fact, Amer. Journ. of Psych. Jan. 1940

POST-SCRIPT   No. 2
Nov. 1944

If I am doomed to live a long time there might some day be another volume added to these manuscripts, entitled perhaps "The Last Lap". But for the present this Post-Script No. 2 will serve to brings things up to date, and it is unlikely that what is yet to happen will ever deserve a separate volume.

Five years have now passed since the event that led to preoccupation with these Memoirs. Although I never exacted to live so long, these years have been very active and in some ways eventful. They seem in fact to have constituted something of a unitary era. Many things begun when this period started have been brought to a conclusion and other things have occurred that will inevitably make life a bit different in years to come.

The events of this period are so recent that account of them now might almost be considered a diary. Certainly they ought to be recalled with greater vividness than the events described in earlier pages. And yet, when I review these years, and begin to sketch their happenings, it is surprising to note how much is already almost forgotten. Partly to refresh my memory for these years, partly just to bring the narrative up to date, and partly for occupation during days when an obstinate lameness keeps me from out-door activity, I am going to write, then, a second post-script, in which the events of the past five years are briefly noted.

APPENDIX

Most striking of all has been the remarkable way in which time has slipped by. It seems incredible that L— has been gone for five whole years,— almost as long as we lived in the reconstructed house at Hollywyck; as long as the whole period of our acquaintance before the day of our marriage. Many things have happened in these years, although I seem to have changed but little. It seems but yesterday that we took that wild ride in the ambulance, on a stormy Sunday in November, from Hollywyck to the Medical Center, where our life plans crashed completely. What have the years contained ?

Marriage

Early in 1946 Josefine was involved in the rather complicated process of taking out final citizenship papers. In spite of numerous difficulties, due chiefly to her classification as an enemy alien, the goal was finally achieved. In June of that year it seemed to us that our life together, which was running smoothly and happily, would be simplified if we should be married. So, after the necessary formalities, we appeared before a local police judge and became husband and wife. This was about two and a half years ago and it was a wise and comfortable thing to do.

We are happy together and feel mutually secure and in a position to take care of each other more easily. Josefine is a congenial and devoted companion. I enjoy the liveliness of her spirit, her range of interests, her artistry, her vitality, her kindness and her courage. ~~[struck through]~~ Living with her has brought me varieties of joy such as come too seldom to men of my age.

In the preceding Post-Script I expressed an impulse to close the books and start somewhere a new life and a new identity. Strangely enough this is almost what has happened. With Josefine as my companion there has come fresh vitality and quiet enthusiasm. New and sweet sources of pleasure have been tapped and even the local infirmities of increasing age have not availed wholly to thwart this rejuvenation of spirit.

Indeed, not only have I acquired a wife and become again a husband,- I also have children, or at least step children, and also a grand child. The lonely old widower has become the patriarchal member of a family. This is in fact a new existence and not far from a new identity, although the old name still hangs on.

Transcriptions

Page 3A:
The Doors of Schermerhorn, A. T. Beals, NY

Page 12A:
With two Early Columbia Playmates—E. K. Strong and A. T. Poffenberger.

Page 14A:
Maundering with W. P. Montague

Page 33A:
Vagabonding in Europe

Page 49a:
The Doors of Milbank

Page 86a:
With Father and Mother on Columbia Campus. Photo by L.S.H. who appears as a shadow.

Page 87a:
On the Adriatic, 1910

Page 91a:
Ruth and L.S.H.

Page 96a:
L S H at 417 West 118th St.

Page 105a:
A Tri-furcated Personality

Page 111a:
The Colony Assembles for a Tournament

Page 112a:
A corner of the "Colony Lake"

Page 116a:
Our original House at Montrose

Page 119a:
Our Tennis Court, L.S.H. Serving

Page 120a:
A Glimpse of "Road Day"

Page 122a:
Some of Our Dogwoods, Photo by L.S.H.

Page 125a:
We Build Our Own Canoe

Page 126a:
Associate Professor 1916

Page 130a:
Chief of Educational and Psychological Service

Page 132a:
Officer of the Day 1918

Page 164a:
Josefine and Virginia

Page 166a:
A Glimpse of Ancestral Derbyshire

Page 167a:
Somewhere in Ireland

Page 183a:
The House at Hollywyck

Page 187a:
At Hollywyck

Page 193a:
L.S.H.

Page 197A:
A bit of Publicity for Barnard

Note: Harry L. Hollingworth has been abbreviated to HLH and Leta Stetter Hollingworth has been abbreviated as LSH throughout the index. All names are included in both the subject index and the name index. An underscore has been inserted where the manuscript did not include the first name of the person.

Hollingworth's maternal and paternal relatives, in-laws, second wife, and step-daughter can be found under "family" in the subject index and their relationships to Hollingworth are defined. Louise Hollingworth is listed in the index as HLH's sister-in-law; it is assumed from contextual clues that she was the wife of his half-brother Ernest. Aurel Hollingworth is similarly assumed to be the wife of his paternal cousin Robert E. Hollingworth and is included under the entry "cousins" in the subject index.

Hollingworth mentions *The Psychology of Conduct* twice in the manuscript; it is likely he is referring to *Psychology and Ethics* (1948).

Name Index

A
Achilles, Edith Mulhall, 196
Ackerman, Carl W., 205
Adams, Lois, 196
Adler, Felix, 10
Anastasi, Anne, 121, 196
Andrews, T. G., 196
Angell, James Rowland, 110e
Anthony, Katherine, 83, 121
Arai, Tsuru, 42

B
Bagster–Collins, E. W., 112, 117, 184
Bailey, Pearce, 32
Barrett, Dorothy M., 196
Bates, Kathryn Murray, 121
Becker, H. C., 7
Bell, J. Carleton, 22d, 83
Bessey, C. E., 43b
Bingham, Walter V., 122
Birchall, Sara, 121
Boas, Franz, 10, 22d
Bolton, Martha Busse, 121
Bolton, Thaddeus L., 1c, 20, 43, 43b, 105, 121, 153, 203
Bond, Guy L., 121
Bonser, Frederick G., 99
Breitwieser, J., 7, 37, 87
Brown, Warner, 8, 9, 22a, 22d
Bryan, William Jennings, 77, 79
Buhler, Charlotte, 121, 196
Bush, Wendall T., 10

C
Carothers, Florence Edith, 155
Cattell, James McKeen, 1c, 3, 6a, 7–8, 10–11, 12–17, 18–20, 22d, 43c, 62, 87, 110f–10g, 111, 119, 121, 161, 174, 218.

Chapman, Dwight W., 121
Chase, Margaret L., 121
Chrislip, A. E., 7
Chrysler, Mattie Spencer 204, 218
Clapp, Elsie R., 7
Clapp, Professor _____, 43b
Clark, Frank Jones, 121
Cox, Harvey, 43b
Crawford, Meredith P., 196
Culler, A. J., 7

D
Dallenbach, Karl M., 121
Dallenbach, Peggy, 121
Dashiell, J. F., 7, 66
Davis, Katherine B., 77, 79
Davison, Ella Spencer, 204
De Frem, Herman, 83
De Fursac, Joseph Rogues, 152
Deady, Henderson, 83
Dell, Floyd, 83
Denio, Ruth E., 121
Dewey, John, 10, 18–19, 22d, 83
Dorr, Rheta Childe, 83
Downs, E. Hall, 121
Dunlap, James M., 121, 221, 223–24
Dunlap, Knight, 51

E
Eastman, Max, 7, 22d, 83
Ebbinghaus, Hermann, 41
Elwin, Adolph, 83
Engelbrecht, Susi, 121
Evans, Muriel, 121, 184

F
Farrand, Livingston, 10, 19
Fernberger, Samuel, 22d

NAME INDEX

Findley, Cleo Scott, 121
Fling, Professor _____, 43b
Foley, John P., 121, 189, 196
Fordyce, Charles, 43b
Fossler, Laurence, 43b
Fox, Dixon R., 5
Frederick, Christine, 83
Frederick, J. George, 83
Freeman, Daniel, 1a
Freeman, Frank, 51
Froeberg, Sven, 7
Fuller, Mary Ben, 121
Fullerton, George S., 10

G

Garret, Henry E., 121
Gates, Arthur I., 11, 81, 117, 121, 183, 223
Gates, Georgina Strickland, 117, 121, 134, 155, 183, 196, 223
Giddings, Franklin, 92
Goldenweiser, Alexander A., 7, 22d
Goodman, Anne Leigh, 121
Goodsell, Wyllistine, 7
Gregory, Menas S., 218
Guilford, J. P., 203
Guy, Florence, 83

H

Hamilton, F. M., 7, 22d
Hamilton, H. C., 196
Hare, Hobart, 61
Hart, Margaret. See Strong, Margaret Hart
Henmon, V. A. C., 7, 22d, 87
Henneman, R. H., 196
Hill, Lawrence, 7
Hinman, E. L., 18, 43b, 105, 163
Hoch, August, 153
Hollingworth, Ernest, 121
Hollingworth, Gertrude, 85, 223
Hollingworth, Irwin, 218
Hollingworth, Leta Stetter, 1c, 2–3, 6, 11, 17, 29–33, 35–37, 41, 43, 45, 50, 53, 72, 80, 82, 86–86a, 87–91a, 96a, 116, 119–20, 122a, 124, 133, 140–41, 150–51, 165–66, 181, 183–84, 193a, 201–9, 220–28, 230
    appointment at Columbia University, Teachers College, 94–95, 122, 136, 139, 164–65, 167, 182, 201
    Chi Omega Sorority, 1c
    death, 2, 97–97a, 120, 151, 204, 210–11, 218–19, 221–28, 235, 244–45
    doctoral degree, 92, 94
    employment in clinical psychology, 93–95
    graduate work, 49, 53, 55, 91, 92–94, 122
    involvement with Coca Cola research, 65–66, 68
    marriage to HLH, 35–40, 200
        impact on career, 138–41, 203
    Memorial Conference on the Gifted in Honor of Leta S. Hollingworth, 97a, 222
    memorial fellowship, 232–33
    public school teacher, McCook High School, 29, 35, 201
    publications, 93, 96–97, 99, 164, 222, 227
    research and involvement with gifted children, 164, 166
    research and involvement with women's rights, 83, 92–93a, 96–97, 220
    writer, 50, 91, 222
Hollingworth, Libbie "Lizzie" J. Andrews, 204
Hollingworth, Louise, 121
Hollingworth, Mittie Gunder, 1f, 85, 86a
Hollingworth, Thomas 1b, 1f, 85, 86a
Holmes, Joseph, 196
Hotchkiss, George Burton, 99, 152
Hull, Helen R., 117, 121, 183
Hunter, Fred M., 201
Hurlock, Elizabeth, 196

I

Irwin, Elizabeth, 83, 121, 218

J

Jackson, Theodore A., 121, 189, 196
James, William, 10
Jastrow, Joseph, 121, 218
Jersild, Arthur T., 11, 117, 121, 184, 196, 223
Jersild, Catherine, 117, 121, 184, 223
Johnson, Enid, 119
Johnson, John H., 121
Judd, Charles, 22d
Jung, Carl, 34–34a

K

Kasner, Edward, 82
Keppel, Frederick P., 112–13, 117, 121d, 184, 218, 227, 234
Koffka, Kurt, 25

L

Landis, Carney, 121
Lane, Margaret, 119

Lee, F. S., 100
Lipsky, Abram, 7
Lord, Harvey G., 10
Lorge, Irving, 121
Lowie, Robert, 22d
Lund, Frederick, 121, 196
Lyon, D. O., 7, 22d

M
MacMurray, Alan, 121
MacMurray, Donald, 121
Marsh, H. D., 22d
Marshall, Henry Rutgers, 22d
Martin, S. H., 121
McComas, Thomas, 22d
McDougall, William, 149, 158
McGeoch, John A., 218
McHugh, Gelolo, 121, 196
McKay, Thomas A., 121, 223–24
Meyer, Adolph, 153
Miller, Dickinson, 10, 19, 62
Mills, Jean, 121
Monroe, Paul, 18, 92
Montague, Helen, 81, 83, 96, 111–12
Montague, William P., 10, 14A, 22d, 51, 69, 81–83, 98F, 111–12
Moore, Gertrude, 121
Mumford, Claire, 218
Munsterberg, Hugo, 99–100, 110e, 149
Murphy, David, 121
Murphy, Gardner, 121

N
Nissen, Henry W., 121, 196
Norsworthy, Naomi, 10–11

P
Pallister, Helen, 196
Parmelee, Maurice, 22d, 83
Parsons, Frank A., 99, 152
Patterson, Professor _____, 43b
Pickup, Nellie B., 121
Pintner, Rudolf, 11, 218
Pitkin, Walter B., 10, 22d
Poffenberger, A. T., 7, 12A, 66, 81, 105–6, 110e–10f, 117, 121, 121e, 183, 189, 218, 223
Poffenberger, Flosie K., 117, 121e, 183, 218, 223
Poffenberger, Helen, 121
Poffenberger, John, 121

Pound, Louise, 43b, 121, 203
Pritchard, Miriam, 221
Puckett, H. W., 121
Puckett, Mary, 121

Q
Quigley, Ruth, 121

R
Reisner, Betty, 121, 124, 184
Reisner, Edward H., 11, 121, 124, 184
Rejall, A. E., 7, 22d
Rice, D. E., 7, 66, 81, 87, 89
Rice, Margaret G., 81, 87–88, 121
Ripin, Rowena, 196
Robinson, Mabel L., 43b, 117, 121, 183
Rodman, Henrietta, 83
Rohe, Alice, 121
Rosanoff, A. J., 127, 152, 218
Ross, E. A., 43b
Rounds, George H., 189
Rowe, Stuart H., 22d
Ruediger, W. C., 7
Ruger, Henry A., 10
Russell, William Fletcher, 111
Rust, Metta Maund, 121, 196

S
Sargent, S. S., 196
Scott, Walter Dill, 101, 103
Scott, Winifred Starbuck, 121
Scripture, E. W., 22d, 87
Seabury, David, 119, 121
Seabury, Florence, 119, 121
Seward, Georgine H., 196
Shaw, William A., 196
Shen, Y., 121
Shuey, Audrey M., 196
Simpson, Ray H., 121, 189, 196
Spragg, Jane T., 121
Spragg, S. D. Shirley, 121, 196
Stecher, Lorle, 134, 196
Stetter, John G., 218
Stetter, Leta A. See Hollingworth, Leta Stetter
Stetter, Ruth, 49b, 85, 88, 91a, 94, 208
Strang, Ruth, 117, 184
Strong, C. A., 10, 18–19, 153
Strong, E. K., 7, 12A, 66, 68, 74, 121, 149, 153, 196
Strong, Margaret Hart, 69, 74, 112
Stuff, Frederick A., 43b, 121, 218

Stuff, Grace, 121
Sturdevant, Sarah, 218

T

Tait, William D., 149
Taylor, Professor _____, 43b
Terman, Lewis M., 121, 149, 227
Thompson, Professor _____, 43b
Thomson, Godfrey, 121
Thorndike, E. L., 9A–11, 18–19, 22d, 73, 92, 112–13, 117, 121j, 184
Thorndike, Elizabeth Moulton, 184
Thorndike, Robert, 196, 227
Tilney, Frederick, 153
Tipper, Harry, 99, 152
Titchener, E. B., 25, 148–49, 199
Todd, J. W., 7
Tombo, Rudolph, 91
Turner, J. P., 7, 22d

V

Valentine, Clarence, 114, 121k–21l
Volkmann, John, 121

W

Wallin, J. E. Wallace, 22d
Ward, H. B., 43b
Warden, Carl J., 121, 218
Warren, Howard C., 22d
Washburn, Margaret Floy, 218
Watermann, _____, 205
Watson, A. T., 121
Watson, Grace, 121
Weischer, Josefine, 164–65, 184, 221, 223, 225–26, 228, 232, 246
Weischer, Virginia, 164–65, 184, 228
Wells, F. L., 7, 9a, 22d
Whipple, G. M., 218
Whitley, M. T., 7
Wickware, F. H., 218
Wiley, Harvey, 61
Willetts, Joseph, 110e
Wissler, Clark, 19, 22d
Woodbridge, Frederick J. E., 10, 18–19, 22d, 83, 112–13, 184
Woodrow, H. H., 7, 22d, 51
Woodworth, Robert S., 3, 4, 10–11, 18–20, 22d, 112, 117, 121, 129, 155–56
Woolston, Howard, 7
Wundt, Wilhelm, 6a, 8

Y

Young, Aurel D., 121
Young, Robert E., 121
Young, Rose, 121
Youtz, Adella, 121
Youtz, Richard E. P., 121, 196

Subject Index

A

Abnormal Psychology (1930), 153, 158, 168, 176, 238
Achilles, Edith Mulhall, 196
Ackerman, Carl W., 205
Adams, Lois, 196
Adler, Felix, 10
Adolescence (LSH), 227
Advertising and Selling (1913), 55–59, 65, 70, 88, 177, 238
Advertising, Its Principles and Practise (1915), 99, 104, 152, 238
agriculture, 1a–1b
alcohol research. *See* applied psychology
American Association for the Advancement of Science, 144
American Association of Applied Psychologists, 110c
American Journal of Sociology, 97
American Philosophical Association, 104, 109
American Psychological Association, 76, 104, 110c, 122–23, 165–66, 174
Anastasi, Anne, 121, 196
Andrews, T. G., 196
Angell, James Rowland, 110e
Anthony, Katherine, 83, 121
applied psychology, 53, 74, 99, 106, 110c–10g, 123, 154, 157
    alcohol research, 154–58, 188
    caffeine research, 61–68, 70, 73, 155–58, 159, 188
    Columbia University extension courses, 54–55, 98, 100, 102, 160, 165–66, 198, 201
    consulting work, 55, 98, 105, 159–63
    New York University School of Business extension courses, 54–55
    psychodynamics of chewing, 178, 188–92
    psychotechnology research in consumer-studies and marketing problems, 105, 107–10b, 122
    public lecturer, 75–79, 177
    salary, 53–54, 62, 68, 92, 122
Applied Psychology (1917), 105, 106, 152, 238
Arai, Tsuru, 42
Archives of Psychology, 24, 65, 71, 190

B

Bagster–Collins, E. W., 112, 117, 184
Bailey, Pearce, 32
Barnard College, 7, 194–99, 227
    appointment, 43, 43h, 51–52, 61, 69, 94, 98, 105, 122, 134, 136, 166, 167, 194, 221
    courses taught, 69, 70–71, 74, 98–99, 139, 168, 173, 176, 186
    Psychology Department, 69, 98, 150, 186, 195–99
    research, 69–74, 99
    salary, 46–47, 48, 52a, 55, 98, 122, 182, 194
Barrett, Dorothy M., 196
Bates, Kathryn Murray, 121
Becker, H. C., 7
Bell, J. Carleton, 22d, 83
Bellevue Hospital, 93–94, 218
Bessey, C. E., 43b
bibliography, 238–43
Bingham, Walter V., 122
Birchall, Sara, 121
Boas, Franz, 10, 22d
Bolton, Martha Busse, 121
Bolton, Thaddeus L., 1c, 20, 43, 43b, 105, 121, 153, 203
Bond, Guy L., 121
Bonser, Frederick G., 99
book reviews, 148–50
Born in Nebraska, 1a, 29, 212, 223–24, 228, 235

SUBJECT INDEX

Breitwieser, J., 7, 37, 87
Brown, Warner, 8, 9, 22a, 22d
Bryan, William Jennings, 77, 79
Buhler, Charlotte, 121, 196
Bush, Wendall T., 10

C

caffeine research, See applied psychology, caffeine research
Carnegie Corporation, 227
Carnegie Institute of Technology, 122
Carothers, Florence Edith, 155
Catastrophobia, 51, 66
Cattell, James McKeen, 1c, 3, 6a, 7–8, 10–11, 12–17, 18–20, 22d, 43c, 62, 110f–10g, 111, 119, 121, 161, 174, 218. *See also* Fort Defiance Hill
Cattell–Fullerton apparatus, 25, 199
Chapman, Dwight W.,, 121
Characteristic Differences between Recall and Recognition (1913), 74, 240
Chase, Margaret L., 121
Cheyenne, WY,
   1901 bicycle trek from Dewitt to Cheyenne for carpentry work, 201
Children Above 180 IQ (1942, LSH), 227
Chrislip, A. E., 7
Clapp, Elsie R., 7
Clapp, Professor _____, 43b
Clark, Frank Jones, 121
Clearing House for Mental Defectives, 93
Coca Cola Research. *See* applied psychology, caffeine research
Colorado College, 7
Columbia Contributions to Philosophy and Psychology, 24
Columbia University, 1c–1d, 4, 6–7, 10–11, 12A, 22c, 26–27, 62, 81, 110e–10f, 111, 134, 136, 149, 198, 199a–99c, 203, 205, 232, 236
   arrival (1907), 1g–1i
   assistantship, 1c, 4, 7–8, 25, 29, 46, 91, 218
   coursework and research, 12, 18–22d, 25–28, 41–42, 43b–43g, 153
      dissertation, 22, 23–28, 40–43, 70, 149, 199
   Department of Anthropology, 10
   Department of Philosophy, 10, 51
   Department of Psychology, 2, 3, 3A, 4, 8, 10–11, 20, 22c–22d, 51, 101, 156

   employment, 53
      summer tutor to James McKeen Cattell's children, 12, 13–14, 15–17
   Low Memorial Library, 1h
   social clubs and organizations, 22c
   Teacher's College, 10, 11, 81, 93a, 100, 198, 218, 223
Cornell University, 25, 148, 199a
Correlation of Abilities as Affected by Practise, The (1913), 73, 240
Cox, Harvey, 43b
Crawford, Meredith P., 196
Culler, A. J., 7
Current History Magazine, 97

D

Dallenbach, Karl M., 121
Dallenbach, Peggy, 121
Dashiell, J. F., 7, 66
Davis, Katherine B., 77, 79
De Fursac, Joseph Rogues, 152
Deady, Henderson, 83
Definition of Judgement (1925), 154, 241
Dell, Floyd, 83
Denio, Ruth E., 121
Dewey, John, 10, 18–19, 22d, 83
DeWitt, NE,
   as hometown and birthplace of HLH, 1a, 204, 224, 226
doctoral degree in psychology, HLH, 40–43. *See also* Columbia University
Donald, Douglas, 218
Dorr, Rheta Childe, 83
Downs, E. Hall, 121
Dunlap, James M., 121, 221, 223–24
Dunlap, Knight, 51

E

Eastern Psychological Association, 22d
Eastman, Max, 7, 22d, 83
Ebbinghaus, Hermann, 41
Economic Psychology Association, 110c–10e, 110g
education,
   The University of Montgomery and Ward and Co., 6a
Education and the Individual (1940, LSH), 97a, 222
Educational Psychology (1933), 168, 176, 178, 238

SUBJECT INDEX

Elwin, Adolph, 83
employment,
    early employment, 1c, 52a
    carpentry, 51
    public school teacher, 17, 43i, 45, 51, 204
    University of Nebraska, 30–31b
Encyclopedia Brittanica, The, 97
Engelbrecht, Susi, 121
Evans, Muriel, 121, 184
Experimental Studies in Judgment (1913), 71, 153, 239

F
family (extended),
    maternal,
        aunts,
            Chrysler, Mattie Spencer, 204, 218
            Davison, Ella Spencer, 204
    paternal,
        aunts,
            Watson, Grace, 121
        cousins,
            Young, Robert E., 121
            Young, Aurel D. [Robert], 121
        uncles,
            Watson, A. T. [Grace], 121
family (immediate)
    father,
        Hollingworth, Thomas, 1b, 1f, 85, 86a
    father-in-law,
        Stetter, John G., 218
    half-brothers,
        Hollingworth, Ernest, 121
        Hollingworth, Irwin, 218
    half-sisters,
        Hollingworth, Gertrude, 85, 223
    mother,
        Hollingworth, Libbie "Lizzie" J. Andrews, 204
    second wife,
        Weischer, Josefine, 164–65, 184, 221, 223, 225–26, 228, 232, 246
    sister-in-law
        Hollingworth, Louise [Ernest], 121
        Stetter, Ruth (LSH's sister), 49b, 85, 88, 91a, 94, 208
    step-daughter,
        Weischer, Virginia, 164–65, 184, 228
    step-mother,
        Hollingworth, Mittie Gunder, 1f, 85, 86a
    wife, see Hollingworth, Leta Stetter

Farrand, Livingston, 10, 19
Fernberger, Samuel, 22d
Findley, Cleo Scott, 121
Fling, Professor _____, 43b
Foley, John P., 121, 189, 196
Fordyce, Charles, 43b
Fort Defiance Hill, Cattell family home, 12–17, 87
Fossler, Laurence, 43b
Fowler & Wells, 102–3
Fox, Dixon R., 5
Frederick, Christine, 83
Frederick, J. George, 83
Freeman, Daniel, 1a
Freeman, Frank, 51
Fremont High School, 1c, 1e, 12, 29, 36, 218
Frequency of Amentia as Related to Sex, The (1913, LSH), 96
Froeberg, Sven, 7
Fuller, Mary Ben, 121
Fullerton, George S., 10
Functional Periodicity (1914, LSH), 93

G
Garret, Henry E., 121
Gates, Arthur I., 11, 81, 117, 121, 183, 223
Gates, Georgina Strickland, 117, 121, 134, 155, 183, 196, 223
General Principles of Redintegration (1928), 174, 241
Giddings, Franklin, 92
Goldenweiser, Alexander A., 7, 22d
Goodman, Anne Leigh, 121
Goodsell, Wyllistine, 7
Great Depression, 86, 121l, 166, 167, 180
Gregory, Menas S., 218
Guilford, J. P., 203
Guy, Florence, 83

H
Hamilton, F. M., 7, 22d
Hamilton, H. C., 196
Hare, Hobart, 61
Hart, Margaret. *See* Strong, Margaret Hart
Harvard University, 199a
health, physical and mental health of HLH, 43h–43i, 140–47, 220, 230–31, 235
Henmon, V. A. C., 7, 22d, 87
Henneman, R. H., 196
Hill, Lawrence, 7
Hinman, E. L., 18, 43b, 105, 163

Hipp Chronoscope, 8
Hoch, August, 153
Hollingworth, Leta Stetter, 1c, 2–3, 6, 11, 17, 29–33, 35–37, 41, 43, 45, 50, 53, 72, 80, 82, 86–86a, 87–91a, 96a, 116, 119–20, 122a, 124, 133, 140–41, 150–51, 165–66, 181, 183–84, 193a, 201–9, 220–28, 230
    appointment at Columbia University, Teachers College, 94–95, 122, 136, 139, 164–65, 167, 182, 201
    Chi Omega Sorority, 1c
    death, 2, 97–97a, 120, 151, 204, 210–11, 218–19, 221–28, 235, 244–45
    doctoral degree, 92, 94
    employment in clinical psychology, 93–95
    graduate work, 49, 53, 55, 91, 92–94, 122
    involvement with Coca Cola research, 65–66, 68
    marriage to HLH, 35–40, 200
        impact on career, 138–41, 203
    Memorial Conference on the Gifted in Honor of Leta S. Hollingworth, 97a, 222
    memorial fellowship, 232–33
    public school teacher, McCook High School, 29, 35, 201
    publications, 93, 96–97, 99, 164, 222, 227
    research and involvement with gifted children, 164, 166
    research and involvement with women's rights, 83, 92–93a, 96–97, 220
    writer, 50, 91, 222
Hollywyck, HLH and LSH country home, 86, 114, 118, 120–21, 121f, 122, 182–87a, 209, 218, 220–21, 225–27, 231–32, 235, 245. *See also* Montrose Colony
Holmes, Joseph, 196
Hotchkiss, George Burton, 99, 152
Hotel Belleclaire, 1h–1i
How We Learn Our Reflexes (1928), 178, 241
Hull, Helen R., 117, 121, 183
Hunter, Fred M., 201
Hurlock, Elizabeth, 196

I

Illusions as a Neuroses, The (1932) [sic], 178, 242
Inaccuracy of Movement, The (1909), 24, 70, 238
Individual Differences as Influence by Practise [sic] (1914), 73, 240
Influence of Caffeine on Efficiency, The (1912), 70, 239. *See also* applied psychology, caffeine research
International Congress of Psychology, 87
Irwin, Elizabeth, 83, 121, 218

J

Jackson, Theodore A., 121, 189, 196
James, William, 10
Jastrow, Joseph, 121, 218
Jersild, Arthur T., 11, 117, 121, 184, 196, 223
Jersild, Catherine, 117, 121, 184, 223
Johnson, Enid, 119
Johnson, John H., 121
Journal of Abnormal and Social Psychology, 156
Journal of Philosophy, 104
Judd, Charles, 22d
Judging Human Character (1922), 153, 238
Jung, Carl, 34–34a

K

Kasner, Edward, 82
Keppel, Frederick P., 112–13, 117, 121d, 184, 218, 227, 234
Koffka, Kurt, 25

L

Landis, Carney, 121
Lane, Margaret, 119
Law of Effect, The [sic] (1931), 178, 242
Lee, F. S., 100
Leta Stetter Hollingworth—A Biography (1943), 97a, 223, 228, 238
Linden Cottage, 221, 225–26, 232
Lipsky, Abram, 7
Logic of Intermediate Steps (1925), 104, 109, 154, 241
Loomis Sanitarium, 88
Lord, Harvery G., 10
Lorge, Irving, 121
Lowie, Robert, 22d
Lund, Frederick, 121, 196
Lyon, D. O., 7, 22d

M

MacMurray, Alan, 121
MacMurray, Donald, 121
Manual of Psychiatry (1920), 152, 238
Marsh, H. D., 22d
Marshall, Henry Rutgers, 22d
Martin, S. H., 121
McComas, Thomas, 22d

McDougall, William, 149, 158
McGeoch, John A., 218
McHugh, Gelolo, 121, 196
McKay, Thomas A., 121, 223–24
Mental Growth and Decline (1927), 168, 173, 176, 238
Meyer, Adolph, 153
Milbank Hall. *See* Barnard College, Psychology Department
Miller, Dickinson, 10, 19, 62
Mills, Jean, 121
Monroe, Paul, 18, 92
Montague, Helen, 81, 83, 96, 111–12
Montague, William P., 10, 14A, 22d, 51, 69, 81–83, 98F, 111–12
Montrose Colony, 111–21q, 182–87, 209, 218, 223
Moore, Gertrude, 121
Morningside Press, The, 110c, 110f, 110g
Mrs. Pilgrim's Progress, 97
Mumford, Claire, 218
Munsterberg, Hugo, 99–100, 110e, 149
Murphy, David, 121
Murphy, Gardner, 121

N
National Research Council, 122
Nature of Learning, The, 178
Nebraska,
    as HLH's hometown and birthplace, 1a–1b, 1i, 6, 16–17, 33, 49b, 79, 180–81, 200, 224, 234
    HLH & LSH return trip, 1938, 203–9
Nebraska Academy of Sciences, 20
Nebraska Wesleyan University,
    Wesleyan Academy, 36, 194, 218
New Experiment in Perception, A (1913), 74, 240
New Woman in the Making, The (1927, LSH), 97
New York, NY, 1a, 22c, 80, 85, 119
Nissen, Henry W., 121, 196
Norsworthy, Naomi, 10–11

O
Obliviscence of the Disagreeable (1910), 73, 131, 239
Omission of Intermediate Steps in Behavior (1930), 178, 241
Outlines for Experimental Psychology (1913), 70, 238

P
Pallister, Helen, 196
parenthood, 85
Parmelee, Maurice, 22d, 83
Parsons, Frank A., 99, 152
Patterson, Professor _____, 43b
philosophy, 6a–6b, 7, 10, 18–19, 69, 72
phrenology, 102–3. *See also* Fowler and Wells
Pickup, Nellie B., 121
Pintner, Rudolf, 11, 218
Pitkin, Walter B., 10, 22d
Plattsburg Army Hospital, 123–35, 153, 159–60, 199
    curative work shop, 126
    psychological testing, 126, 127, 129–31
    reconstruction service, 123–24, 126
    war neuroses, 123, 130, 134–36, 152–53, 158, 177, 199
Poffenberger, A. T., 7, 12A, 66, 81, 105–6, 110e–10f, 117, 121, 121e, 183, 189, 218, 223
Poffenberger, Flosie K., 117, 121e, 183, 218, 223
Poffenberger, Helen, 121
Poffenberger, John, 121
politics, 13–14, 32, 79, 84, 213, 215–16, 219–20
Pound, Louise, 43b, 121, 203
poverty, 1b, 45–49, 49b–52, 84, 110A
Prairie Years (1940, LSH), 222
Pratt Institute of Technology, 89
Princeton University, 199a
Principles of Advertising (1920), 152, 238
Pritchard, Miriam, 221
Psychodynamics of Chewing, The (1939), 178, 188–92, 238
Psychological Bulletin, 26, 56–60
Psychological Corporation, 110c, 110f–10g
Psychology, 4, 6a–6b, 7, 10, 18–20, 25–27, 30, 61, 69–71, 75, 77, 95, 104–5, 109, 124, 128, 135–36, 149–53, 168, 171–72, 174–76, 181, 197. *See also* applied psychology; Barnard College, Department of Psychology; Columbia University, Department of Psychology
Psychology of Conduct, The (1948), 230, 238
Psychology of Drowsiness, The (1911), 72, 239
Psychology of Functional Neuroses, The (1920), 135–36, 152, 168, 176–77, 238
Psychology of the Audience, The (1935), 79, 168, 177, 238
Psychology of the Family (LSH), 97

Psychology of Thought (1926), 154, 168, 171–72, 238
Psychology, Its Facts and Principles (1928), 168, 175–76, 238
Psycho–physical Continuum, The [sic] (1923), 104, 109, 154, 241
Public Addresses of Leta S. Hollingworth (1941), 222
publications. *See* Bibliography
Puckett, H. W., 121
Puckett, Mary, 121

Q
Quigley, Ruth, 121

R
recreation, 80–83
Reisner, Betty, 121, 124, 184
Reisner, Edward H., 11, 121, 124, 184
Rejall, A. E., 7, 22d
research, 20, 24, 70–74, 97–97a, 99, 100–101, 104–6, 152–54, 156, 158, 168–72a, 173–79, 186–87, 190, 223, 228, 230. *See also* applied psychology, Barnard College, and Columbia University
Rice, D. E., 7, 66, 81, 87, 89
Rice, Margaret G., 81, 87–88, 121
Ripin, Rowena, 196
Robinson, Mabel L., 43b, 117, 121, 183
Rodman, Henrietta, 83
Rohe, Alice, 121
Rosanoff, A. J., 127, 152, 218
Ross, E. A., 43b
Rounds, George H., 189
Rowe, Stuart H., 22d
Ruediger, W. C., 7
Ruger, Henry A., 10
Russell, William Fletcher, 111
Rust, Metta Maund, 121, 196

S
Salesmanship Magazine, 102
Sanitary Corps, 160
Sargent, S. S., 196
Schermerhorn Hall. *See* Columbia University, Department of Psychology
Science, 20
Scott, Walter Dill, 101, 103
Scott, Winifred Starbuck, 121
Scripture, E. W., 22d, 87

Seabury, David, 119, 121
Seabury, Florence, 119, 121
Sense of Taste, The (1917), 105, 106, 238
Seward, Georgine H., 196
Shaw, William A., 196
Shen, Y., 121
Shuey, Audrey M., 196
Simpson, Ray H., 121, 189, 196
Social Devices for Impelling Women to Bear Children (1916, LSH), 97
Speyer School, 203, 221, 224, 227
Spragg, Jane T., 121
Spragg, S. D. Shirley, 121, 196
St. Olaf's College, 7
Stecher, Lorle, 134, 196
Stetter, Leta A. *See* Hollingworth, Leta Stetter
Strang, Ruth, 117, 184
Strong, C. A., 10, 18–19, 153
Strong, E. K., 7, 12A, 66, 68, 74, 121, 149, 153, 196
Strong, Margaret Hart, 69, 74, 112
Stuff, Frederick A., 43b, 121, 218
Stuff, Grace, 121
Sturdevant, Sarah, 218
Symbolic Relations (1926), 154, 238. *See also Psychology of Thought, The*

T
Tait, William D., 149
Taylor, Professor _____, 43b
Teachers College. *See* Columbia University Teachers College
Teachers College Contributions to Education, 93
Terman, Lewis M., 121, 149, 227
Theology, 6–6a
Thompson, Professor _____, 43b
Thomson, Godfrey, 121
Thorndike, E. L., 9A–11, 18–19, 22d, 73, 92, 112–13, 117, 121j, 184
Thorndike, Elizabeth Moulton, 184
Thorndike, Robert, 196, 227
Tilney, Frederick, 153
Tipper, Harry, 99, 152
Titchener, E. B., 25, 148–49, 199
Todd, J. W., 7
Tombo, Rudolph, 91
travel,
  personal,
    Europe, 165–67a
    Scandinavia, 225, 227

travel (cont.)
    United States, 203–9
  professional,
    Europe, 32–35, 87–90
    United States, 38, 200–9, 226
Turner, J. P., 7, 22d

U

Union College, 6
University of California, 8, 51
University of Denver, 201
University of Kansas, 31a–31b
University of Nebraska, 1b–1c, 4, 6a–6b, 29, 136, 153, 194, 199a, 200–203, 218
University of Nebraska
  Alpha Tau Omega Fraternity, 1c, 9a, 201
  assistantship, 1c
  course work, 1c, 8, 20–21, 32, 43a, 153, 163
  honorary degrees for HLH and LSH, 202–3, 205, 207
  Phi Beta Kappa, 32
University of Wisconsin, 7

V

Valentine, Clarence, 114, 121k–21l
variability, 96
Variations in Suggestibility [sic] (1931), 178, 242
Variations on Efficiency During the Working Day (1914), 73, 240
Vicarious Function of Irrelevant Imagery (1911), 72, 239
Vocational Aptitudes of Women (1916, LSH) 97, 99, 238. See also Vocational Psychology
Vocational Psychology (1916), 97, 99, 104, 153–54, 238
Vocational Psychology and Character Analysis (1928), 154, 168, 238
Volkmann, John, 121

W

Wallin, J. E. Wallace, 22d
Ward, H. B., 43b
Warden, Carl J., 121, 218
war neuroses, See Plattsburg Army Hospital
Warren, Howard C., 22d
Washburn, Margaret Floy, 218
Watermann, _____, 205
Wells, F. L., 7, 9a, 22d
Wharton School, 110e
Whipple, G. M., 218

Whitley, M. T., 7
Wickware, F. H., 218
wife. *See* Hollingworth, Leta Stetter and Weischer, Josefine
Wiley, Harvey, 61
Willetts, Joseph, 110e
Wissler, Clark, 19, 22d
Woodbridge, Frederick J. E., 10, 18–19, 22d, 83, 112–13, 184
Woodrow, H. H., 7, 22d, 51
Woodworth, Robert S., 3, 4, 10–11, 18–20, 22d, 112, 117, 121, 129, 155–56
Woolston, Howard, 7
World War I, 103, 105, 110, 110p, 123–36, 154, 177, 199
World War II, 199, 218–19, 225, 232, 234. *See also* Plattsburg Army Hospital
Wundt, 6a, 8
Wyuka Cemetery, 204, 211

Y

Yale University, 199a
Young, Rose, 121
Youtz, Adella, 121
Youtz, Richard E. P., 121, 196